Animals and Objects In and Out of Water

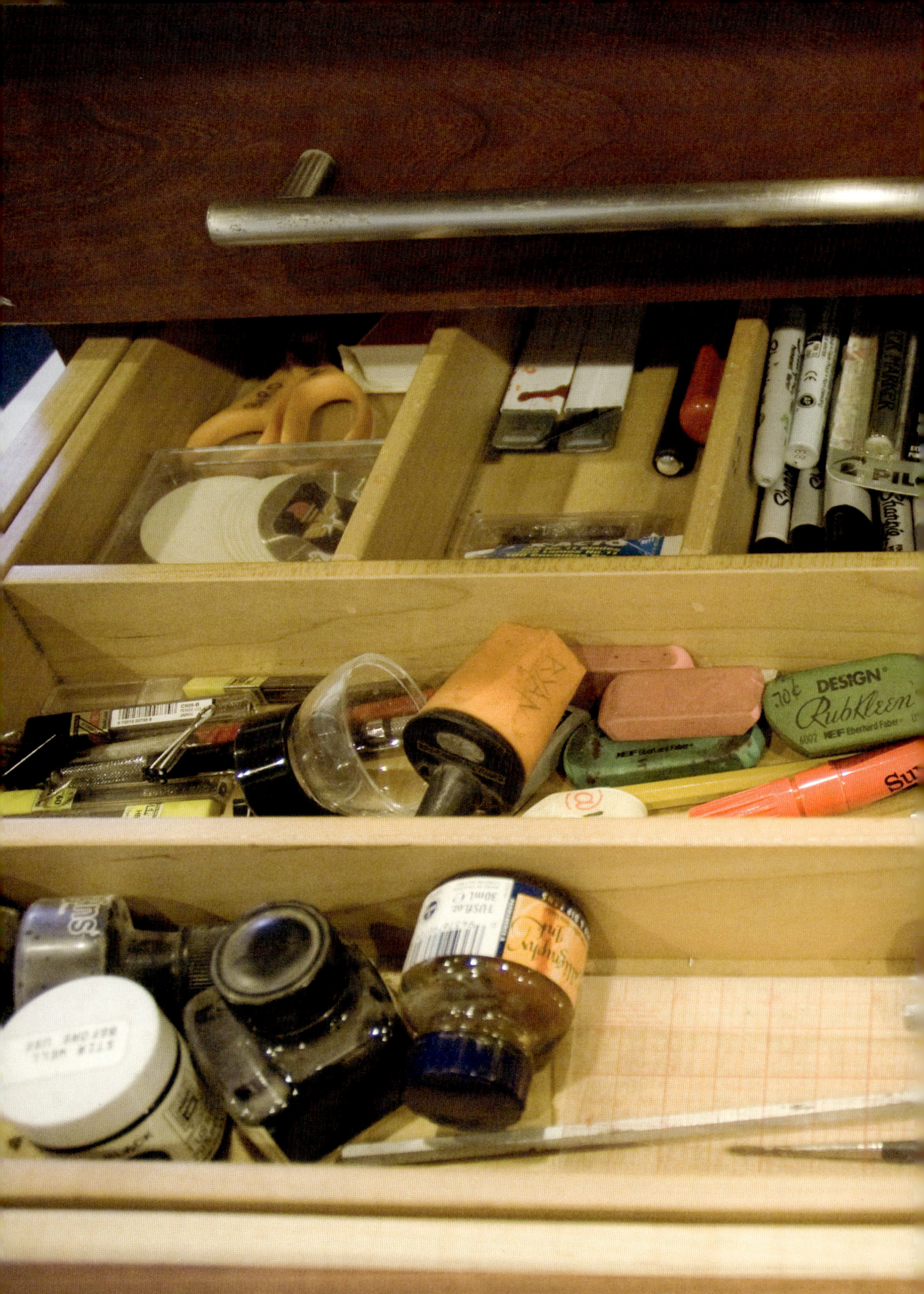
70¢
DESIGN®
RubKleen
Eberhard Faber
Sharpie

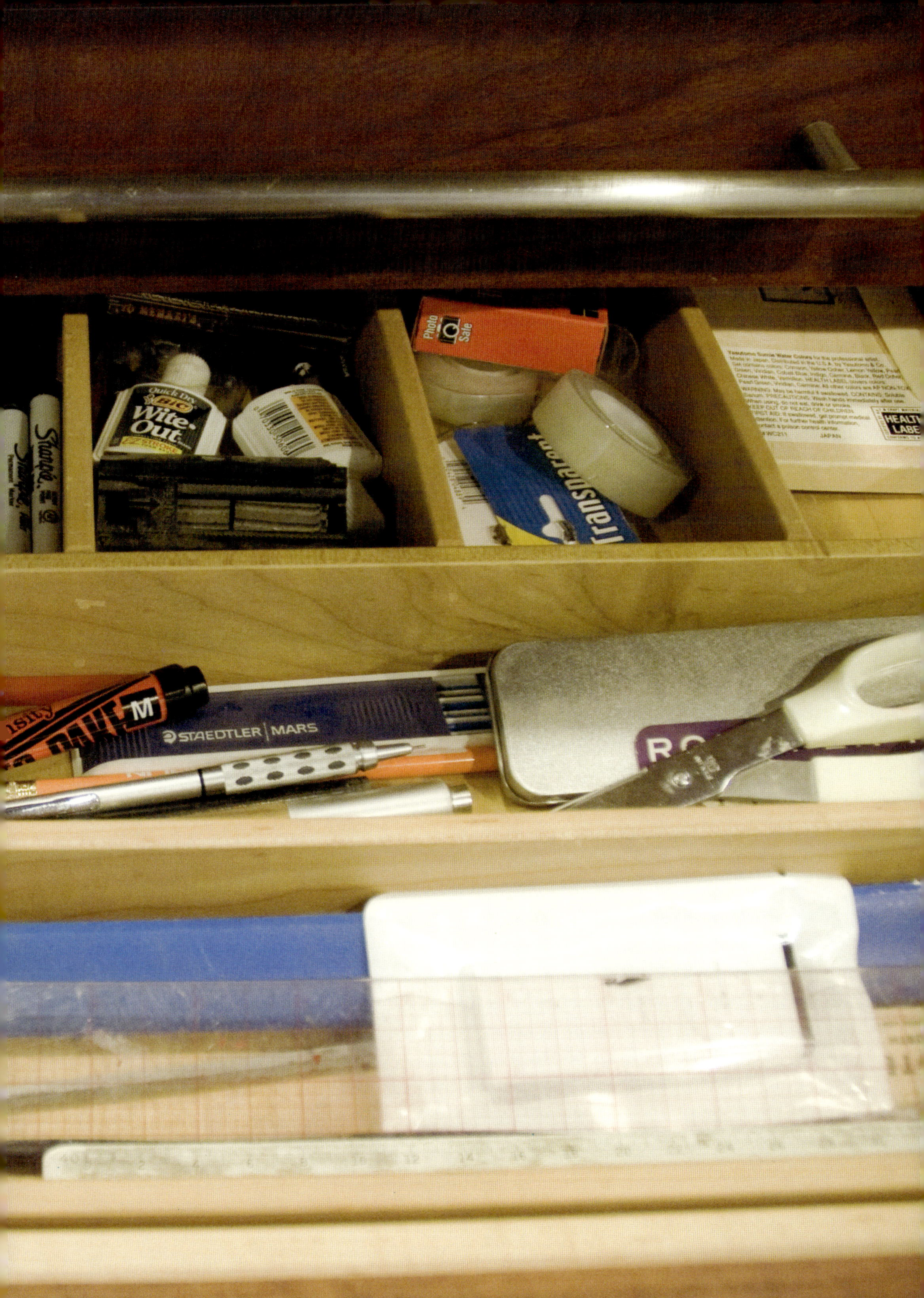
Quick Dry
BIC
Wite-Out
Sharpie
Photo
Sale
STAEDTLER | MARS

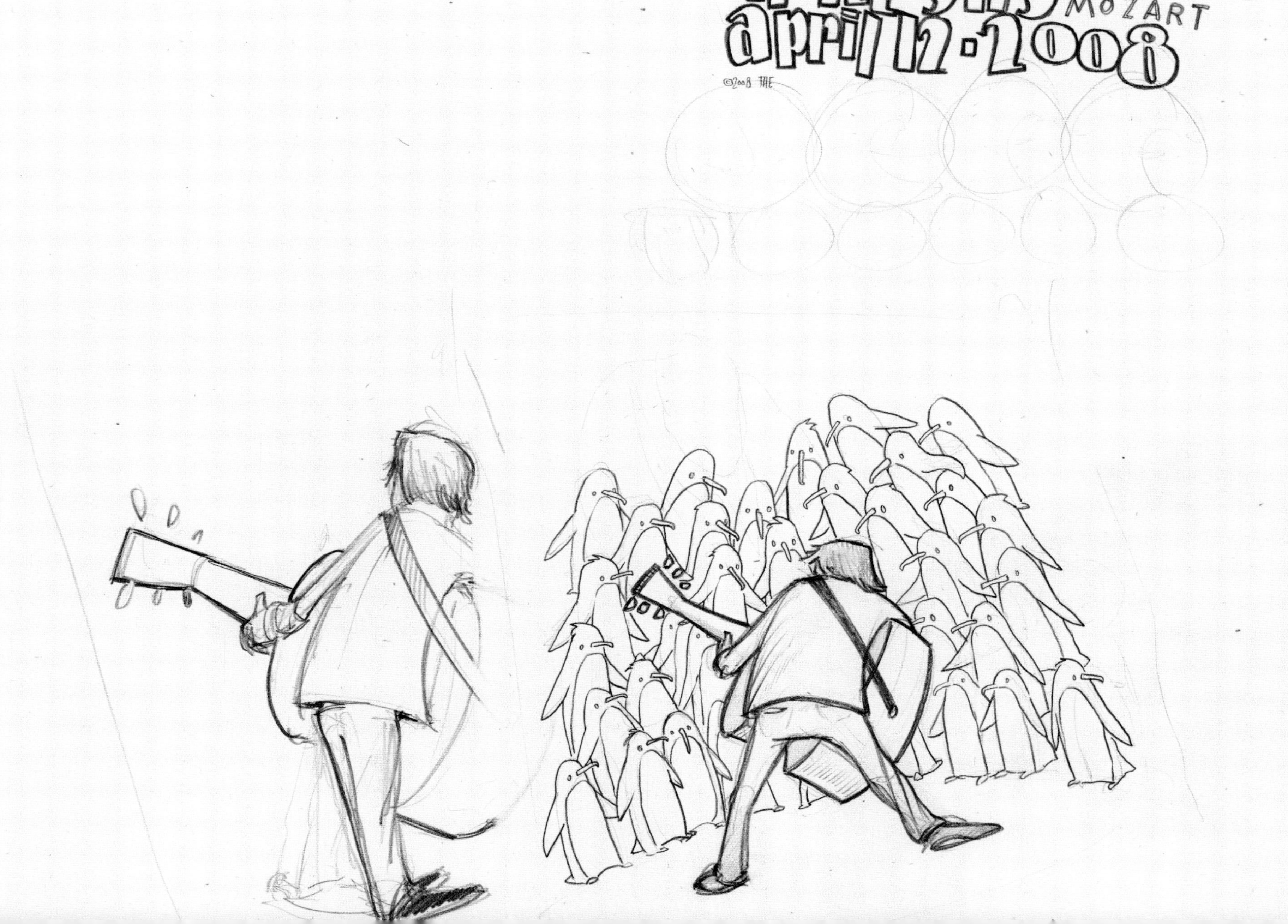
1625 N MOZART
april 12 · 2008
©2008 THE

Animals and Objects In and Out of Water

Posters by Jay Ryan 2005–2008

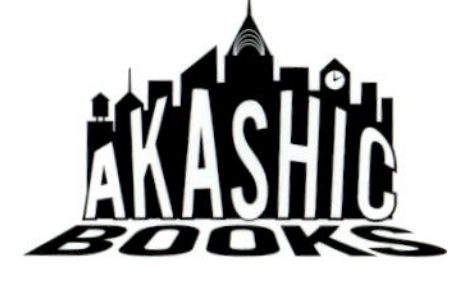

Published by Akashic Books

Book design by Jason Harvey
Photography by Nathan Keay
Edited by Fred Sasaki

ISBN-13: 978-1-933354-92-7

Library of Congress Control Number: 2009922938

First printing

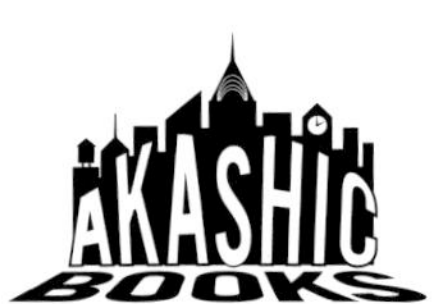

Akashic Books
PO Box 1456
New York, NY 10009
info@akashicbooks.com
www.akashicbooks.com

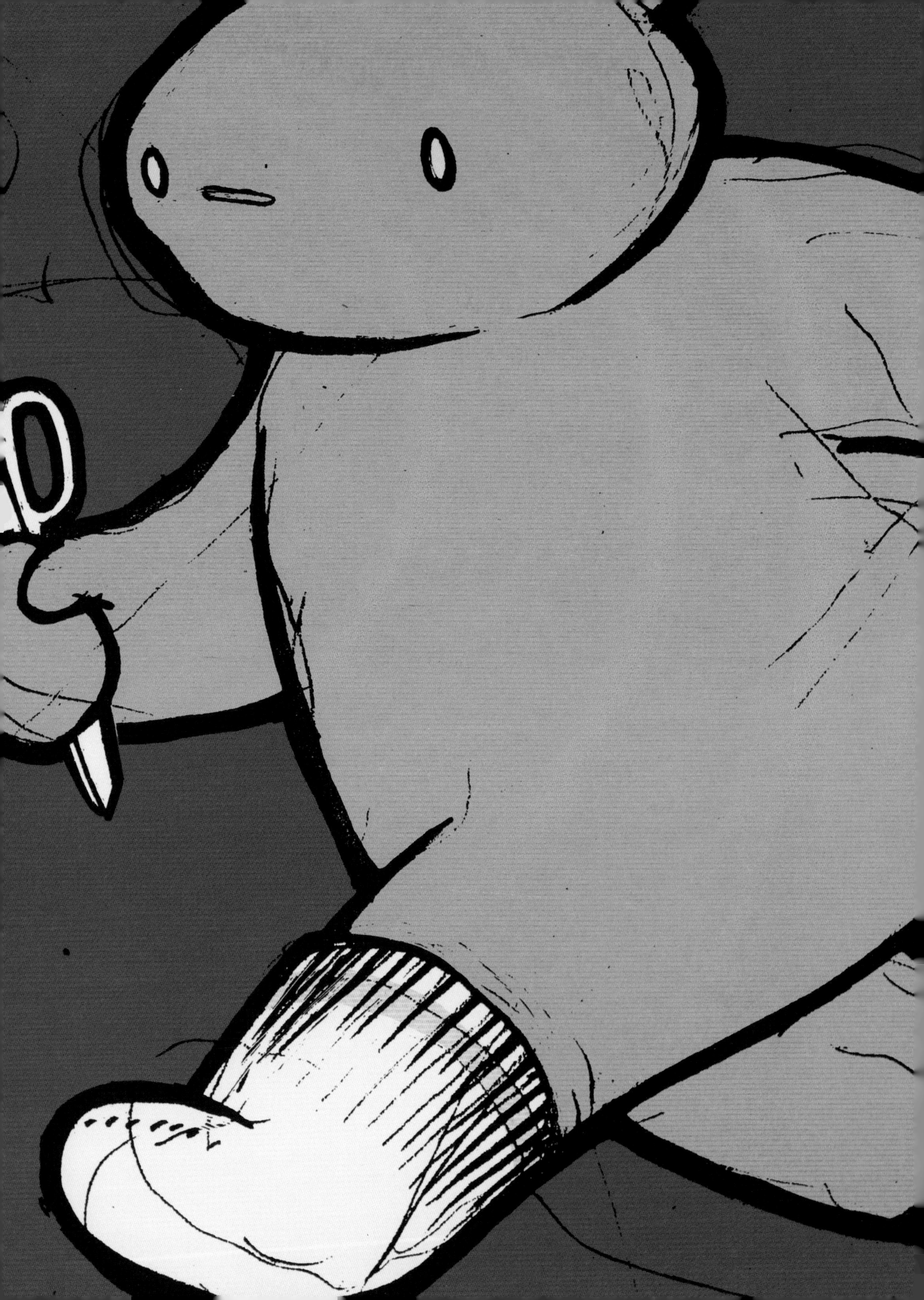

Foreword by Andrew Bird

I met Jay back in 1996 when he was working at Steve Walter's Screwball Press in Chicago, then on Western Avenue. The print shop was a busy collective of young illustrators and designers who hand-pulled screenprints for their friends' indie bands and all of the best Chicago venues. I was pretty knocked out by the work I saw there. Each painstakingly hand-printed piece reached beyond the band's music. The posters marked a moment in time—functional art to be washed off a telephone pole—and asked people to leave their homes and gather in a dark room to drink and sweat and breathe in each other's vapors. They were invitations to commit unwitting acts of intimacy among strangers.

I was twenty-three then and a little insecure about where I fit in to the Chicago music scene. I was fresh out of music school and into early-twentieth-century jazz and cabaret and British folk, and therefore convinced that everyone would hate my music, and me, because I could play and liked fancy music. Anyway, Jay was alarmingly friendly. We met when I was in the Screwball space, getting CD covers letterpressed at Fireproof Press. He showed me what he was working on, and then he reached up and grabbed a CD off the shelf and asked, "Have you ever heard of these guys?" It was the Handsome Family's *Through the Trees*. He played me a song called "The Giant of Illinois"—a heartbreaking true-story song about an oversized boy who "died from a blister on his toe." Brett Sparks sings Rennie Sparks' words: "Delirious with pain his bedroom walls began to glow / and he felt himself soaring up through falling snow / and the sky was a woman's arms."

Rennie takes the story past what happened to what the boy might have felt. Are the woman's arms the promise of someone he'll never know in his mortal life? I don't know what it means, exactly, but the words cut right through and make me exhale in a half laugh, half heart-panging sigh; like a field mouse with tiny boxing gloves has gently pummeled me in the diaphragm so I go "Huh" without the question mark. That's the reaction I have to a lot of Jay's work. There are subtle details in his posters that cause me to cruckle. The question isn't "Why is that bear running intently with scissors?" It's "Why is that bear wearing socks?"

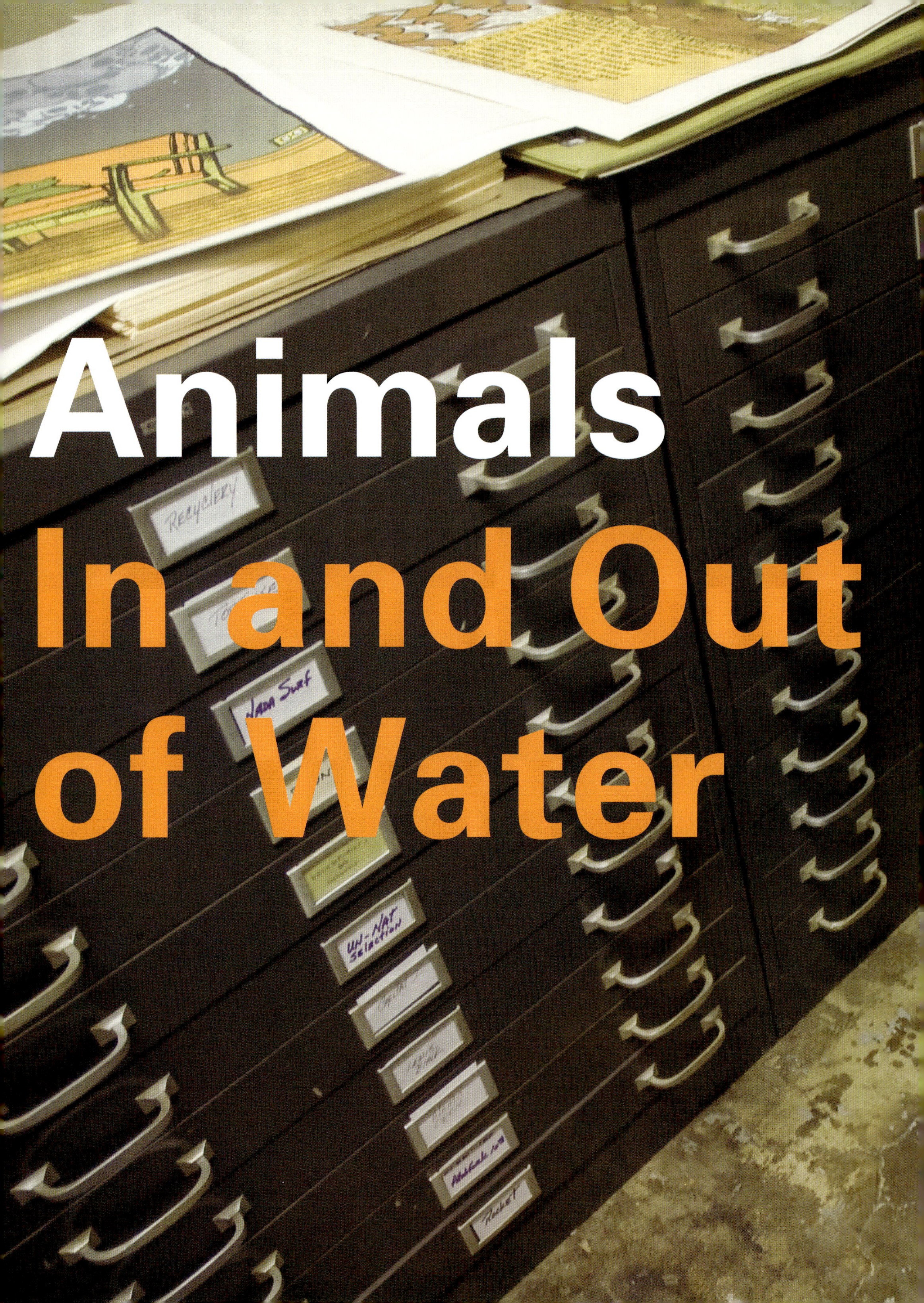

Animals In and Out of Water

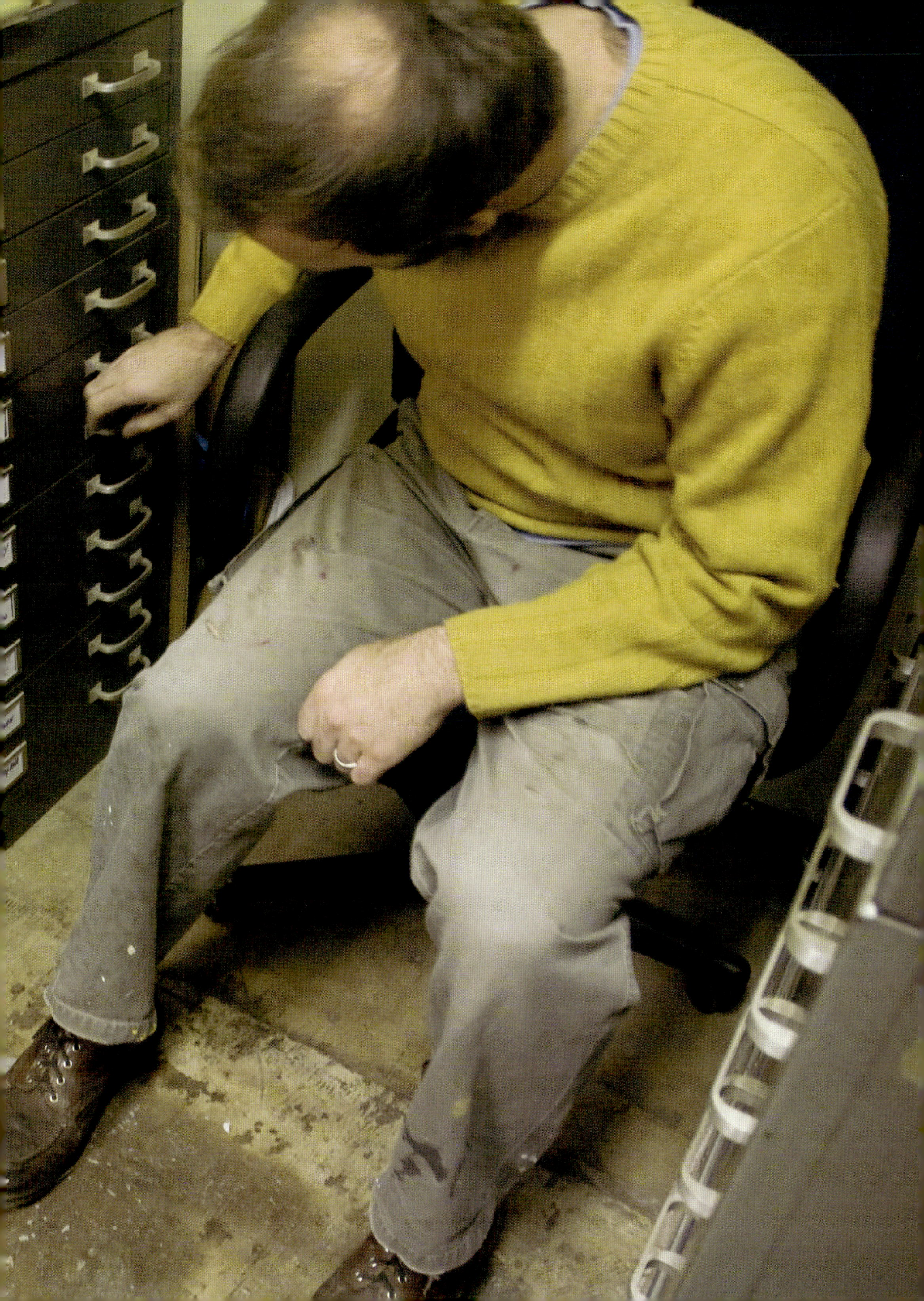

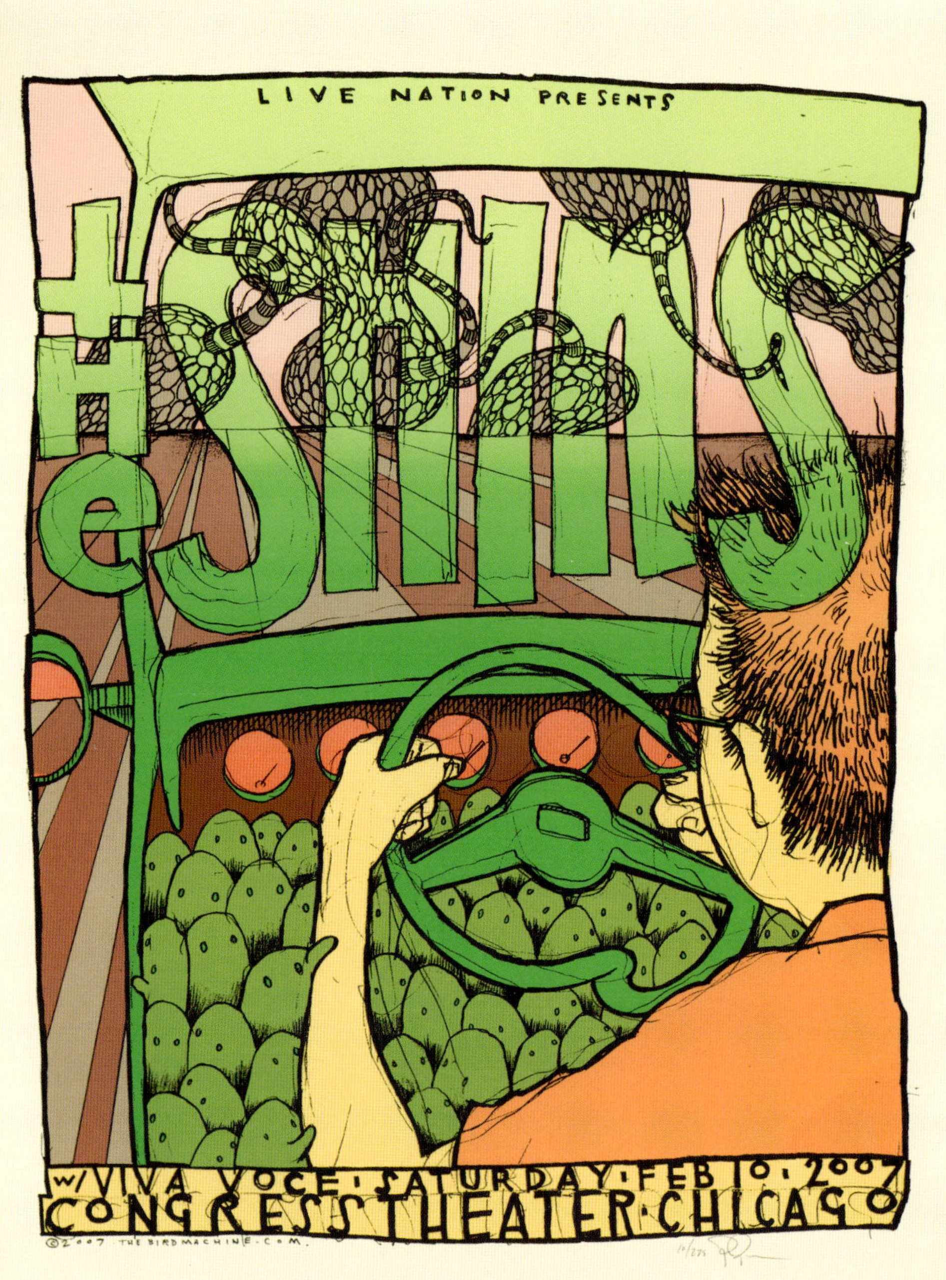

The Shins
2007
18 x 24 inches
5 screens

In the "New Slang" video, the Shins reference the album cover of *Double Nickels on the Dime*, and this print references their reference, while also touching on the organic elements on the cover of *Wincing the Night Away*. The driver needs to sleep.

Chicago Short Film Bridage 2008 Series
2008
13 x 20 inches
6 screens

The Chicago Short Film Brigade is a nonprofit concern which promotes the medium of smaller films, curated and screened in a couple events throughout the year. The Brigade's identity, as well as the first year's posters, were designed by Diana Sudyka. For this print, in the festival's second year, the organizers requested some continuity with the five characters which had appeared in Diana's work.

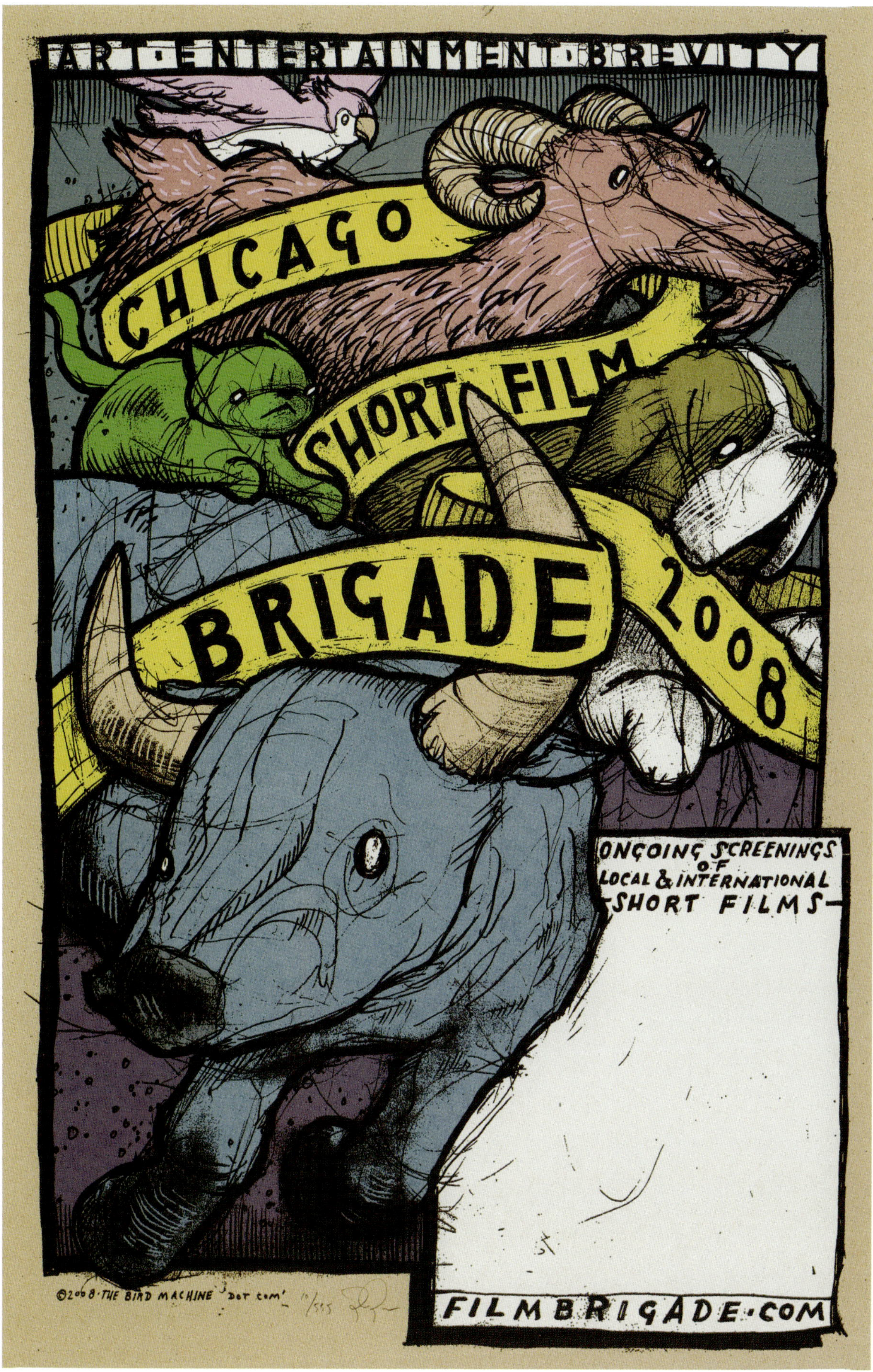

ART • ENTERTAINMENT • BREVITY
CHICAGO
SHORT FILM
BRIGADE
2008
ONGOING SCREENINGS OF LOCAL & INTERNATIONAL -SHORT FILMS-
©2008 · THE BIRD MACHINE 'DOT COM'
FILMBRIGADE·COM

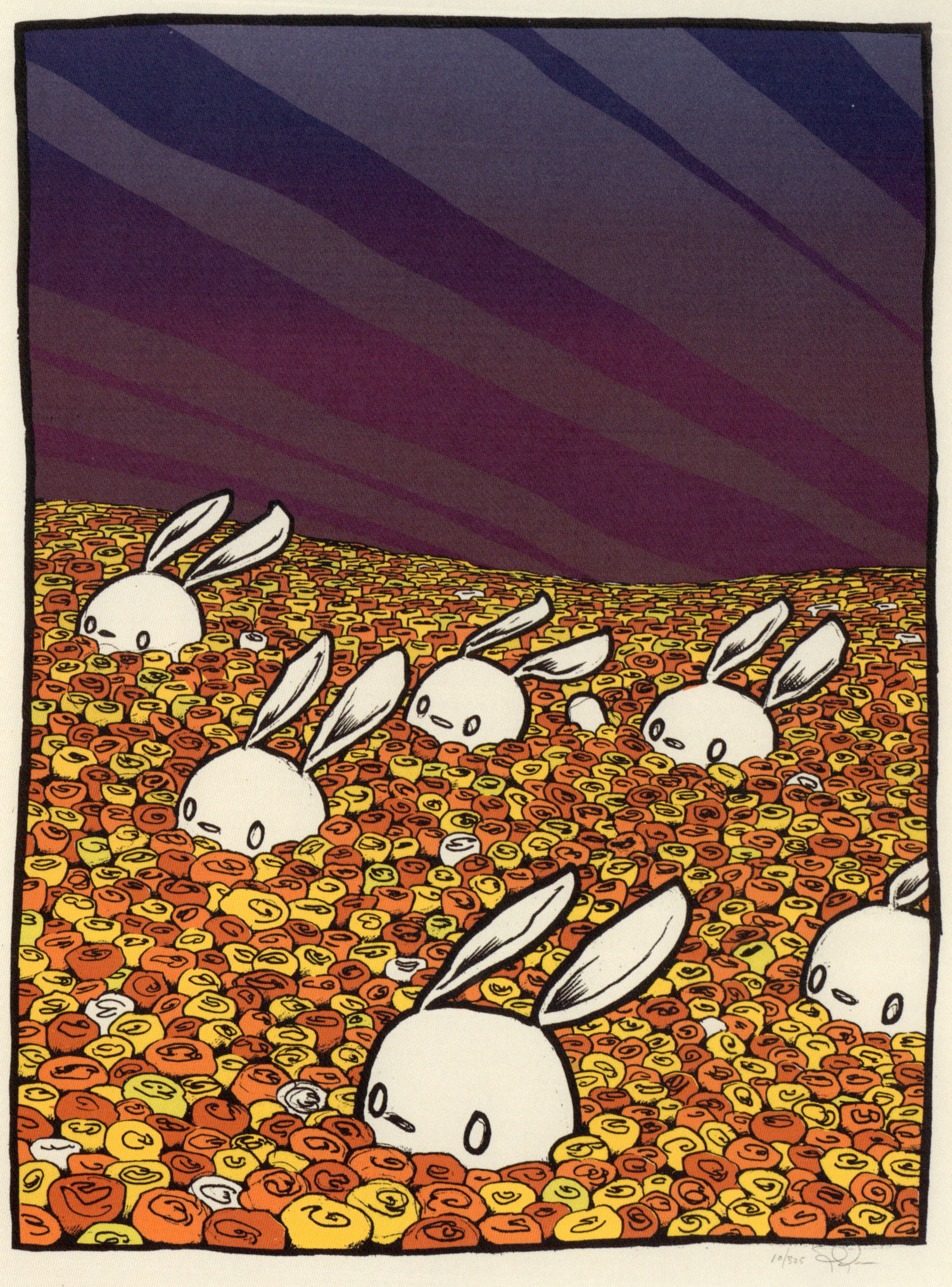

Rabbits in Flowers
2006
18 x 24 inches
8 screens

These rabbits keep coming back to bed down in this field of flowers.

Death Cab for Cutie
2006
18 x 24 inches
6 screens

Cats are usually the first ones to know when things are going wrong.

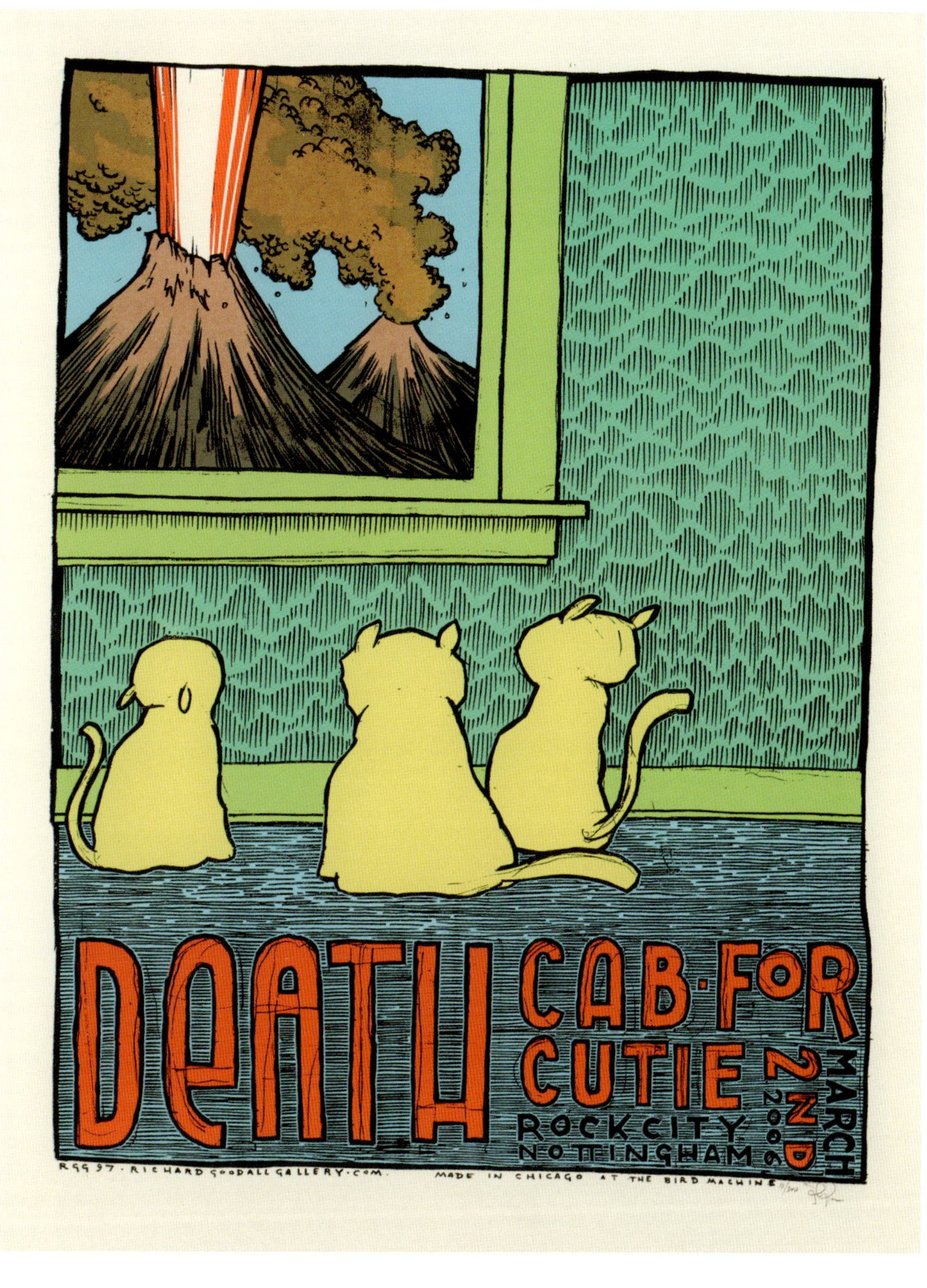

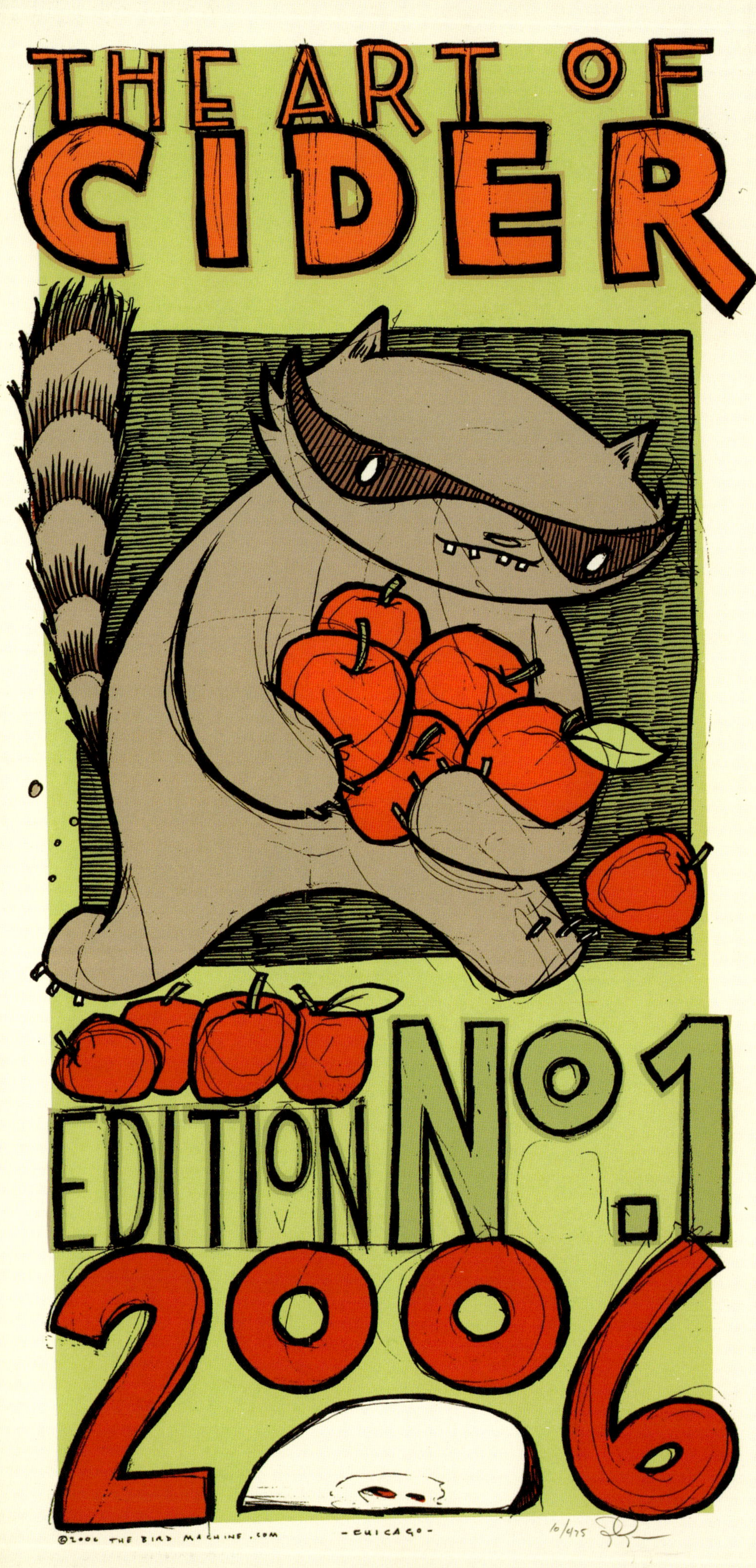

The Art of Cider

2006

12 x 24 inches

4 screens

There is a small cider press called "most of apples" in Hamburg, Germany, which makes wonderful alcoholic drinks using only the purest apples and the sharpest wit. Bernd and Christiane, whose company name is a play on the ingredients of their ciders, as well as the German word for fermenting apple juice, consulted me about my particular tastes, which were used as ingredients (vanilla, chilis, lavender) in this batch of cider. I designed the labels, and printed posters to accompany each bottle. Dieser Kleine Waschbär is obviously up to no good.

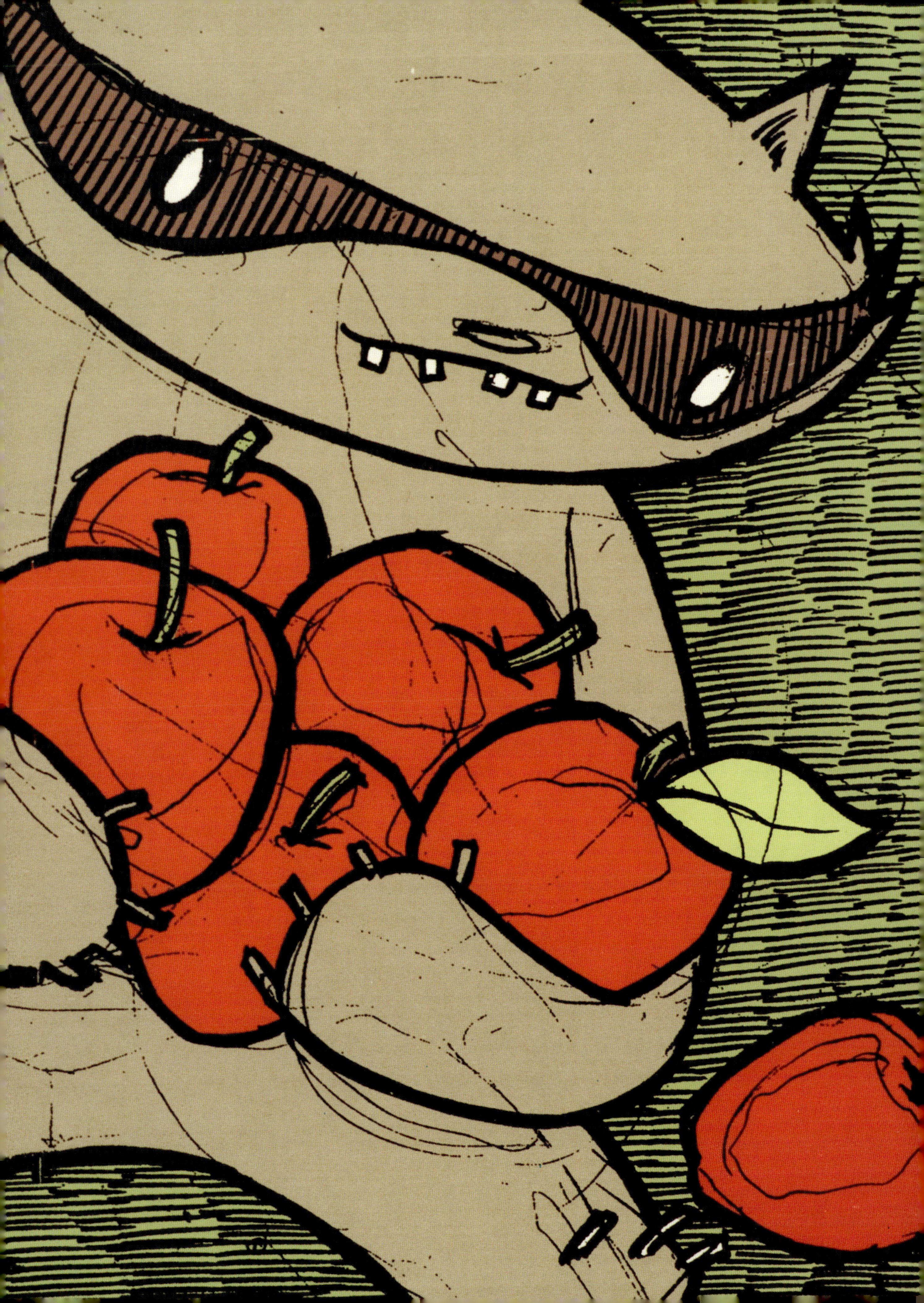

The Recyclery
2008
20 x 26 inches
4 screens

The Recyclery is a nonprofit organization which rebuilds discarded and donated bikes in Evanston, Illinois. They asked that their poster embody the concept of multigenerational community and teaching, and they took no issue with my inclusion of a chimp on a touring bike.

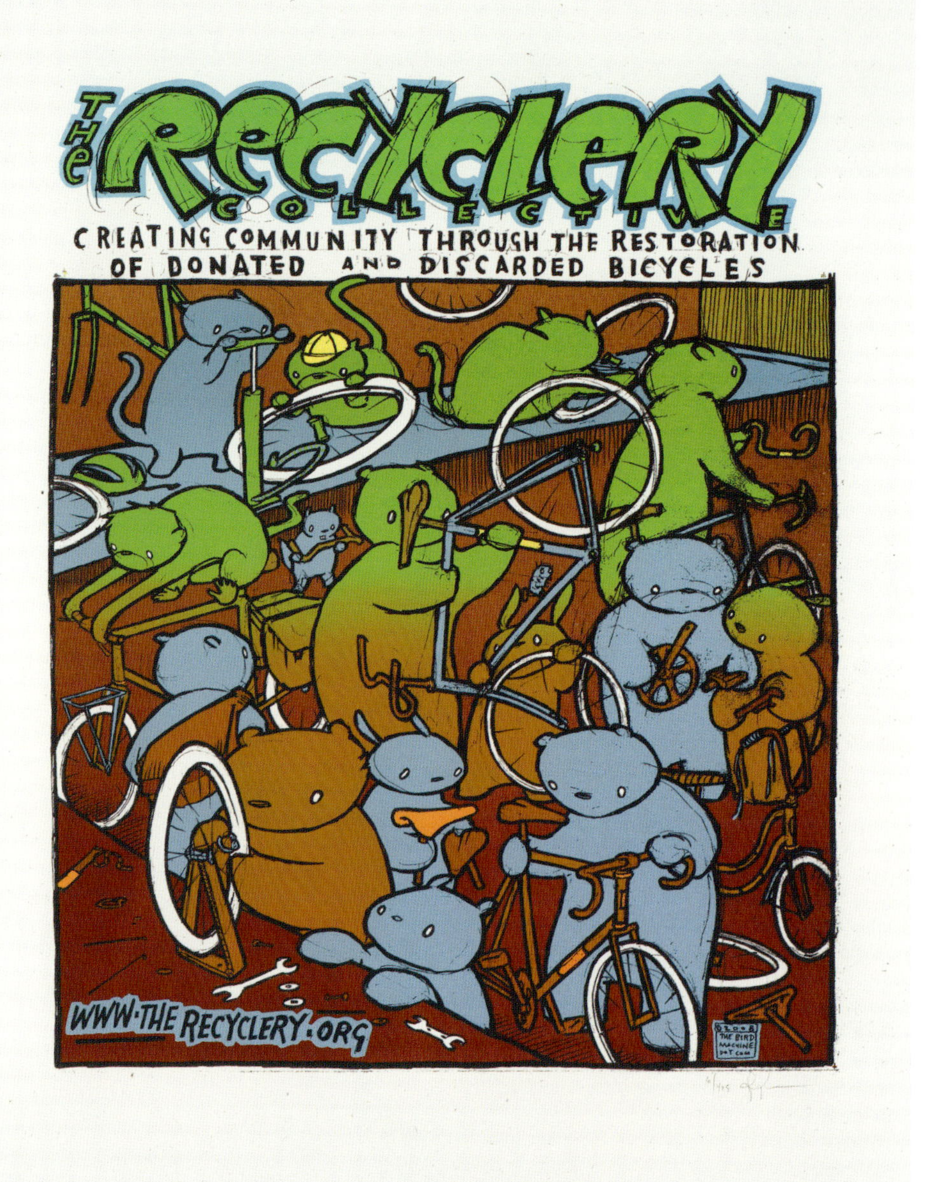

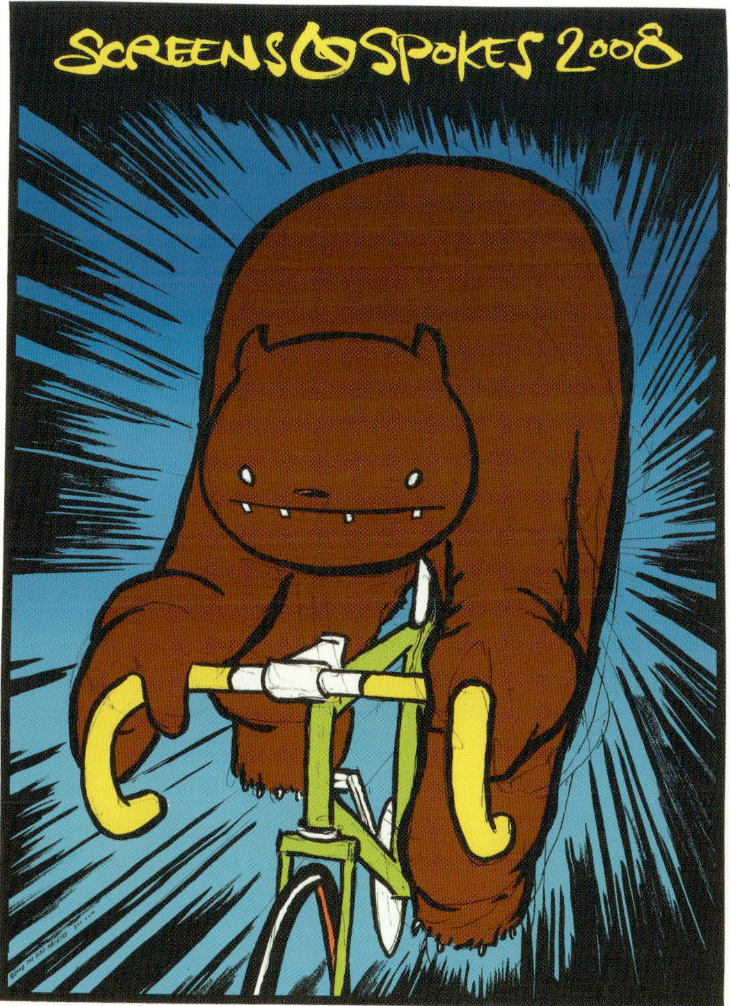

Screens & Spokes 2008

2008

25 5/8 x 33 3/8 inches

4 screens

A different kind of bear attack.

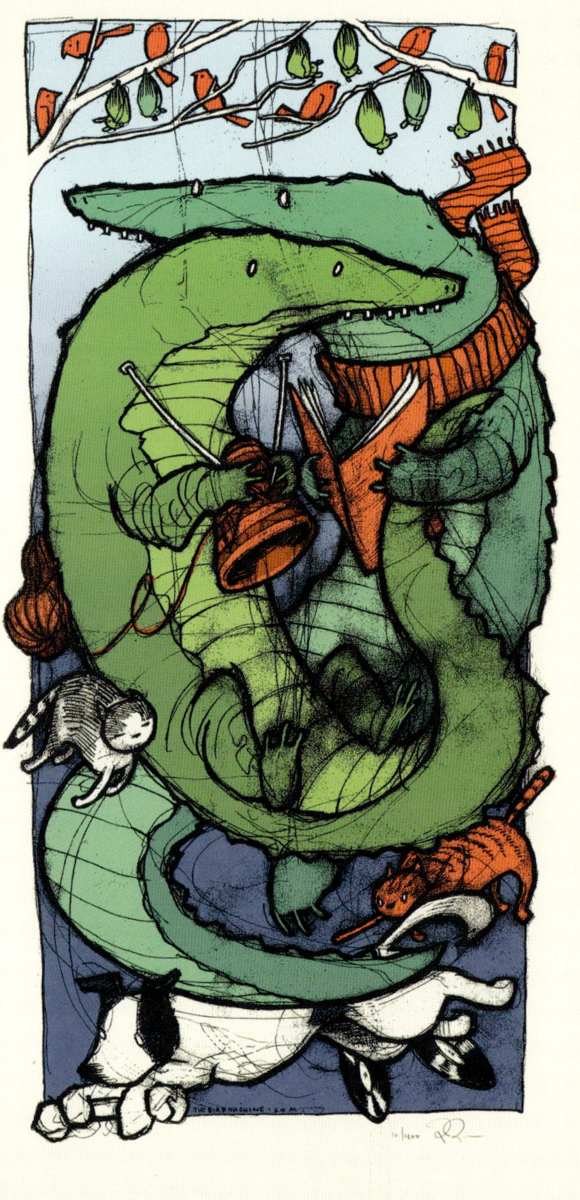

The Alligators
2006
12 x 24 inches
5 screens

The Alligators was an art print made about some friends who got married, and depicts their specific details and interests, as well as the family pets. These may be the cutest bats I have ever drawn.

Jay Ryan Print Demo and Lecture
2007
8.5 x 28.5 inches
3 screens

The student lounge at Minot State University in Minot, North Dakota ("why not Minot?") is called the Beaver Dam, which is where my print demonstration was held during a visit to the university. This little guy is at home, enjoying a pleasant evening alone with his bass guitar.

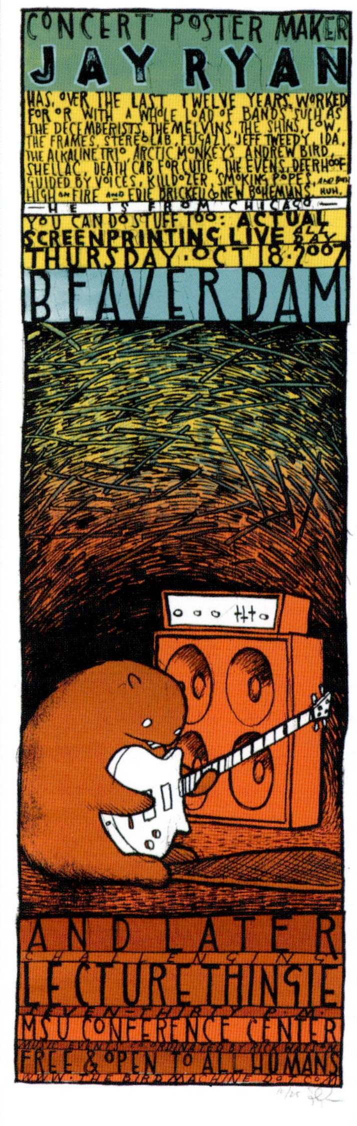

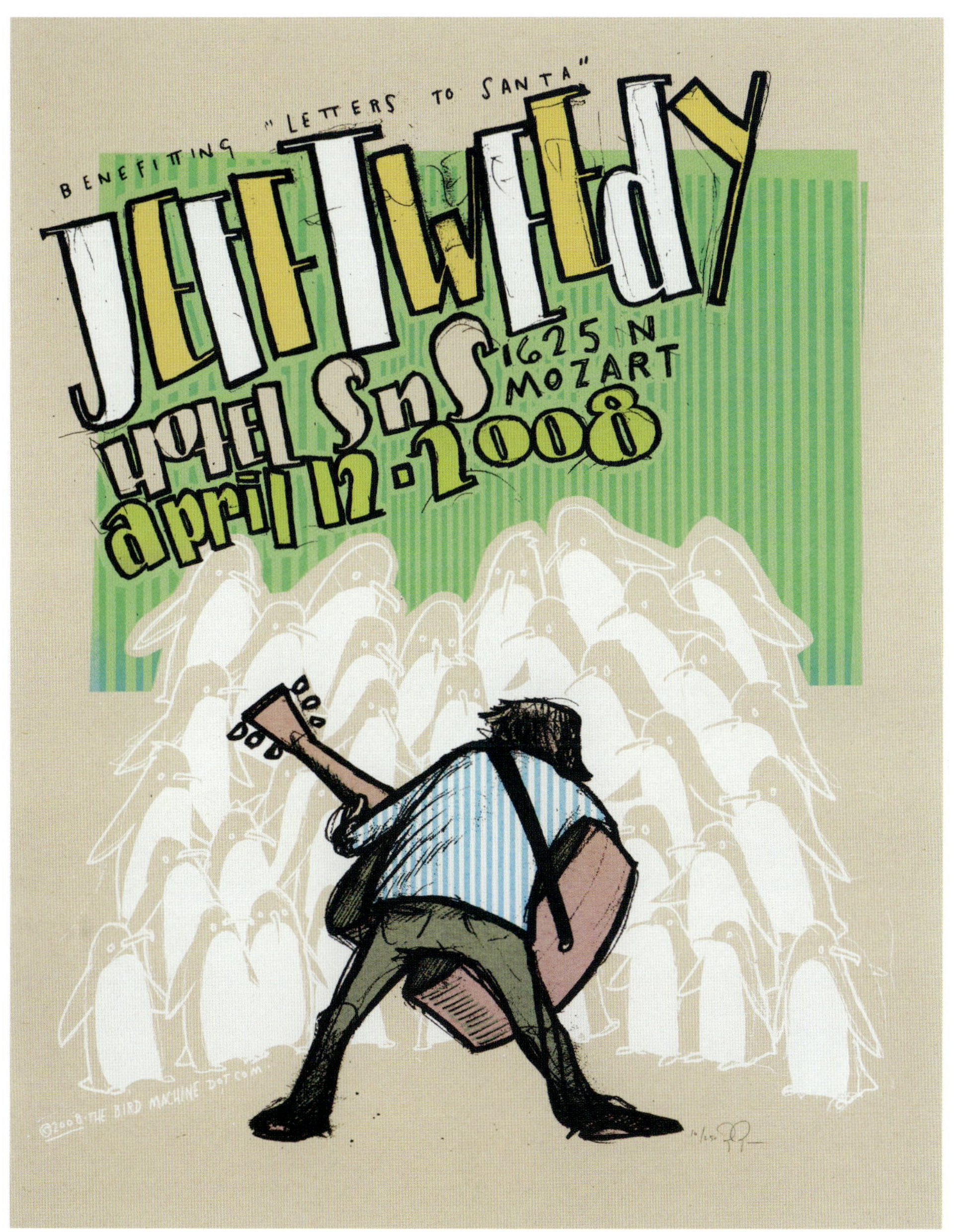

Jeff Tweedy
2008
20 x 26 inches
5 screens

The best way to make penguins pay attention to Jeff Tweedy's solo performances is to give him a larger guitar.

Lewis Black

2007

18 x 24 inches

3 screens

Lewis Black is said to have liked this print, but he became exasperated and yelled at me anyway.

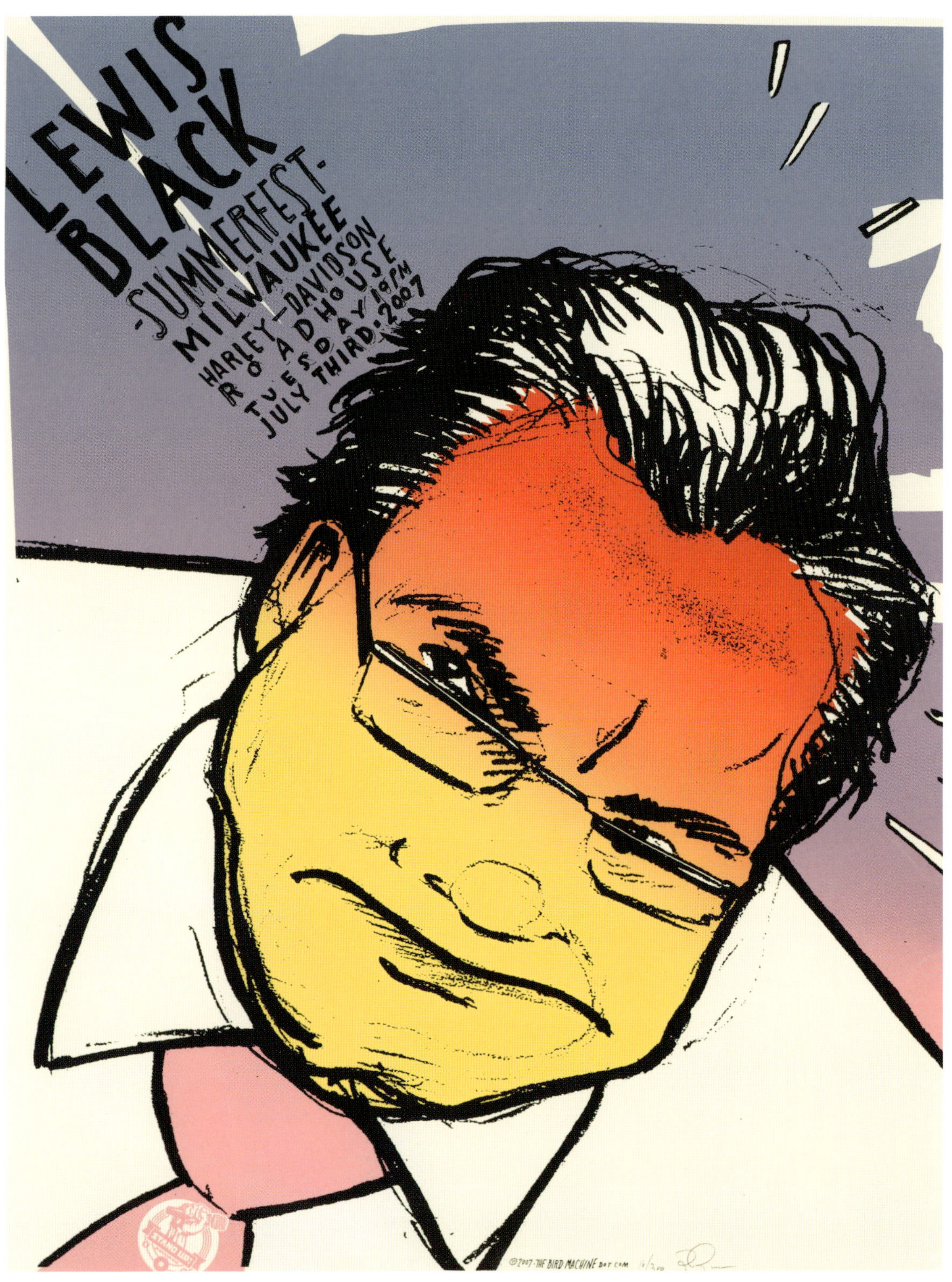

Mudhoney

2008

20 x 26 inches

5 screens

Mudhoney is one of the bands which my friends and I were into at the beginning of college, just before "Seattle" became an adjective to describe the kind of music which these guys pioneered. Twenty years after the release of *Superfuzz Bigmuff,* this print was loosely based on the song "Mudride," with a trip for two on a one-way ride.

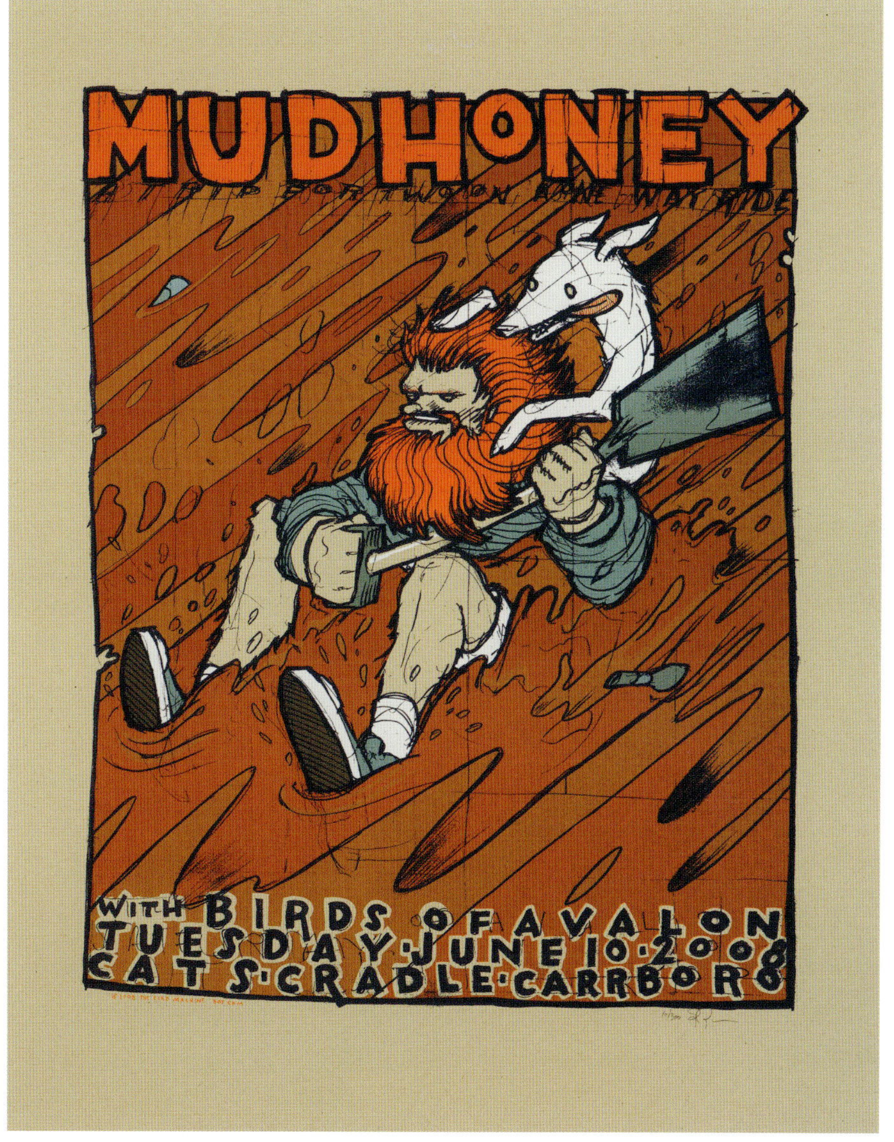

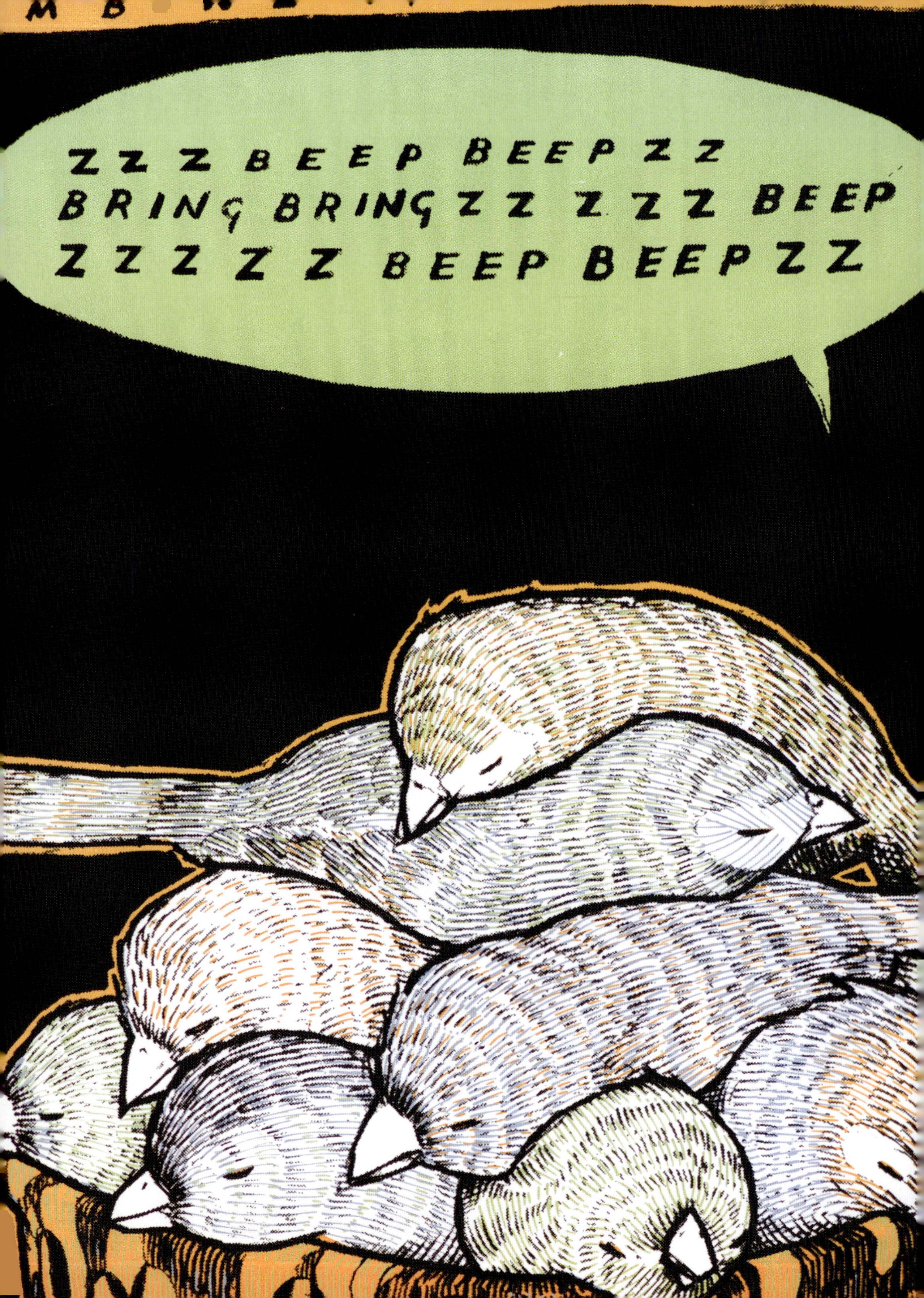
ZZZ BEEP BEEP ZZ BRING BRING ZZ ZZZ BEEP ZZZZZ BEEP BEEP ZZ

Warm Bowl of Sleeping Birds
2008
8.25 x 18 inches
5 screens

I took Seth the dog to the pet store to buy cat litter (for the cats) late one night. At the pet store, he stopped (as he often does) to look at the birds. Off to one side, a cage of finches had all bedded down for the night in their feeding bowl, like some floral arrangement, with their heads all facing outward. A few weeks later, I drew this while in Germany, which somehow influenced the electronic noises I have added to this otherwise reality-based image.

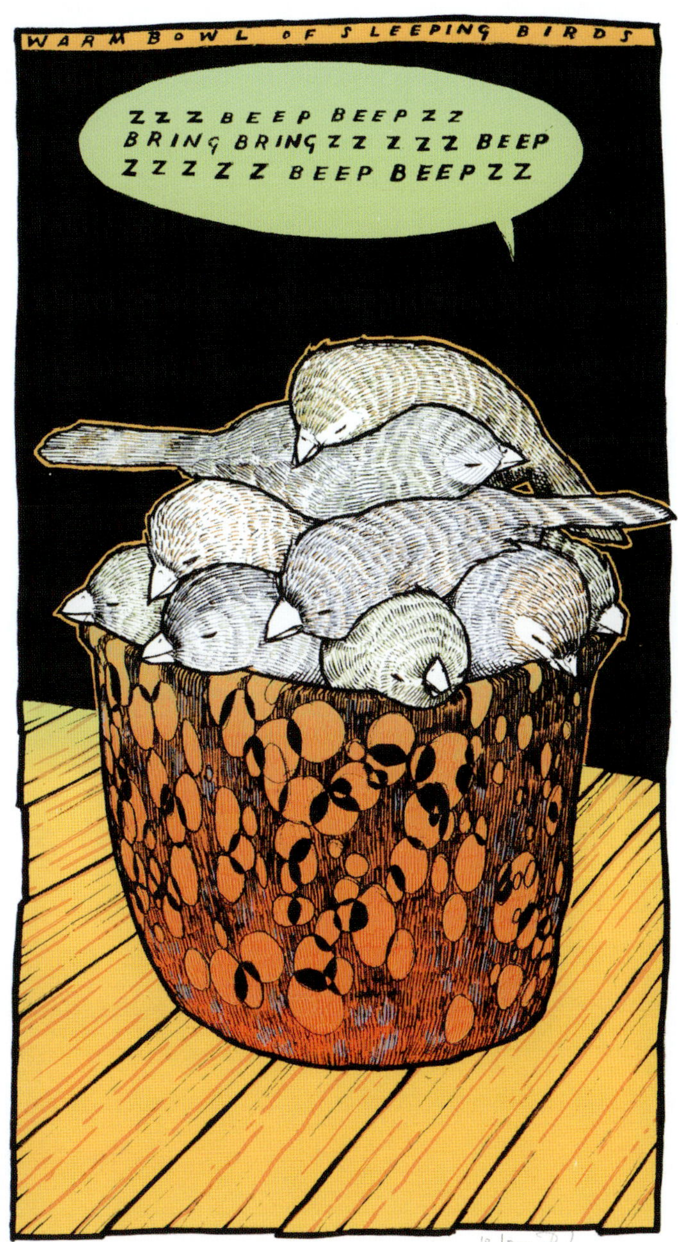

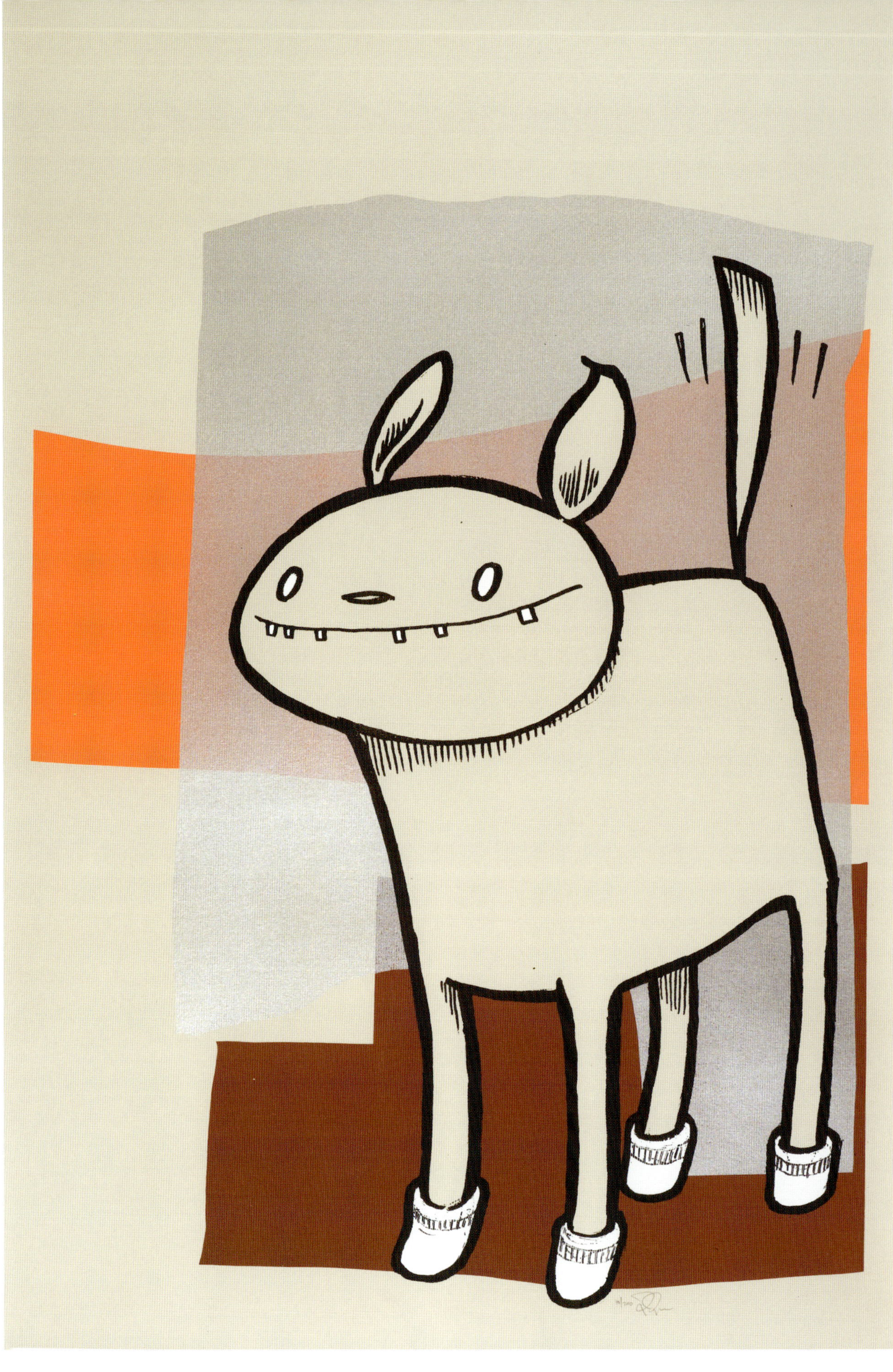

Dog in Socks

2006
23 x 35 inches
5 screens

This good dog is very proud of his nice clean socks, as you can see.

A Bear and His Dog

2006
18 x 24 inches
3 screens

These two buddies were originally made as part of a print demo at a university, but they turned out to be well-behaved, so we soon made a normal run of this print back at the shop.

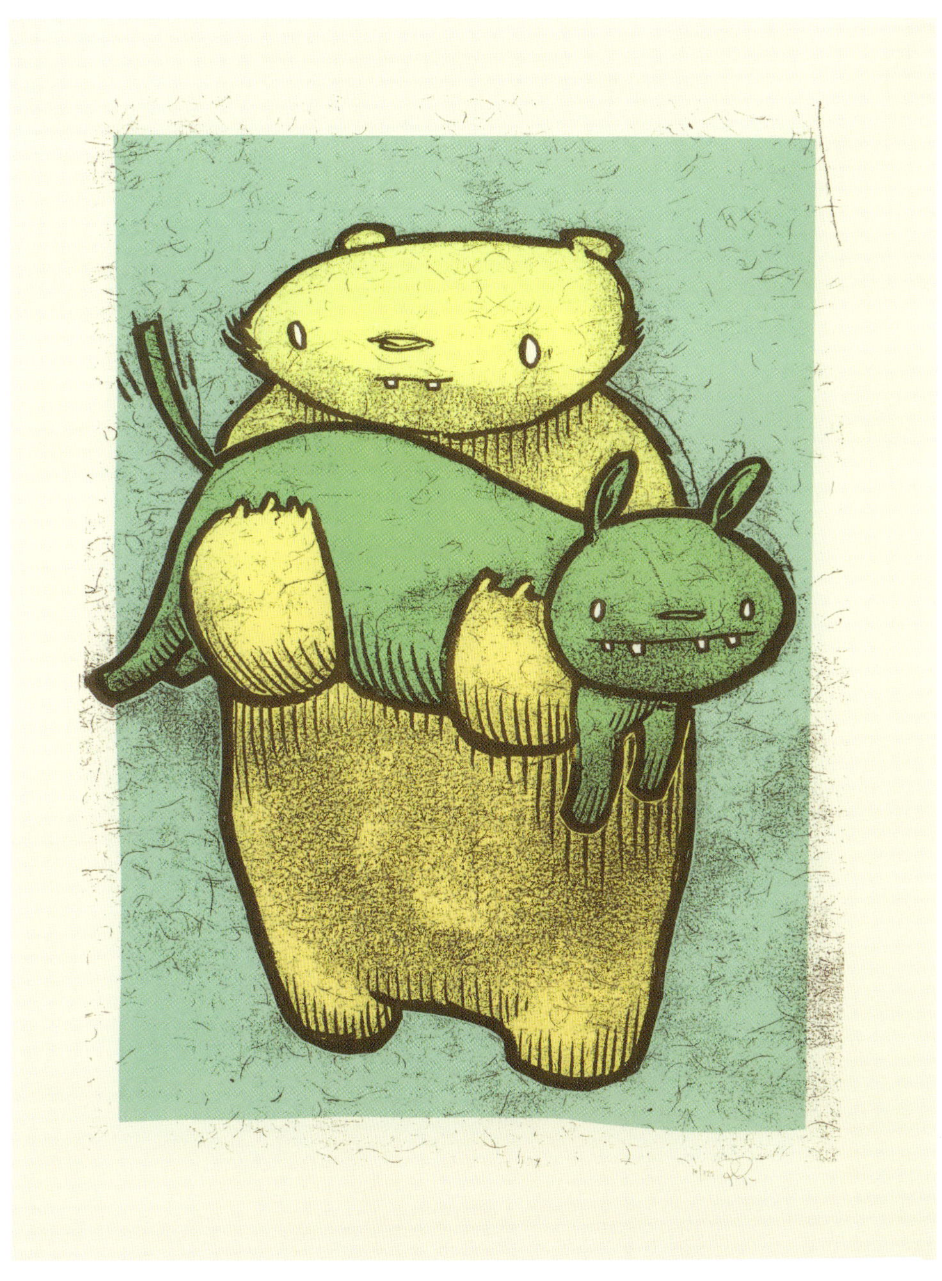

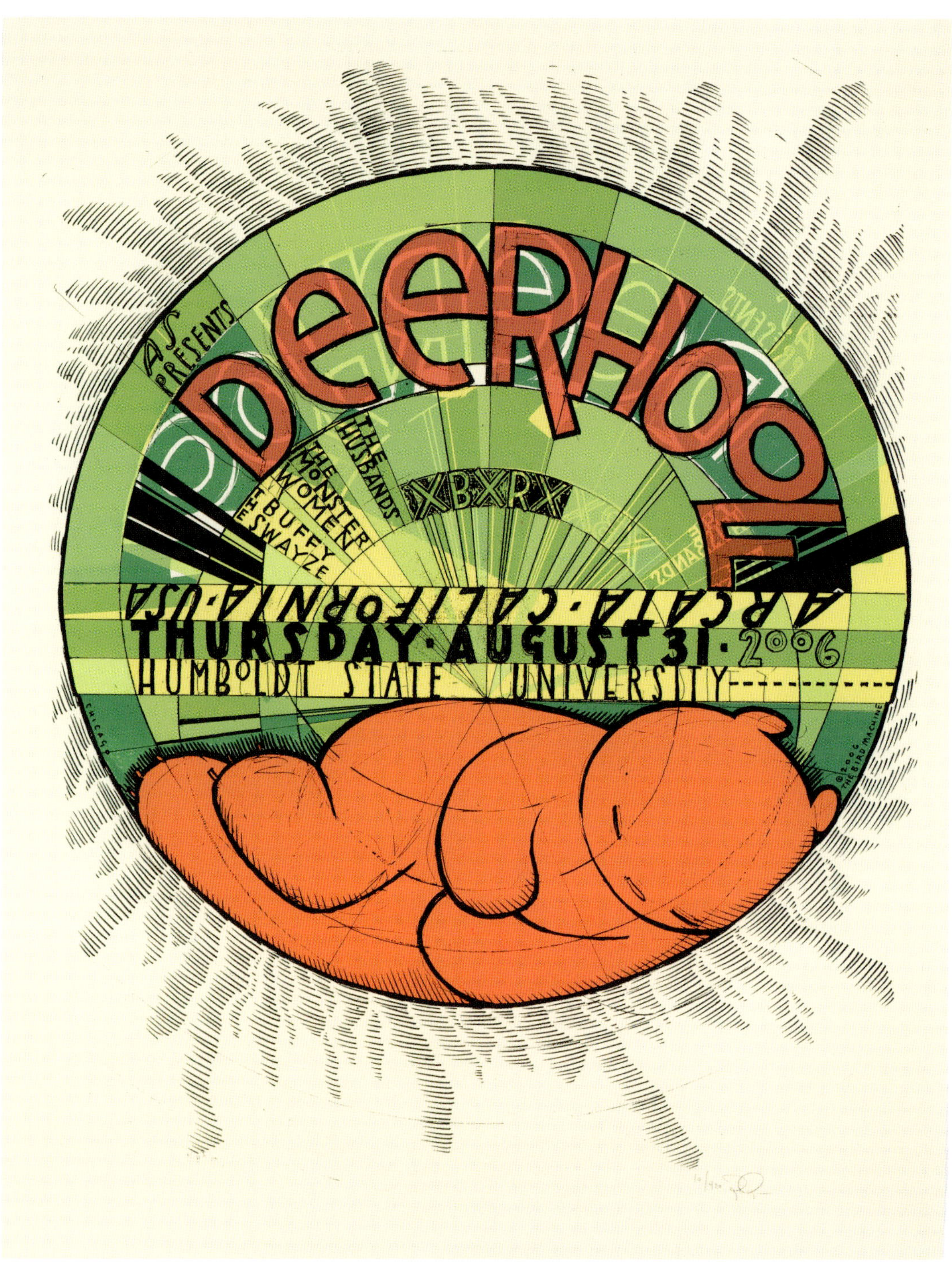
AS PRESENTS
DEERHOOF
THE HUSBANDS
THE MONSTER WOMEN
BUFFY THE SWAYZE
XBXRX
ARCATA · CALIFORNIA · USA
THURSDAY · AUGUST 31 · 2006
HUMBOLDT STATE UNIVERSITY

Deerhoof

2006

18 x 24 inches

5 screens

This sleepy bear doesn't come from a Deerhoof song, but he should.

Flatstock 13

2007

18 x 24 inches

4 screens

Functional posters are usually a reflection of the time when they are made, and Flatstock posters are usually a reflection of stupid Internet jokes. This print from 2007 would have been a headscratcher in 2005, and seems old now.

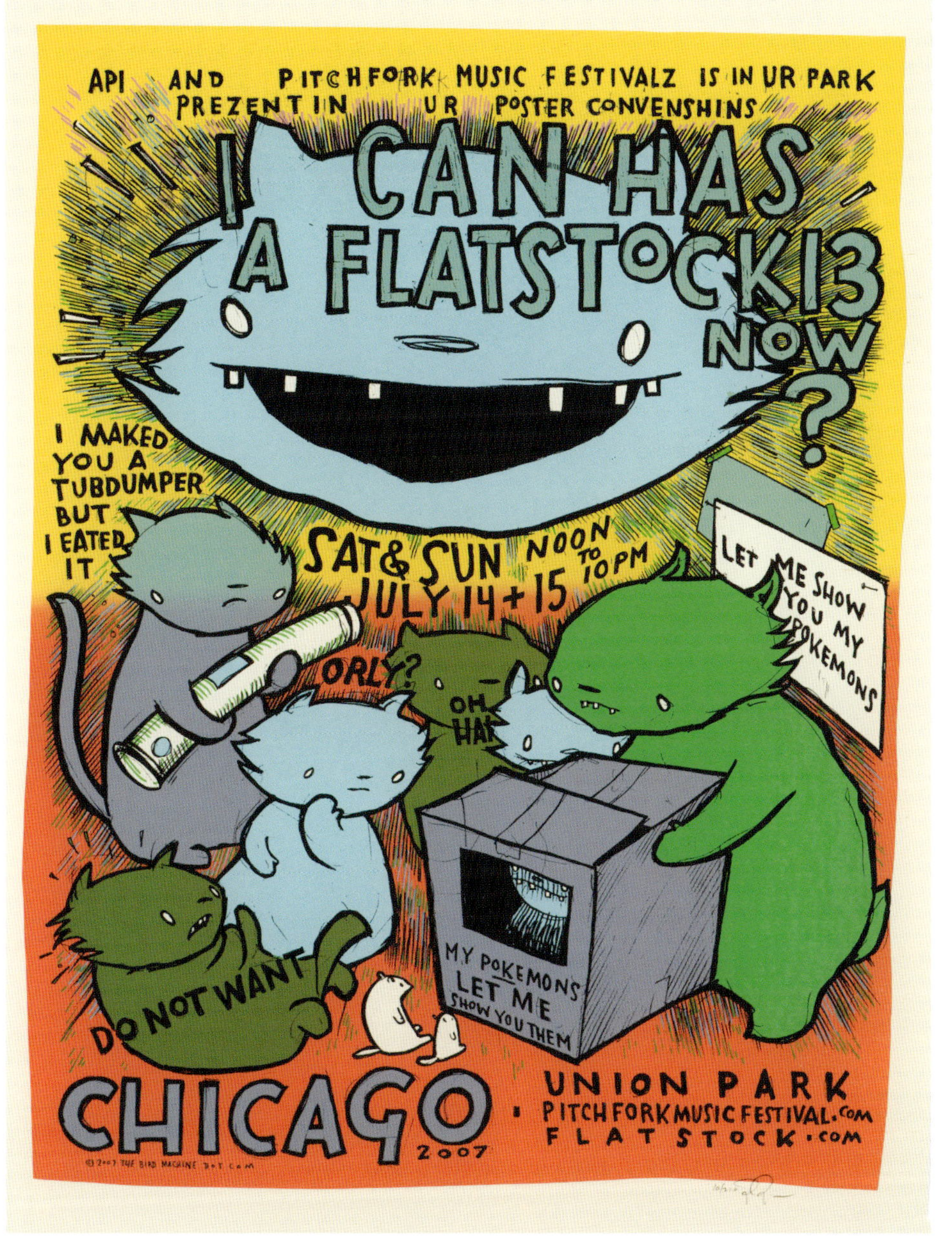

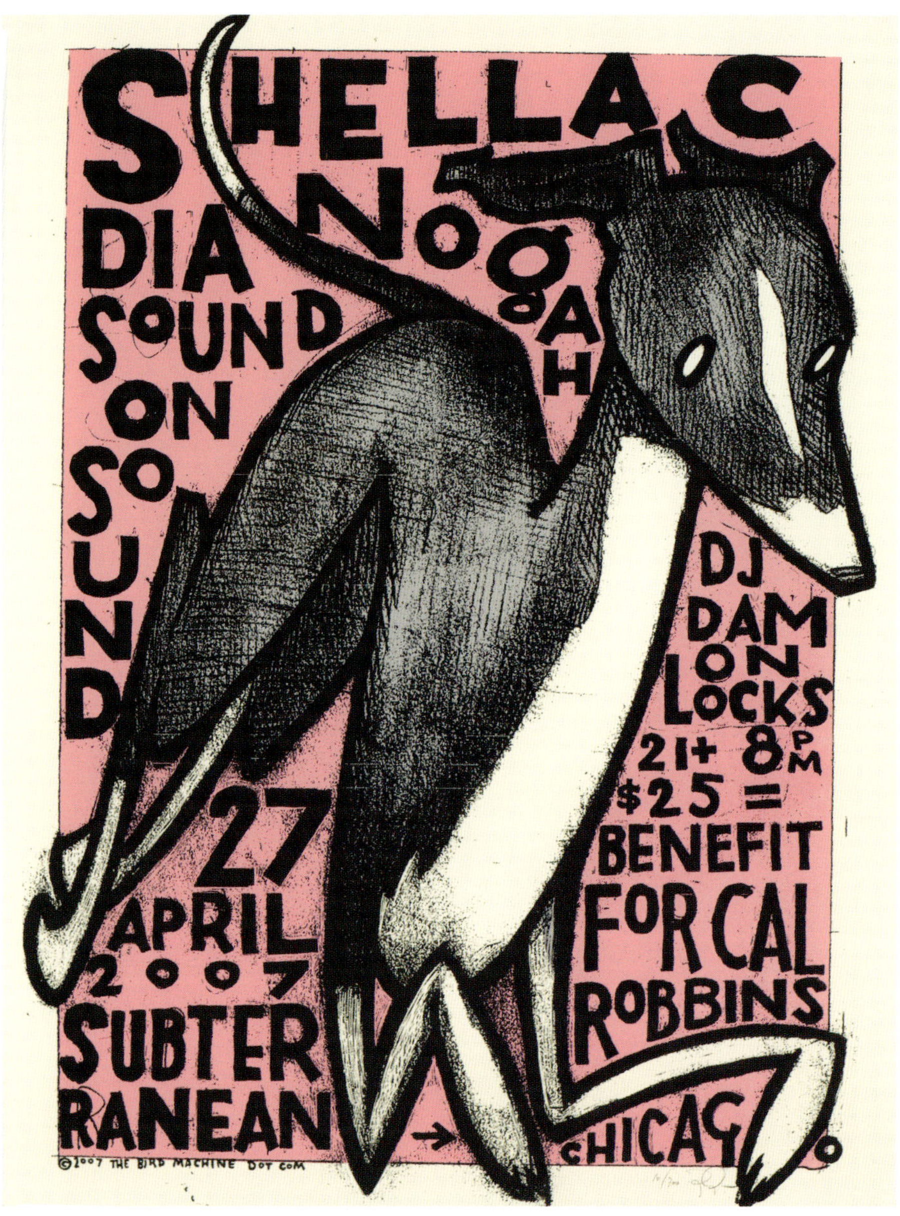

Shellac, with Dianogah

2007

18 x 24 inches

3 screens

Shellac released their album *Excellent Italian Greyhound* in spring 2007, and asked me to draw part of the sleeve. This dog, Uffizi, lives with Todd, Shellac's drummer. The show was a benefit concert for Cal Robbins, a little guy in Baltimore who was born with Spinal Muscular Atrophy.

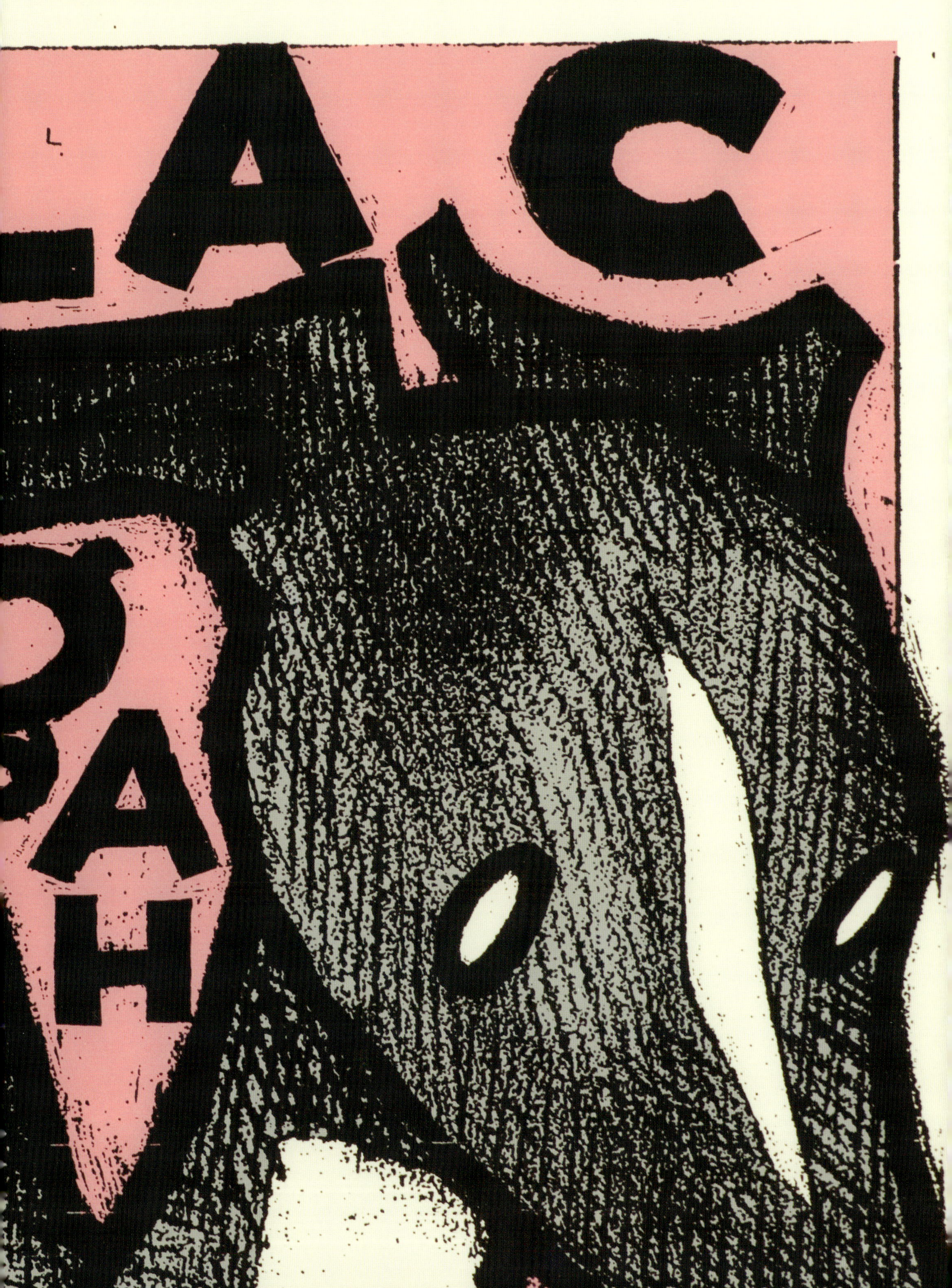

Pitchfork Music Festival 2008
2008
20 x 26 inches
4 screens

Please note that on a whim, I put the band Boris on an arrow which is pointing both inward and outward, while the rest of the bands are named on arrows which only point inward. I was amazed by the number of e-mails I received wondering what I was trying to say about the band, and why I would choose to single Boris out so oddly. This reaction makes me wonder what other nonsensical details I have included during my career, and how many people I have accidentally upset.

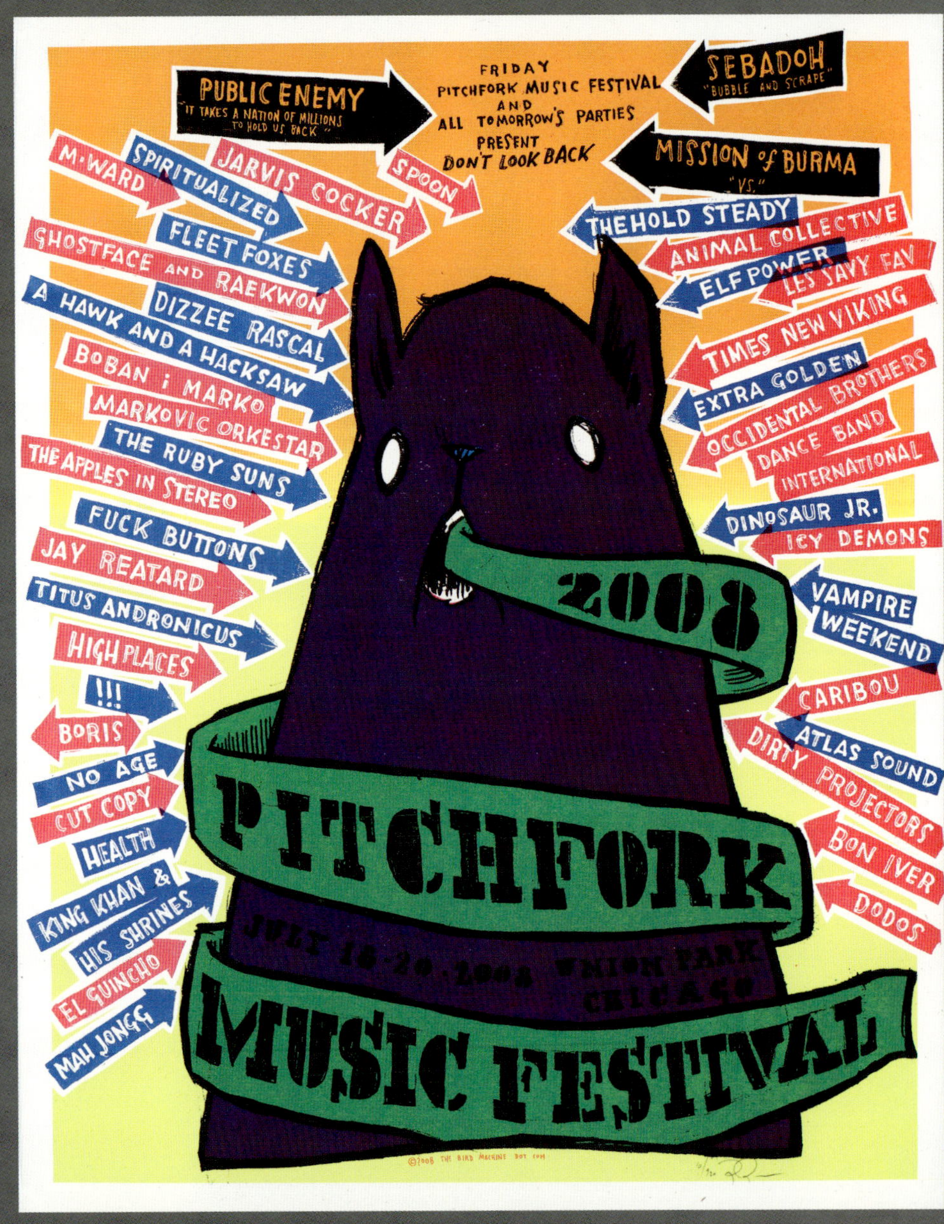

Sound Opinions Radio Show
2007
20 x 26 inches
5 screens

Sound Opinions, which claims to be "the world's only rock-and-roll talk show," is broadcast weekly on public radio in Chicago. The staff encouraged me to include some combative animals in the print, but there was no specific intent to style either of these bumper-car drivers after either of the show's hosts.

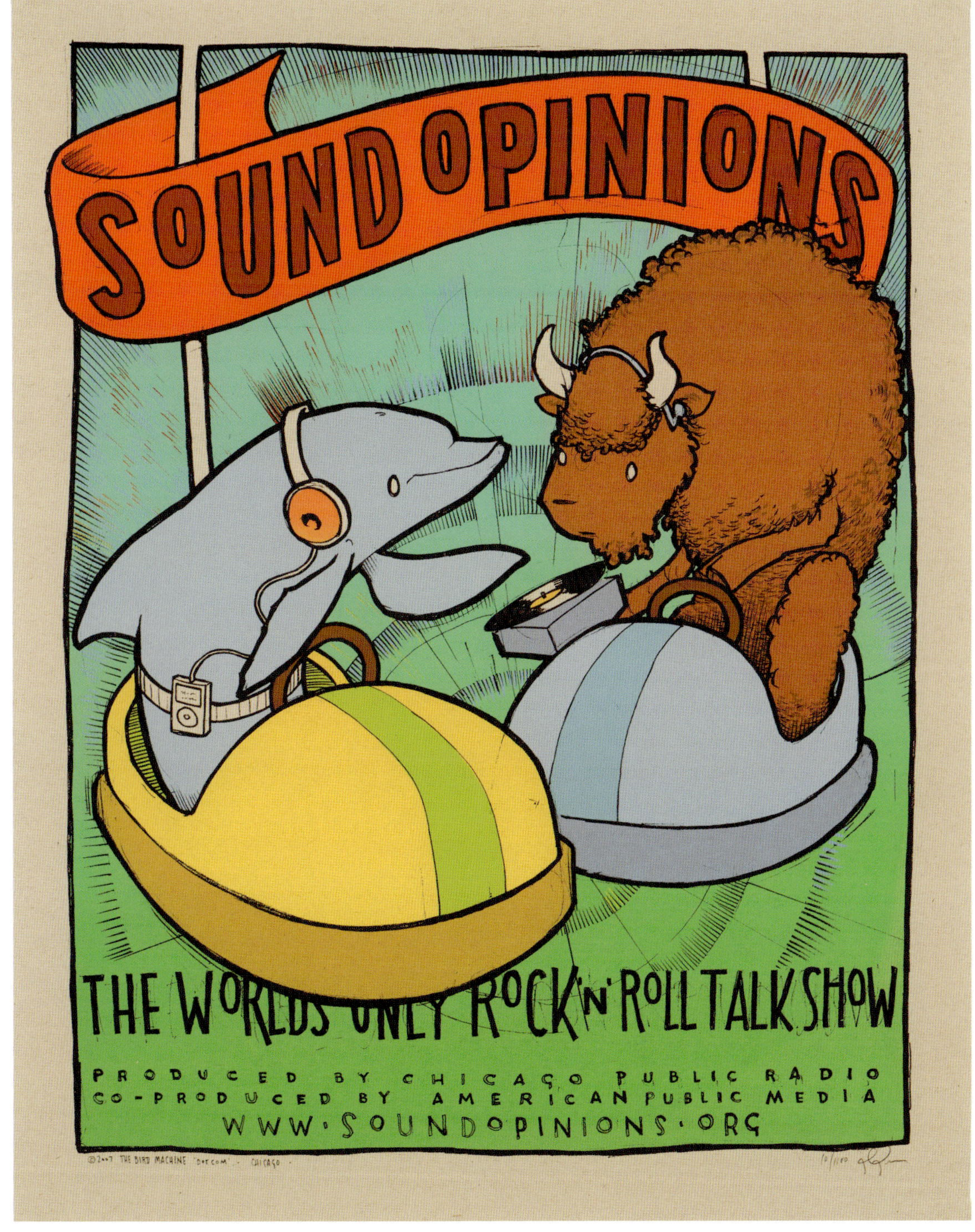

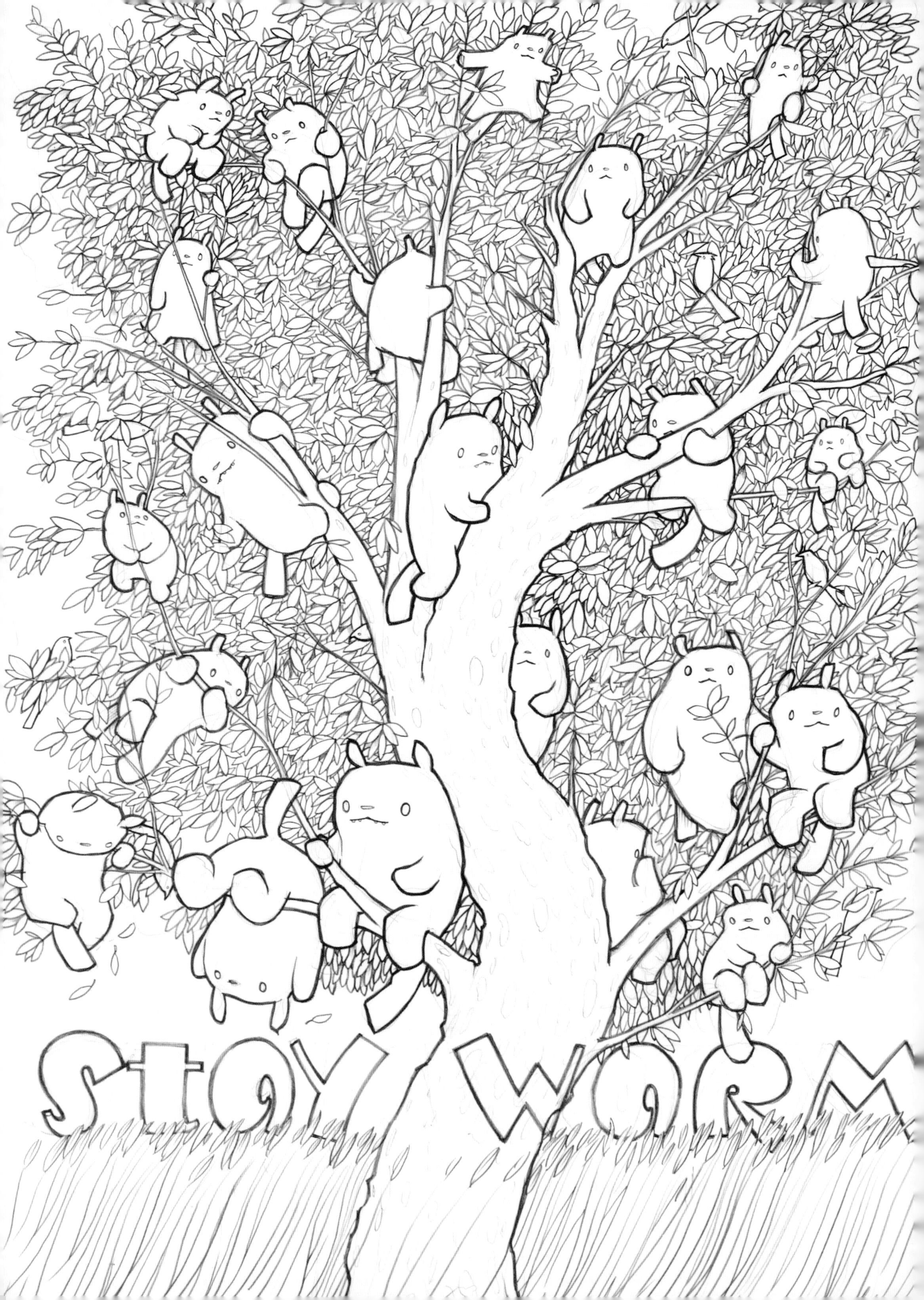
STAY WARM

Intercontinental

2007

20 x 26 inches

6 screens

This tree full of undifferentiated mammals was commissioned to hang in all of the rooms of a new hotel built outside of Chicago.

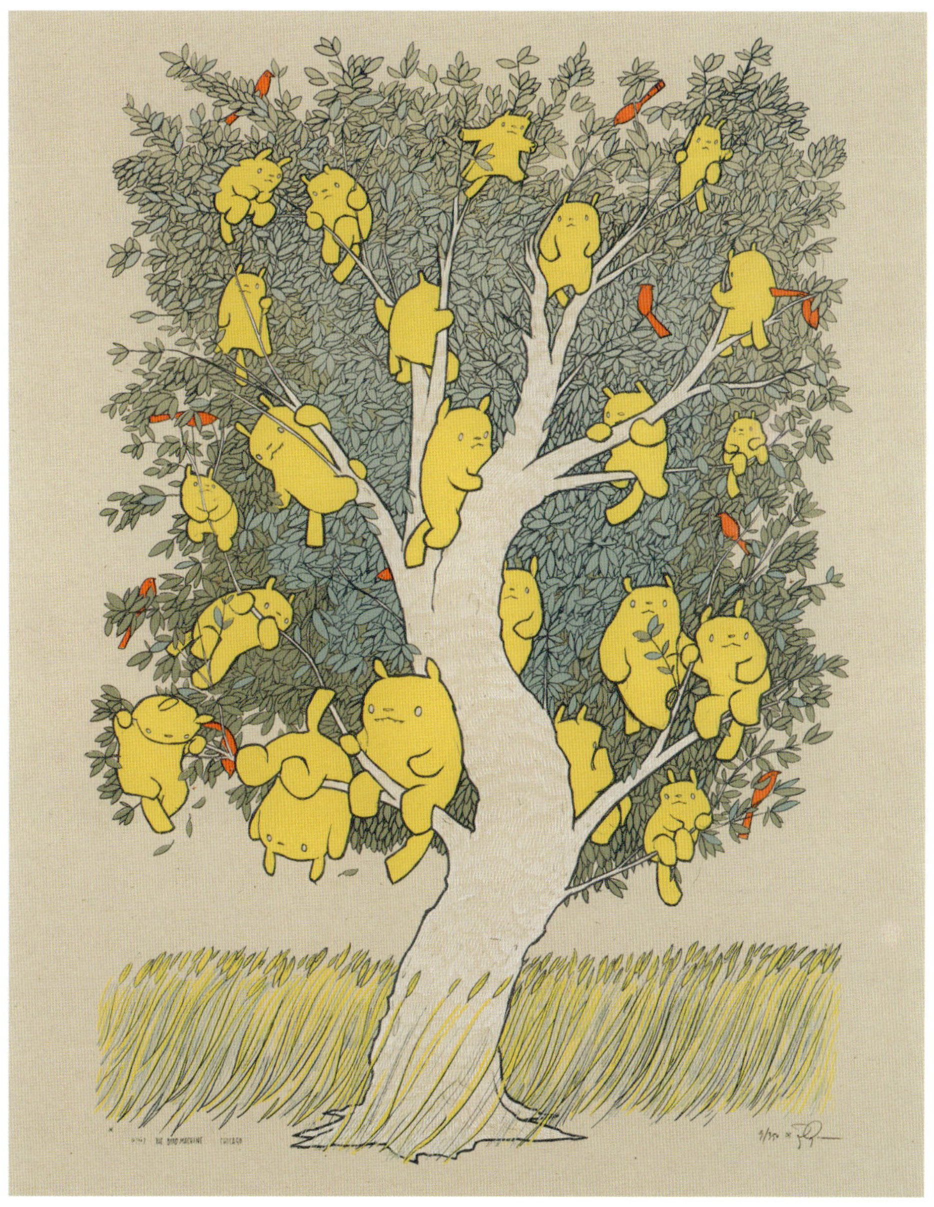

Ice Cream Man

2008

20 x 26 inches

5 screens

Ice Cream Man travels the country giving out free ice cream to people. I think this is one of the few jobs which is more fun than my own.

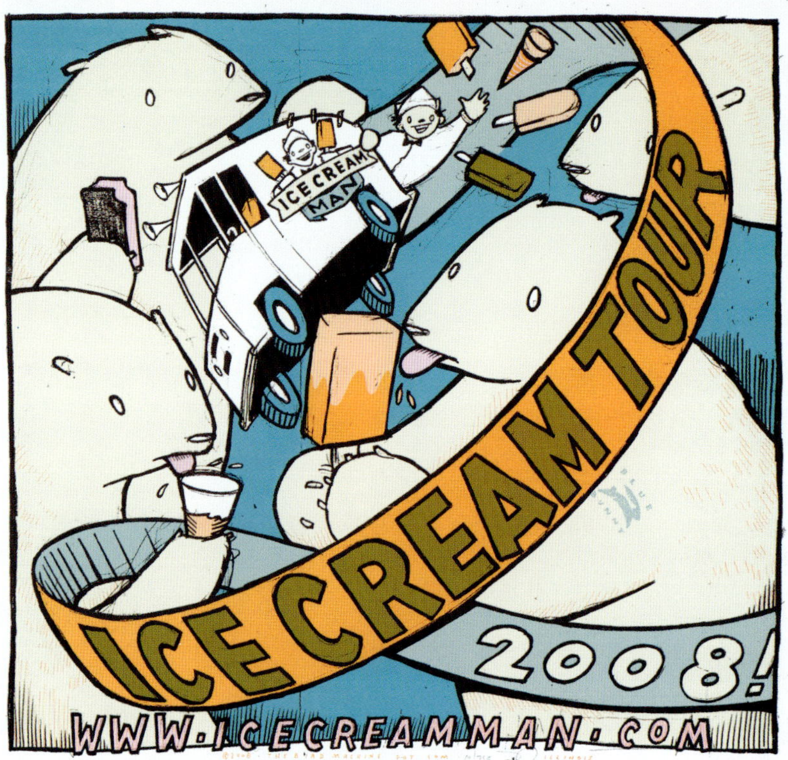

The Melvins (Goat Heads)
2006
18 x 24 inches
5 screens

These are some of the less-menacing demons, depicted using a pretty cool double-key-plate trick involving silver ink printed under the dark brown outlines.

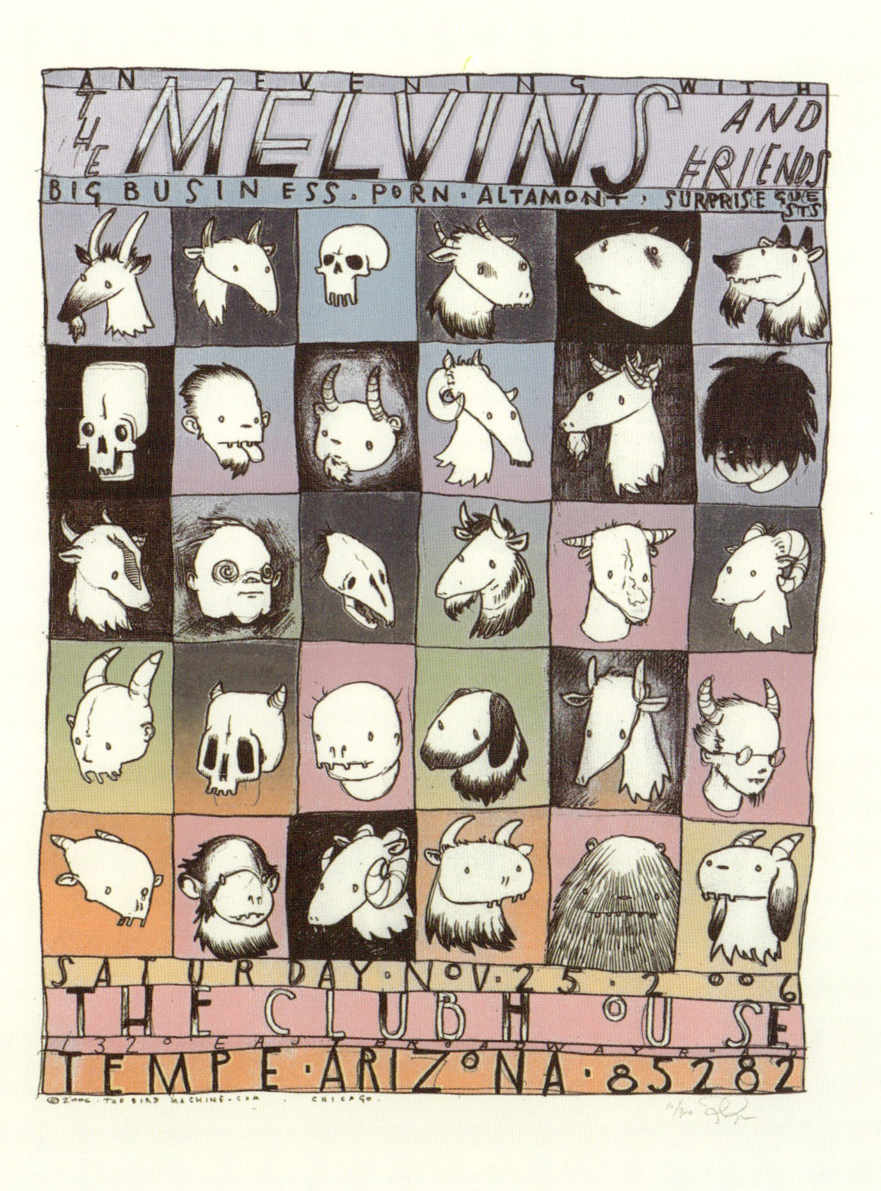

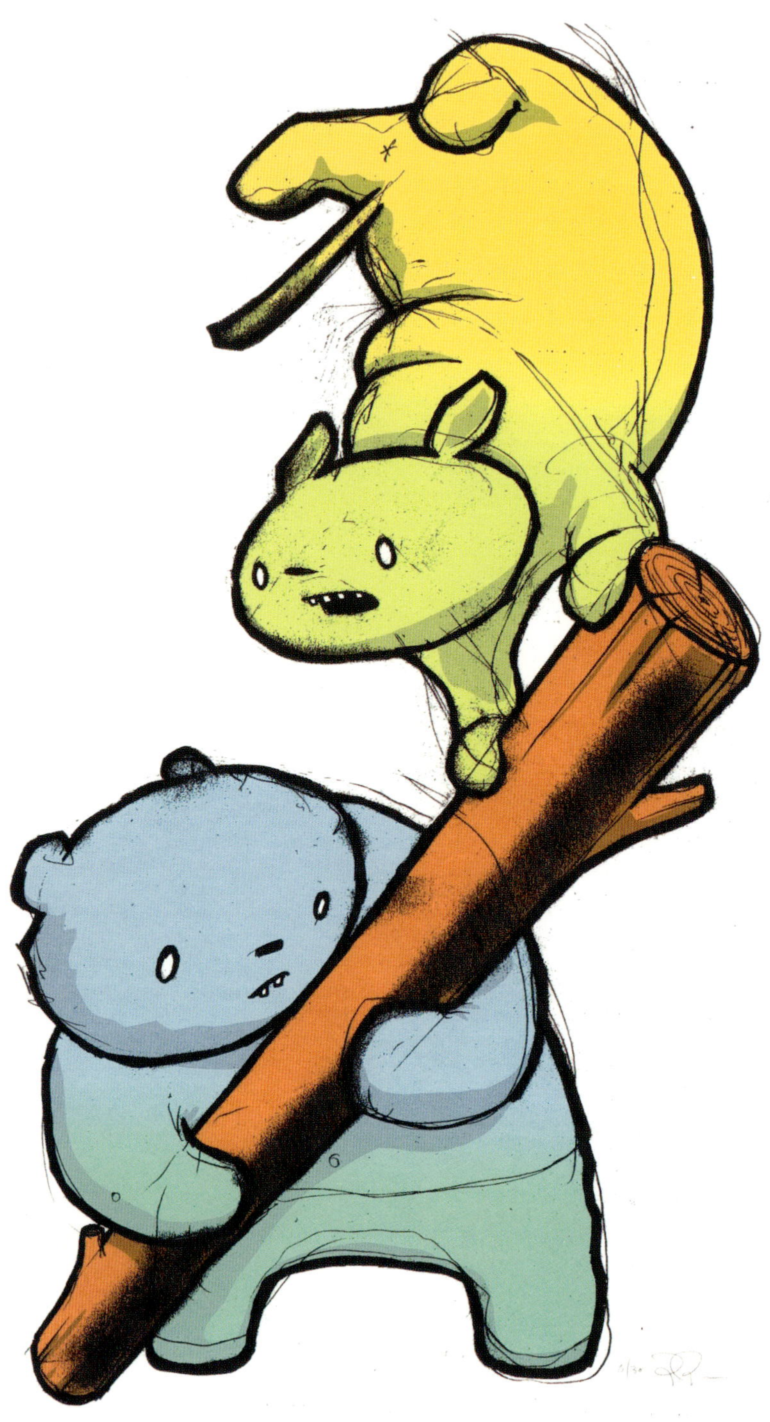

Log Trick

2006
22 x 30 inches
5 screens

This bear and his cat have devised a little gig they like to call the Log Trick. They tried to get a skateboard company to use the trick for a deck, but it was rejected, so they came to me to make a print.

Cat on Bike

2007
23 x 35 inches
9 screens

I was building myself a new bike, when Coudal Partners called and asked me to make a print specifically for their "Swap Meat" online event. Ocho the cat held the flying trackstand pose while I sat and drew.

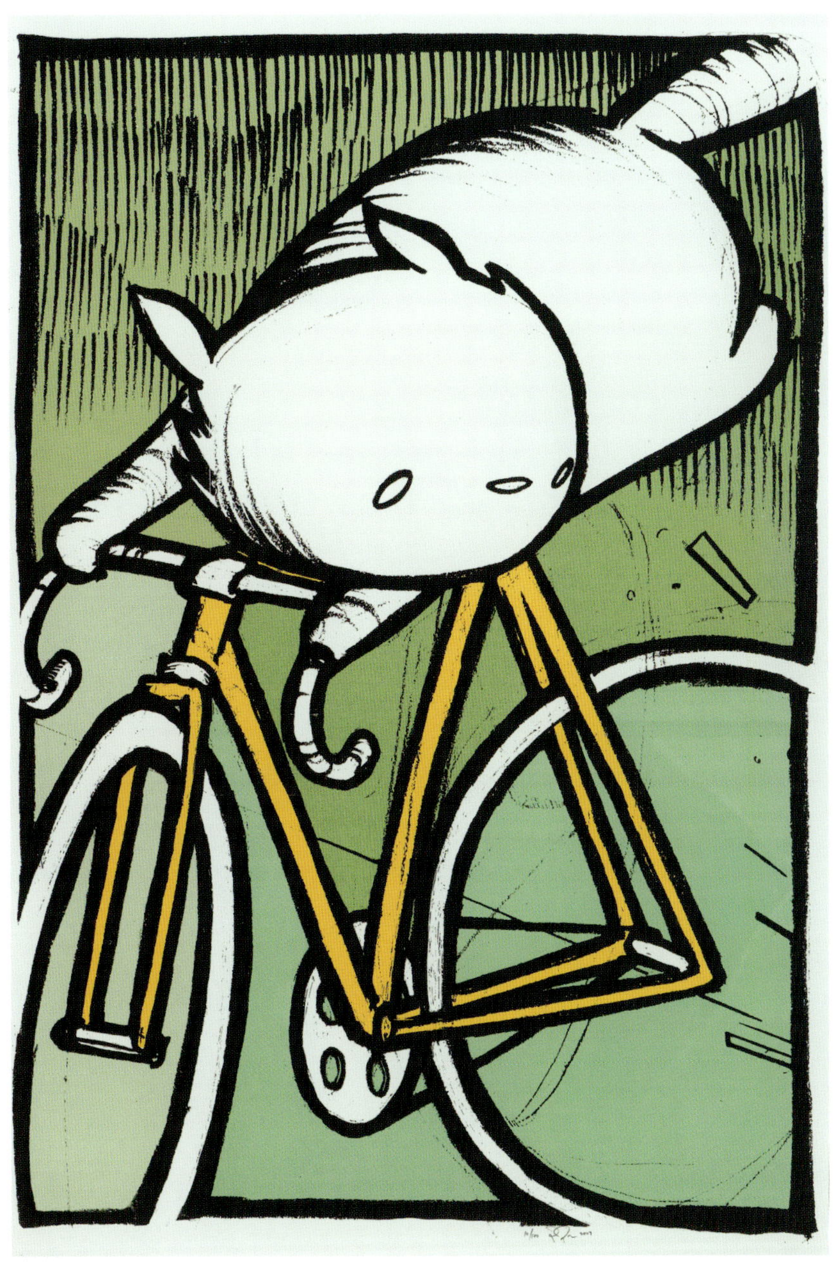

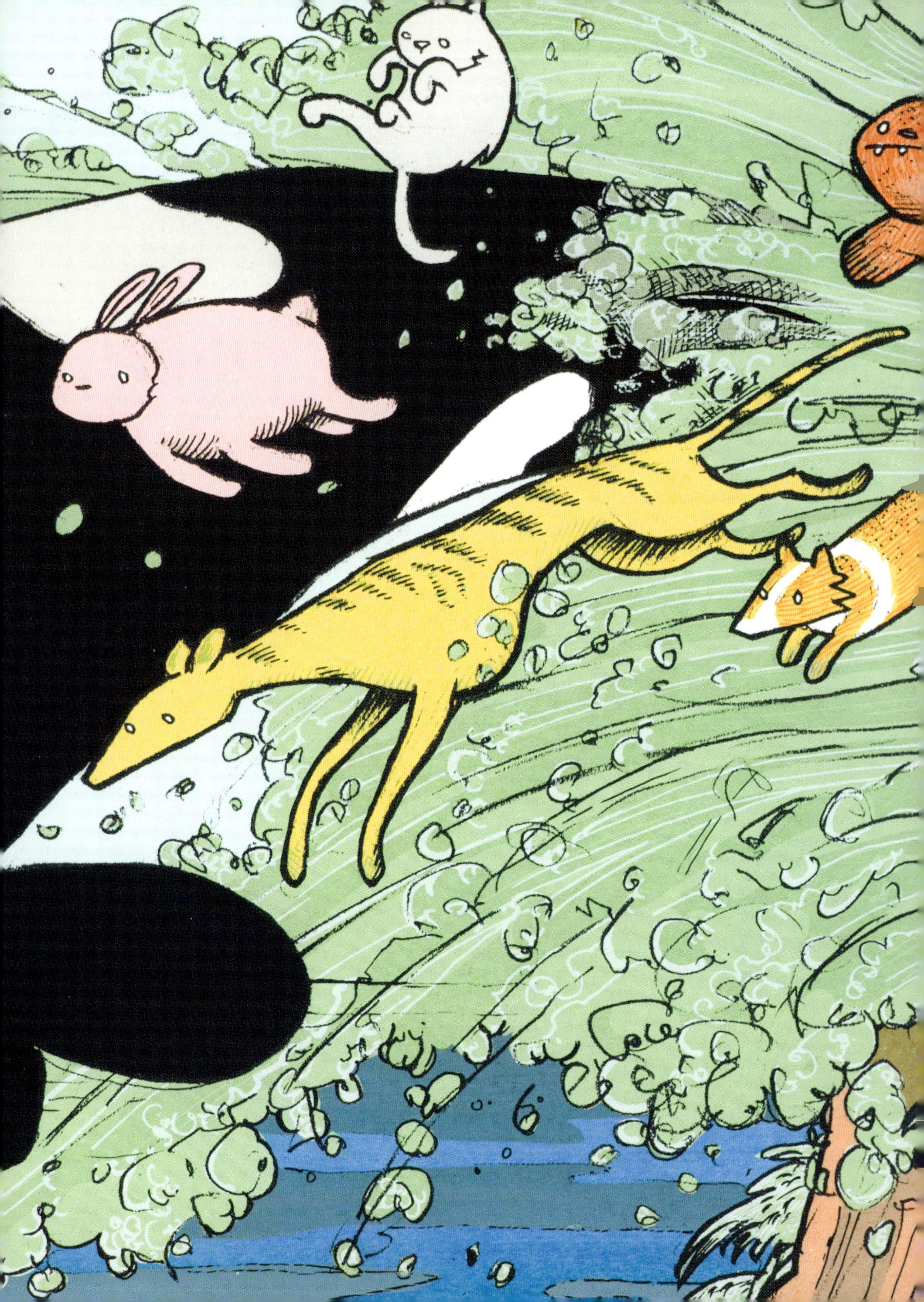

The New Pod
2006
22 x 30 inches
15 screens

This image, loosely related to *Orca and Friends*, was made with the Decoder Ring Design Concern in Austin (see page 47). The fellows at DRDC wanted to start a visiting artist print series, and foolishly selected me as the guinea pig to see how it would work. They encouraged me to hand-print 15 screens, several of which are gloss varnishes in the water. The series has taken off, with other collaborators such as James Victore, Tara McPherson, Gary Baseman, Aesthetic Apparatus, Nick Butcher, and others putting in their time in Austin thus far, with amazing results.

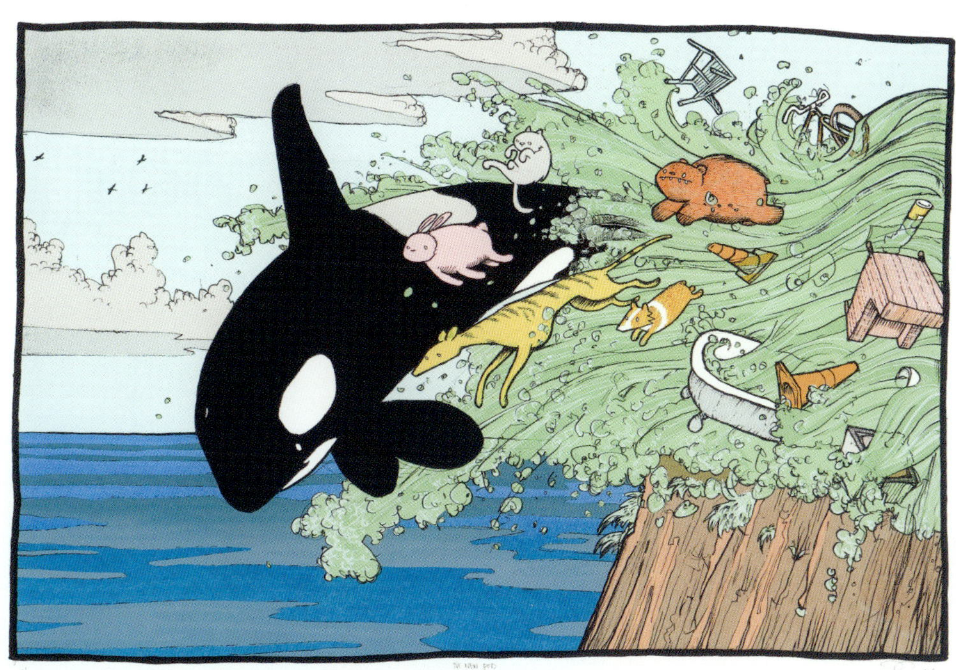

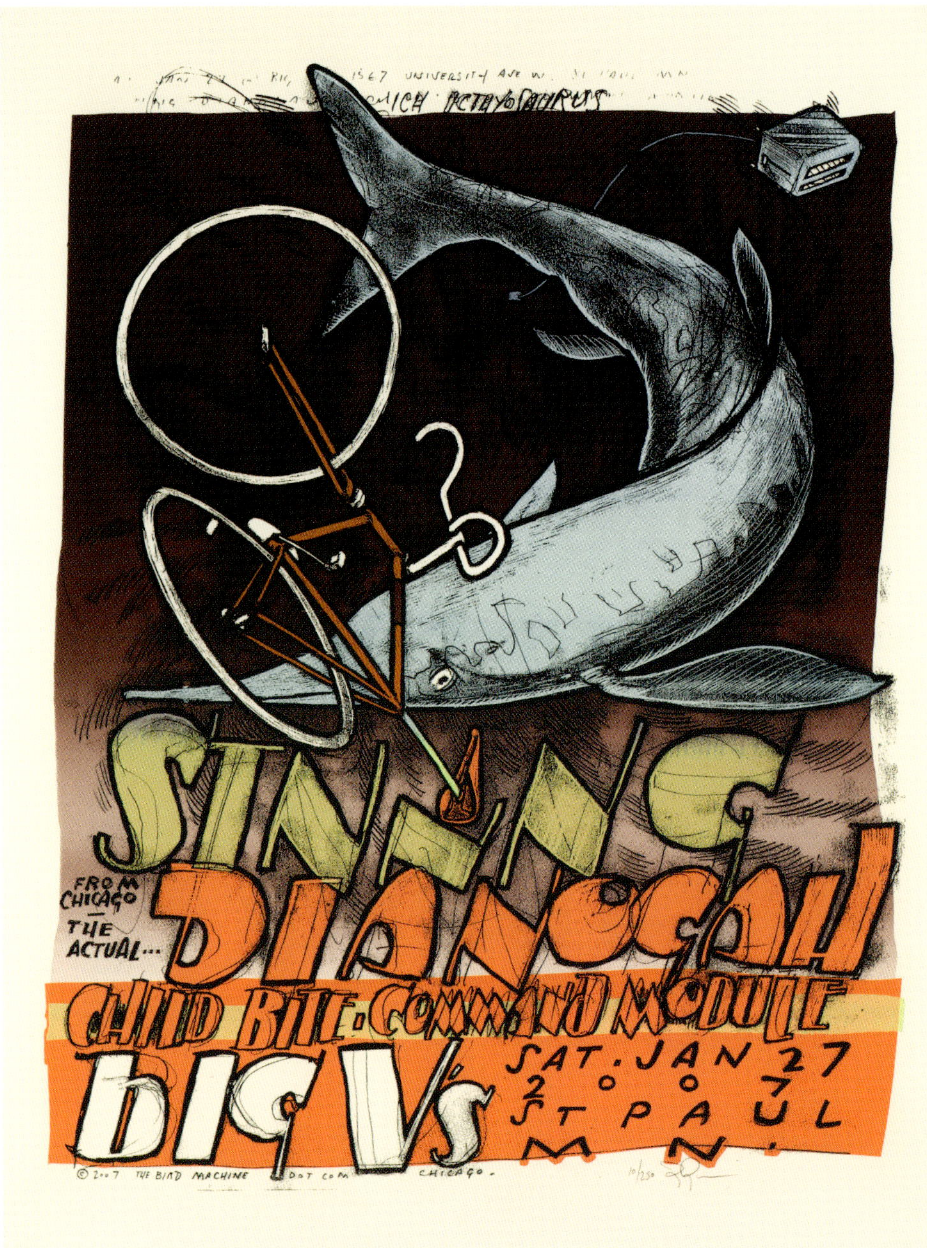

Stnnng / Dianogah

2007

18 x 24 inches

4 screens

I was building a new bike while making this print, so I drew a bike. Then I drew a fat man being thrown from the bike, but replaced him with a dolphin, but soon felt the dolphin didn't fill the space appropriately, and didn't really make sense, anyway. I replaced the dolphin with an icthyosaurus, and added a toaster to tie the whole composition together.

Flatstock 14

2007

12 x 24 inches

3 screens

"Now you've done it!"—this salmon has found a way to avoid swimming from the Puget Sound into Lake Washington via the fish ladder at the Ballard Locks: he's built up another Schwinn single-speed bike.

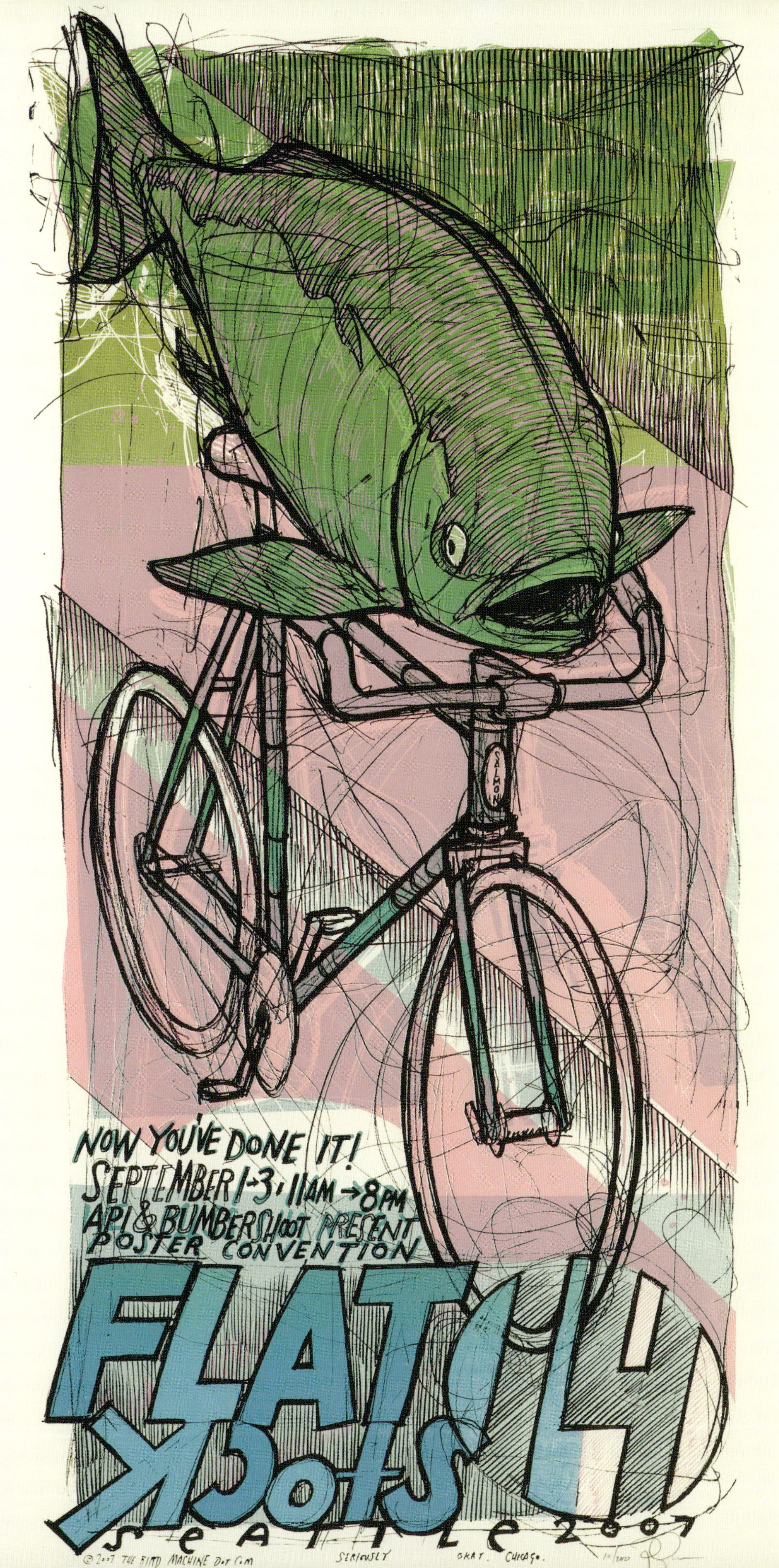
NOW YOU'VE DONE IT!
SEPTEMBER 1→3, 11AM→8PM
API & BUMBERSHOOT PRESENT
POSTER CONVENTION
FLATSTOCK 14
SEATTLE 2007
© 2007 THE BIRD MACHINE DOT COM
SERIOUSLY
OKAY. CHICAGO.
10/200

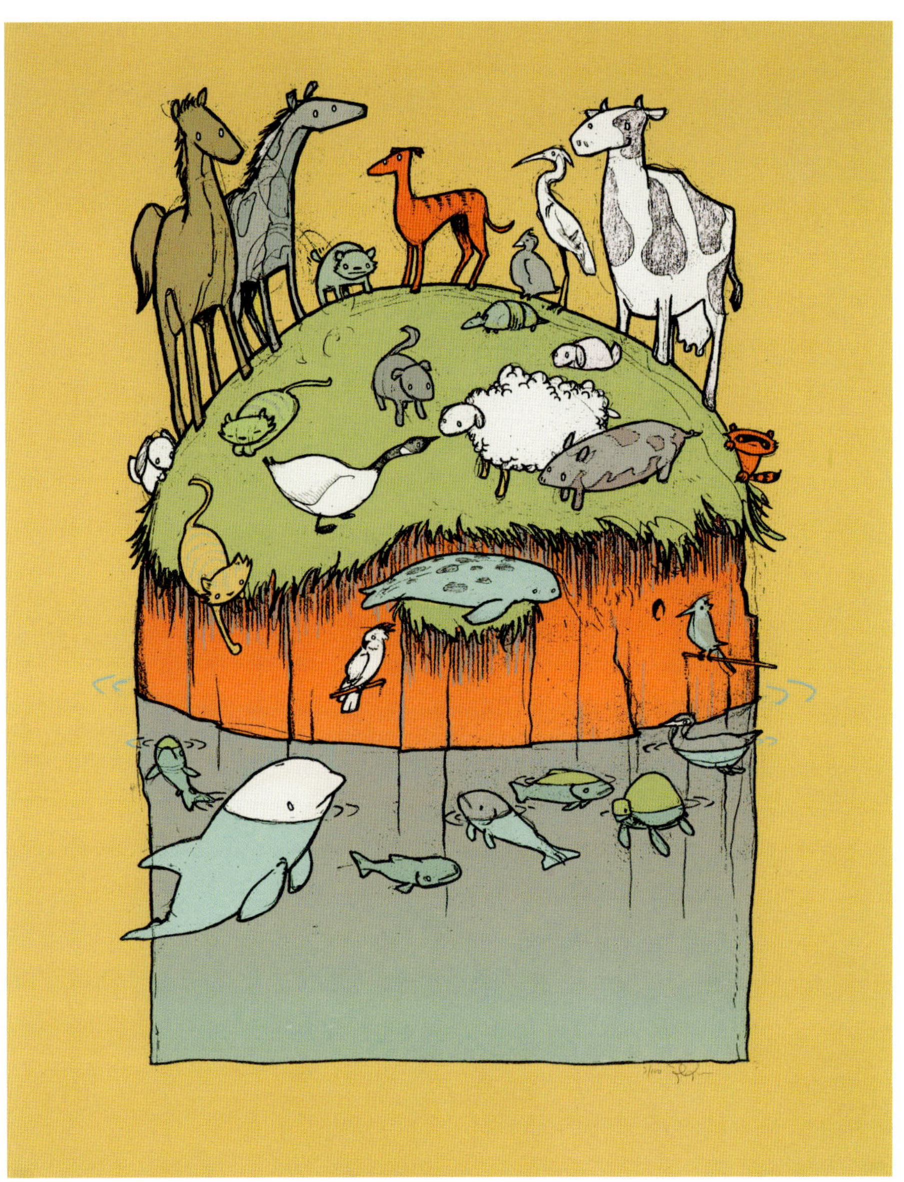

Animals of Prince Edward Island 2006

2006

19 x 25 inches

6 screens

The Atlantic Veterinary College at the University of Prince Edward Island had commissioned prints as gifts for their graduating classes in 2003, and contacted me again about making prints for the 2006 class. This time, they were more specific as to which animals should appear in the print, and we got them all in or around this microcosm of the red-soiled island. Seth the greyhound is in the middle at the top.

Screens & Spokes
2007
19 x 27 inches
5 screens

This is a text-free version of a print made for the art show associated with a fundraising bike ride. Fun fact: due to miscalculated film preparation, the little Muntjac deer in the upper right corner has five legs.

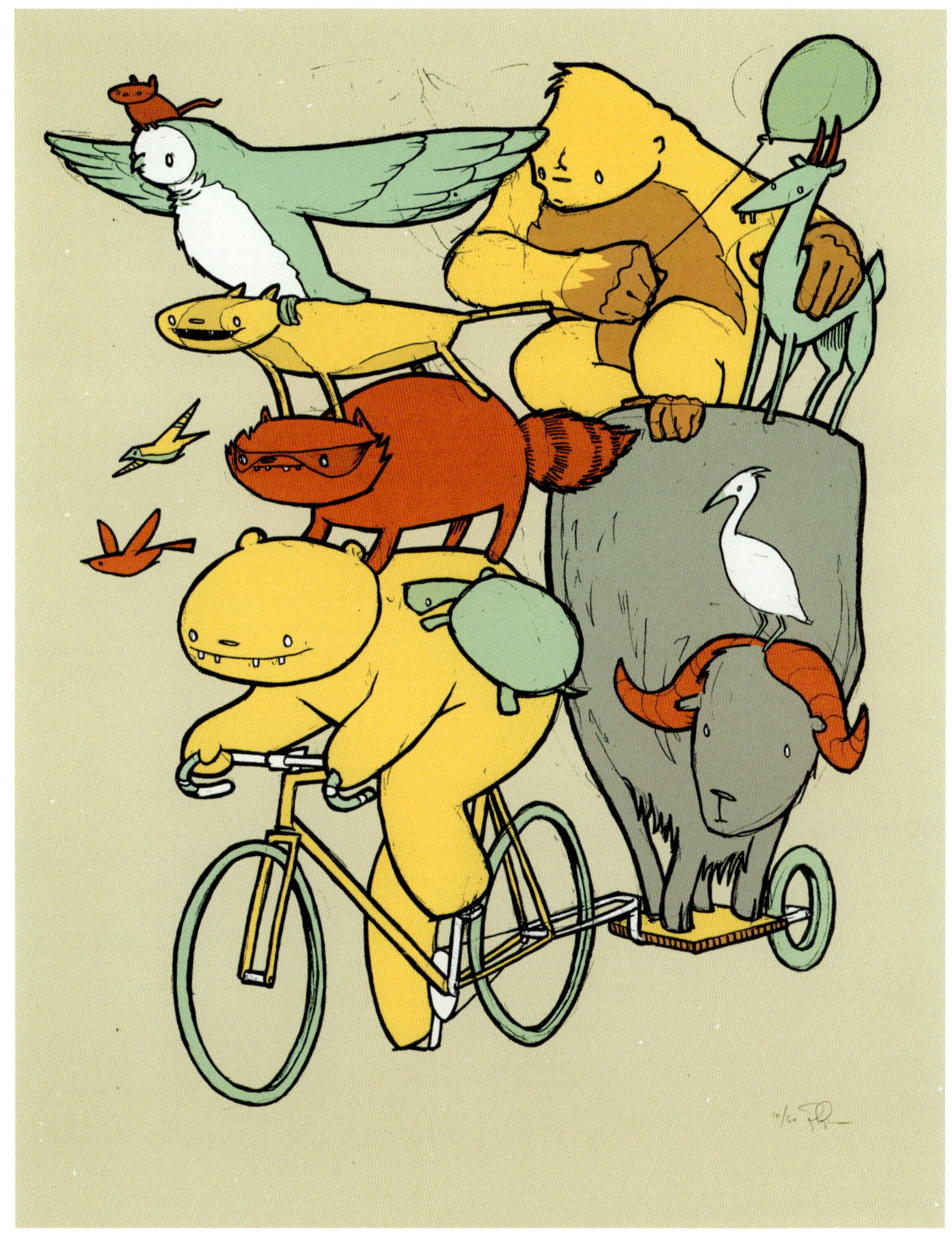

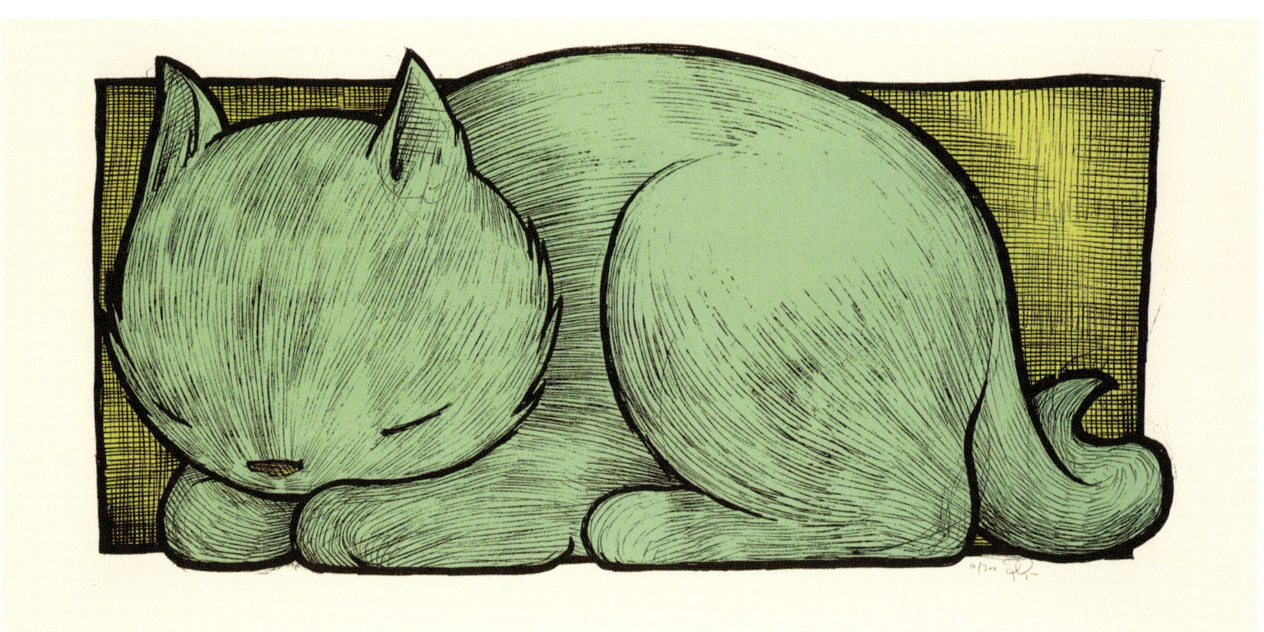

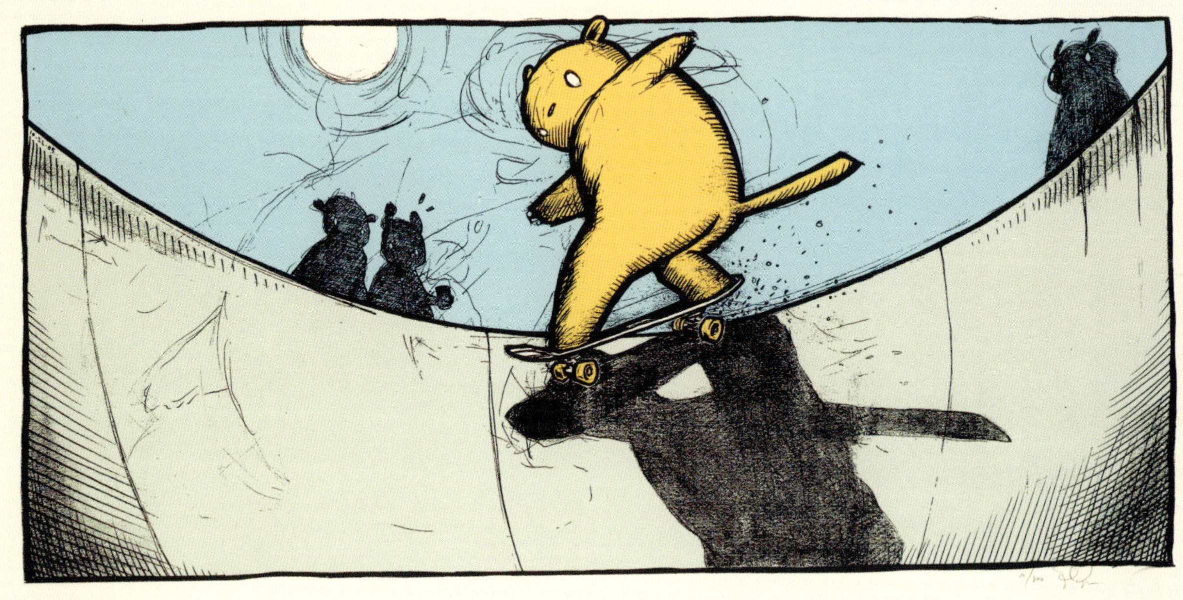

Sleeping Akiko
2005
12 x 24 inches
3 screens

This was one of four prints I made in a large format during a couple visits to AIR in Pittsburgh, and then reprinted at a smaller and more affordable size once the large prints were gone. This is my cat, who also appears in the *She Protects Us* print elsewhere in this book. Jason Harvey, designer of this book, has twin sons who somehow managed to pull the large-size print of this image off the wall, fold it up, and proudly bring it to Daddy one day when they were three.

Frontside Smith Grind
2005
12 x 24 inches
4 screens

Another print made at AIR in Pittsburgh. This cat is impressing his friends by bashing the coping under the hot sun.

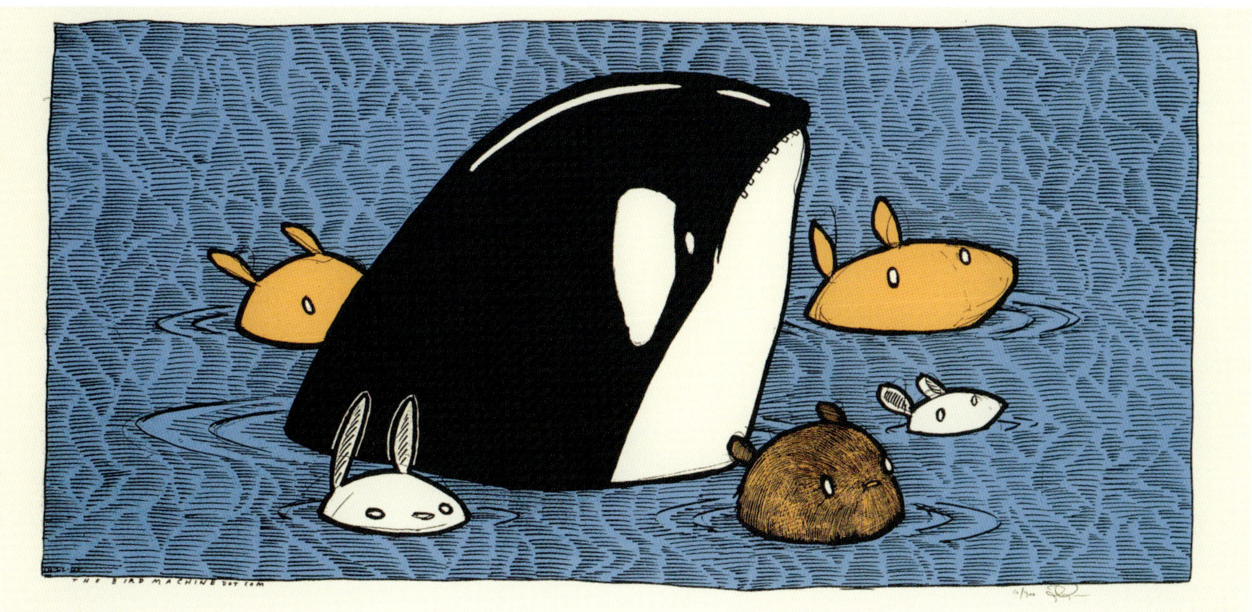

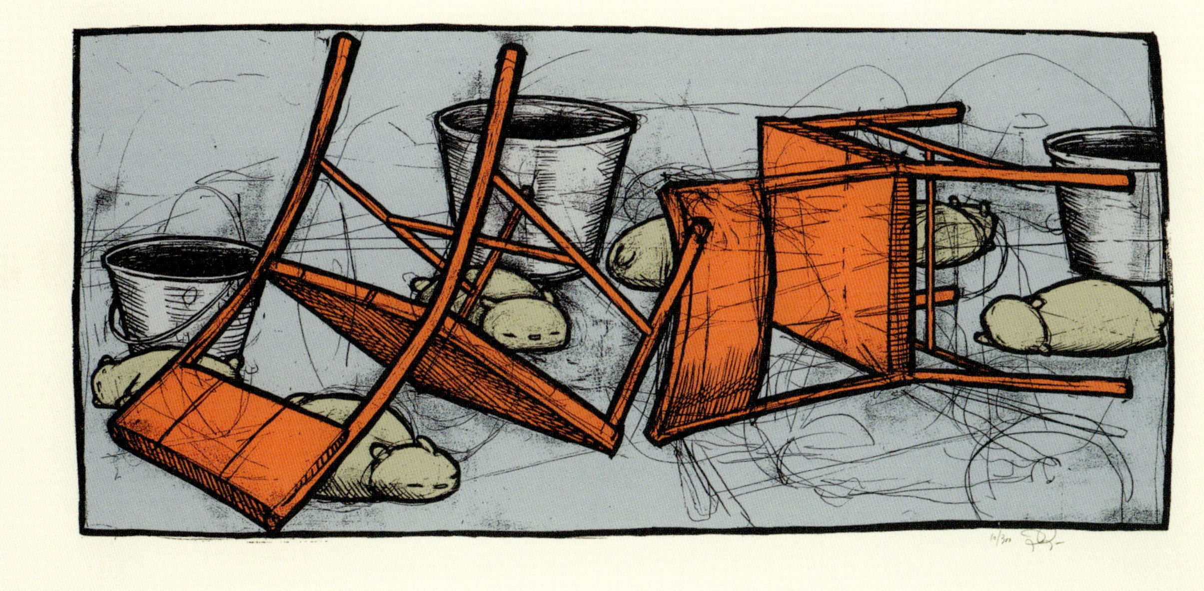

Orca and Friends
2005
12 x 24 inches
3 screens

The San Juan Islands of Washington have three resident pods of orcas, which Diana and I watch when we go there. The whales are social with each other, and occasionally curious about humans. We were discussing how our greyhound, Seth, would react to seeing these whales up close, since I had seen a photo of an orca spy-hopping to go nose-to-nose with a dog in the back of a boat. The scenario played out in my mind with a group of dogs and cats being washed out to sea in *The New Pod*, with this print being the result. This was the third of four prints made at AIR in Pittsburgh during one stint.

Marmots, Chairs & Buckets
2005
12 x 24 inches
5 screens

This, the fourth print from the 2005 stint at AIR, depicts the aftermath of the type of parties to which I used to never be invited.

Murky Waters

2007
20 x 23.5 inches
7 screens

These murky waters were originally drawn as the cover of an Australian magazine, but were rejected. This is one of the very few times that I've digitally assembled individual hand-drawn elements into a single composition for the purpose of screenprinting. The true focus of the image is the cake being stalked in the center of the frame.

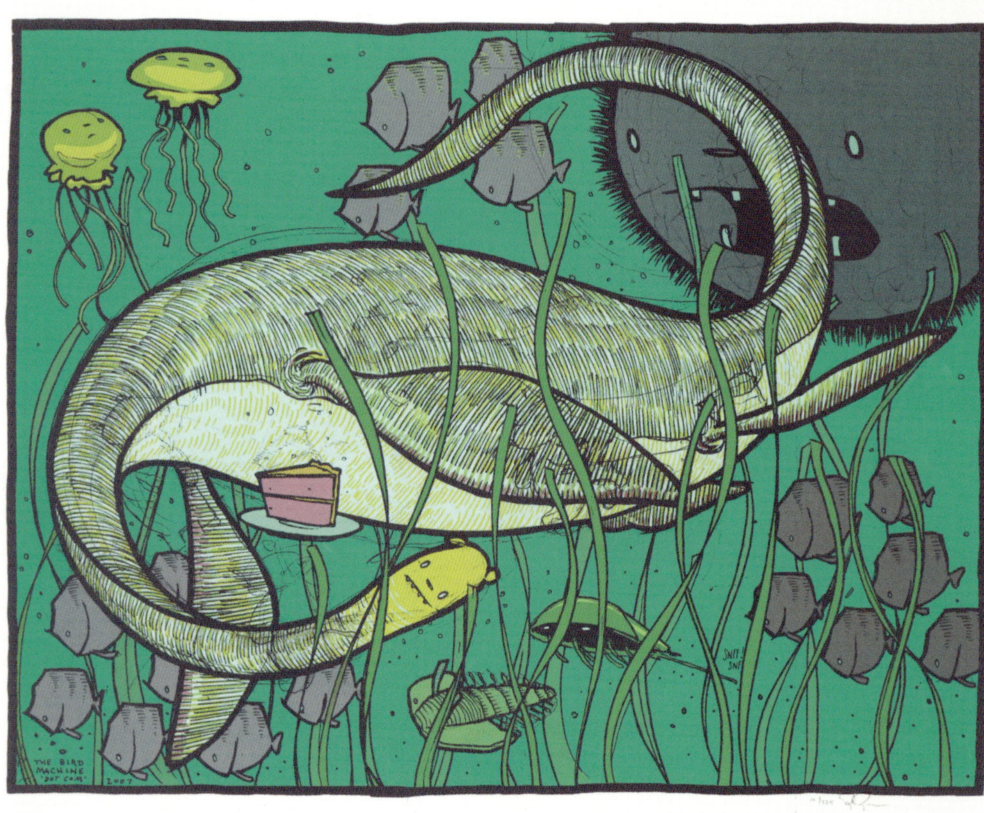

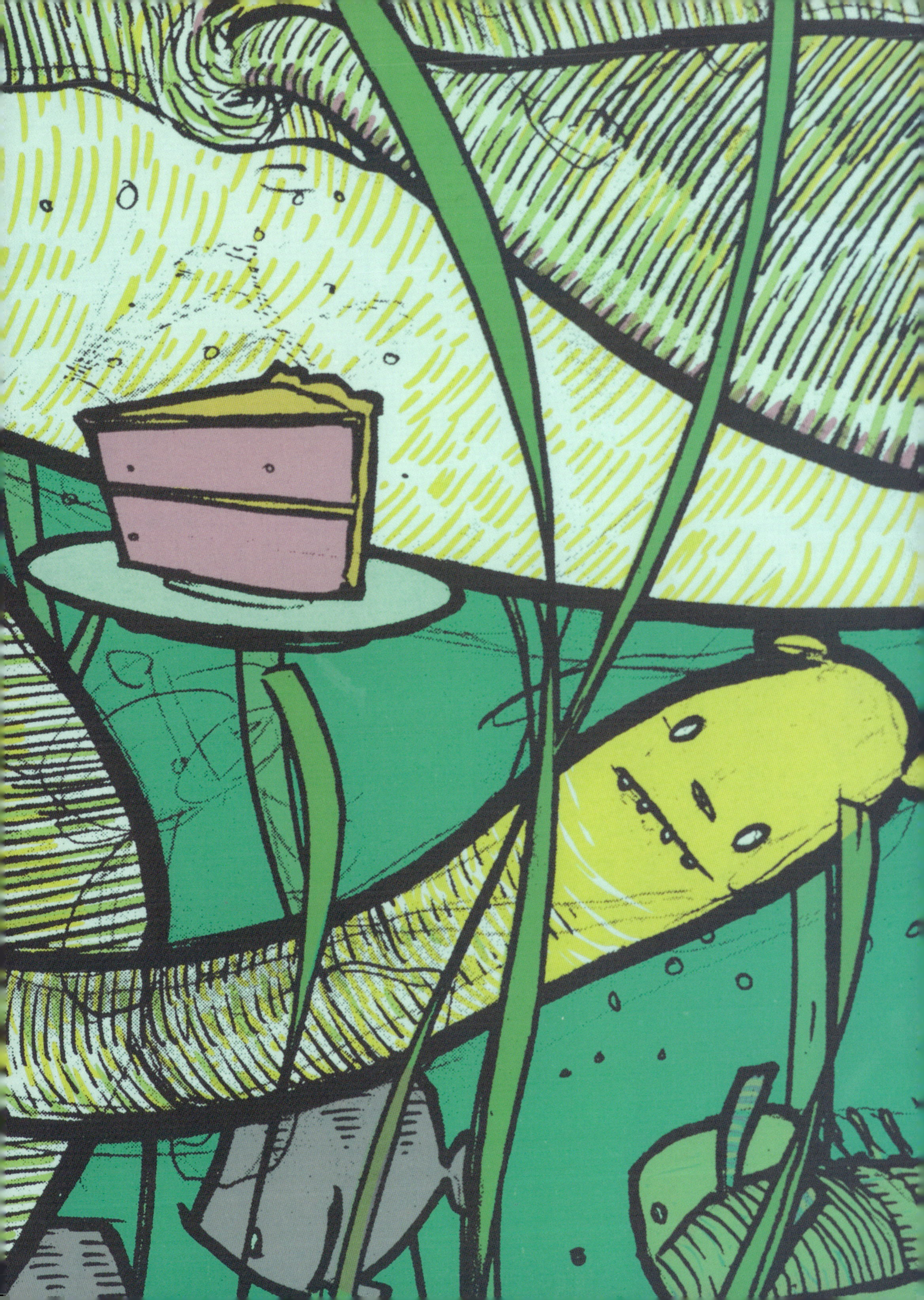

Blue Planet (Orca)
2008
20 x 26 inches
3 screens

The BBC had a nature series called *Blue Planet* in 2001 and 2002, which contained intense, high-definition footage of various aquatic ecosystems across the globe. In 2008, the series was condensed into a two-hour projected film, which had a live symphonic score. The film and the symphony toured the UK for seven performances in five cities. The producers of the film commissioned this series of seven prints, and asked that specific scenes from the series be included.

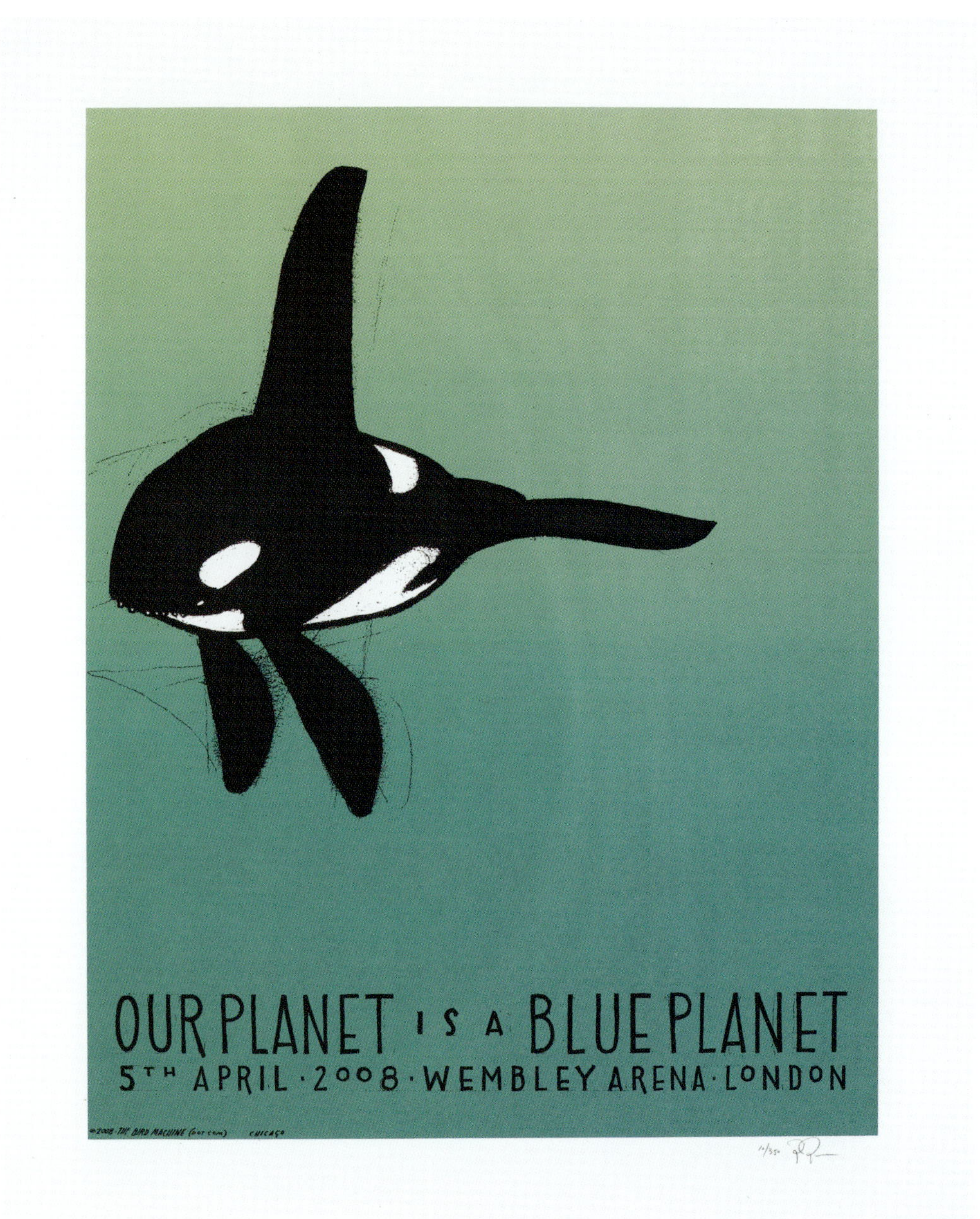

Blue Planet (Rays)
2008
20 x 26 inches
4 screens

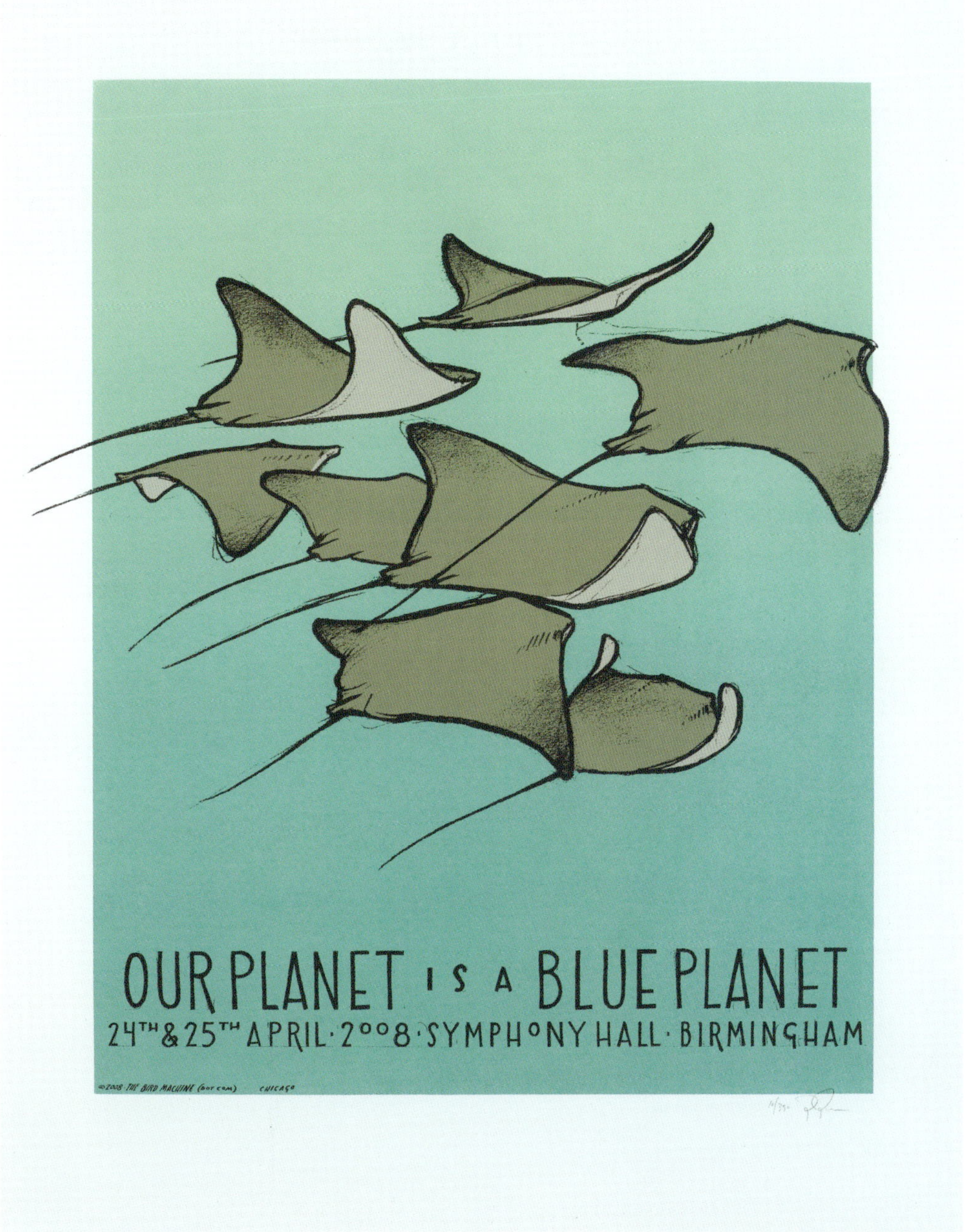

Blue Planet (Polar Bear)

2008

20 x 26 inches

3 screens

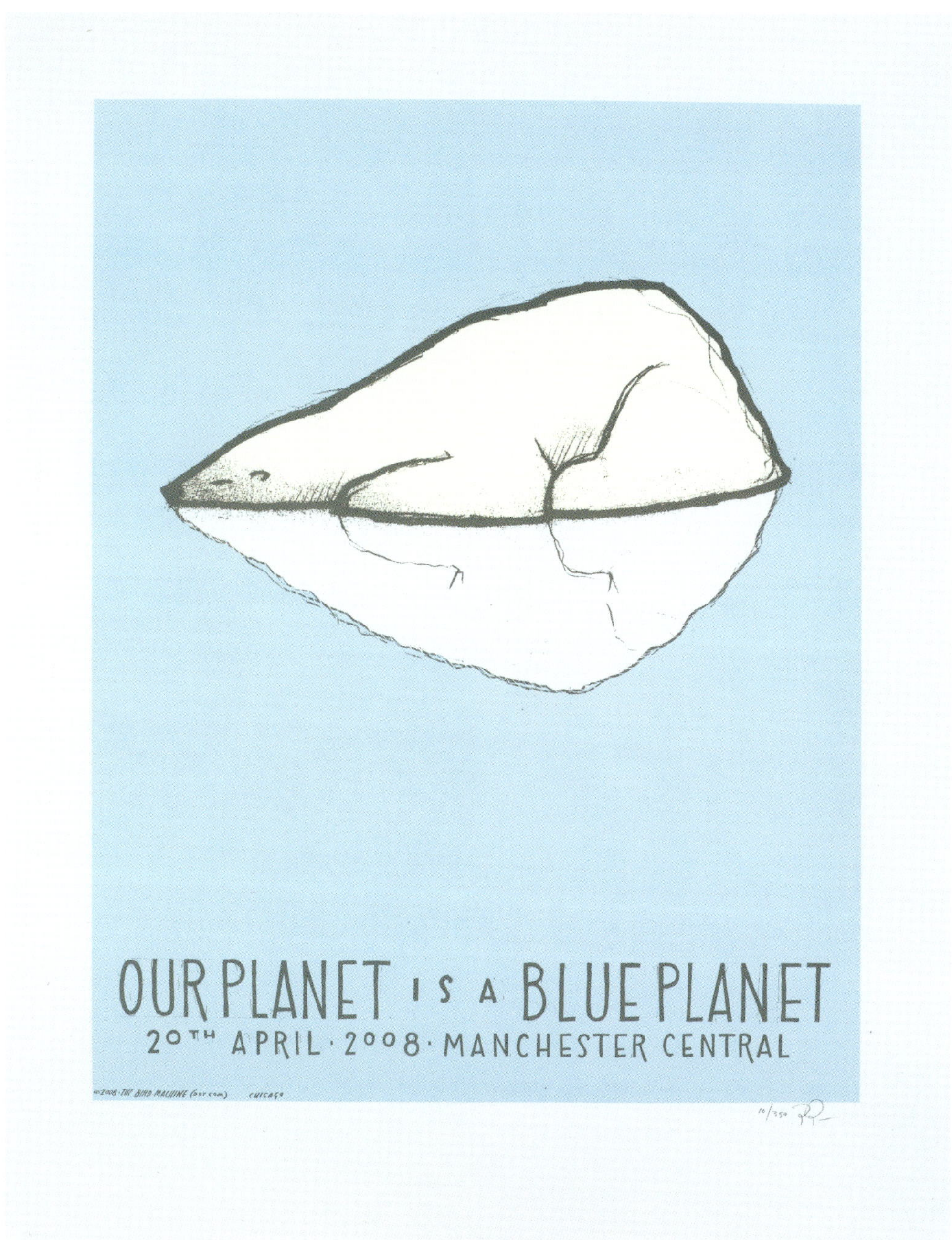

Blue Planet (Blue Whale)
2008
20 x 26 inches
4 screens

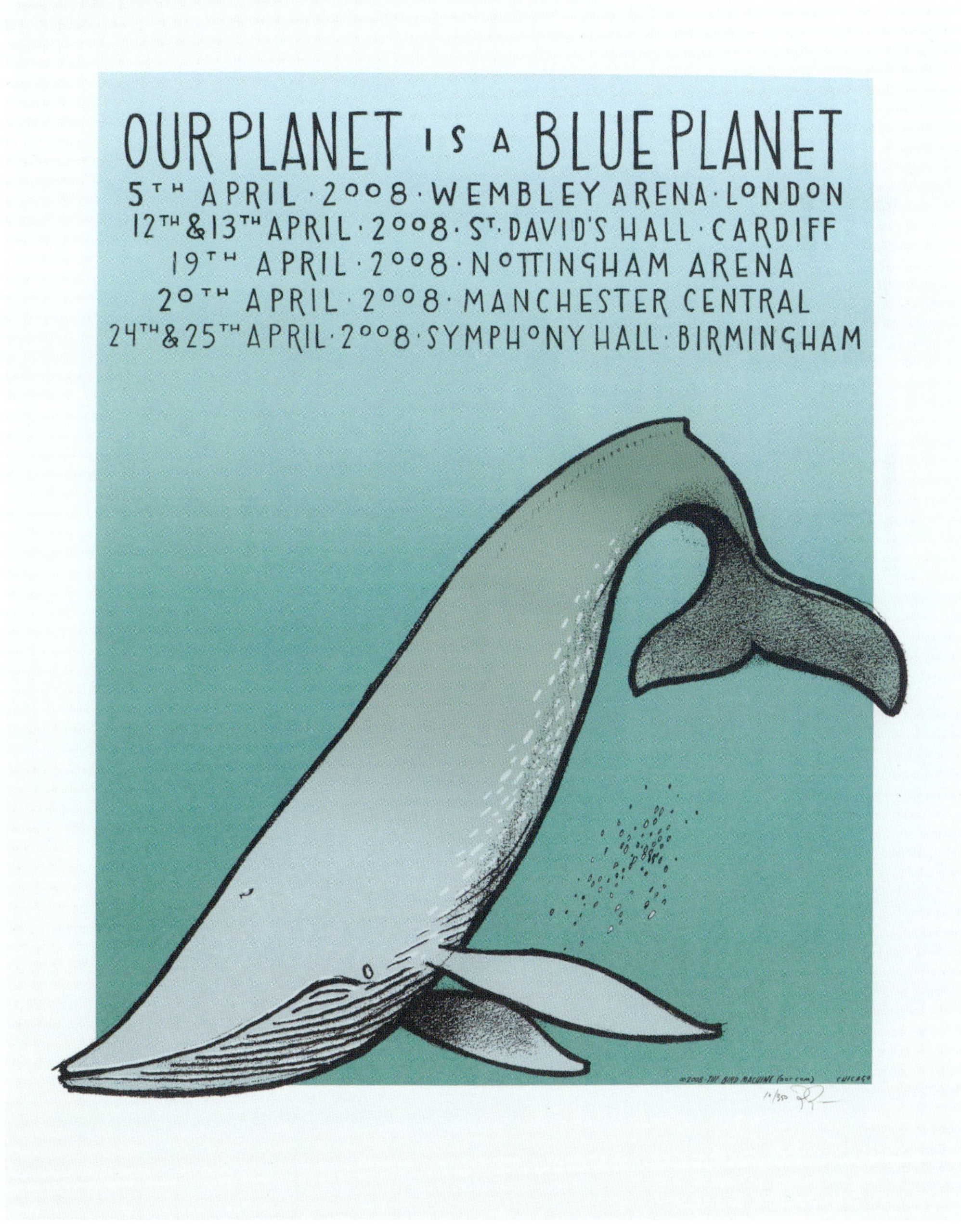

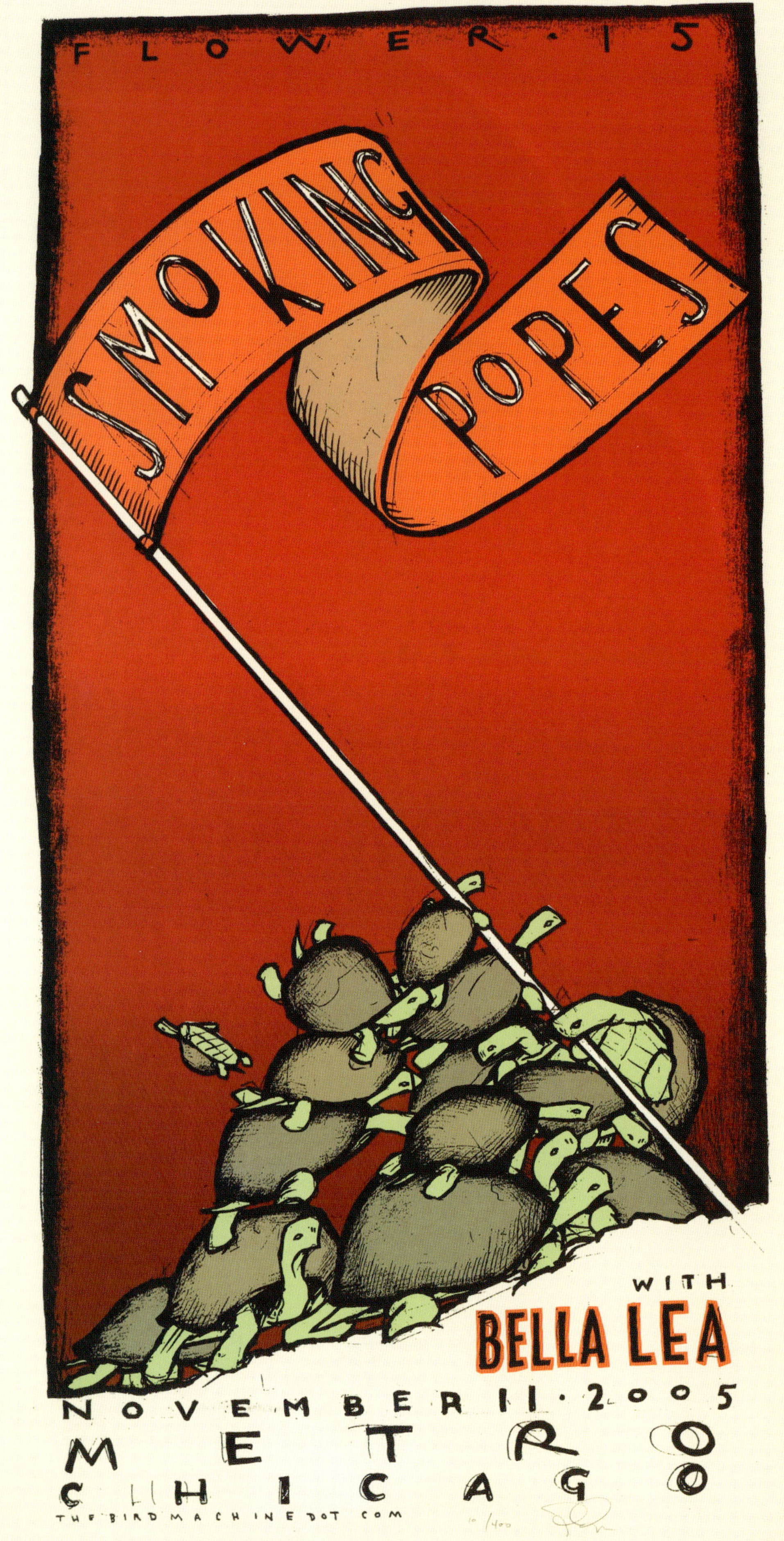
FLOWER · 15
SMOKING POPES
WITH
BELLA LEA
NOVEMBER 11 · 2005
METRO
CHICAGO
THEBIRDMACHINEDOT COM

Smoking Popes
2005
12 x 24 inches
4 screens

This was the Popes' triumphant return to the stage after several years disbanded. The group used this image as the cover of their live DVD after the show was over.

Smoking Popes
2006
12 x 24 inches
5 screens

This show, soon after the Iwo Jima image, was supposed to have a visual continuity from the last print. This time, the central turtle is being played to by various band members in boats.

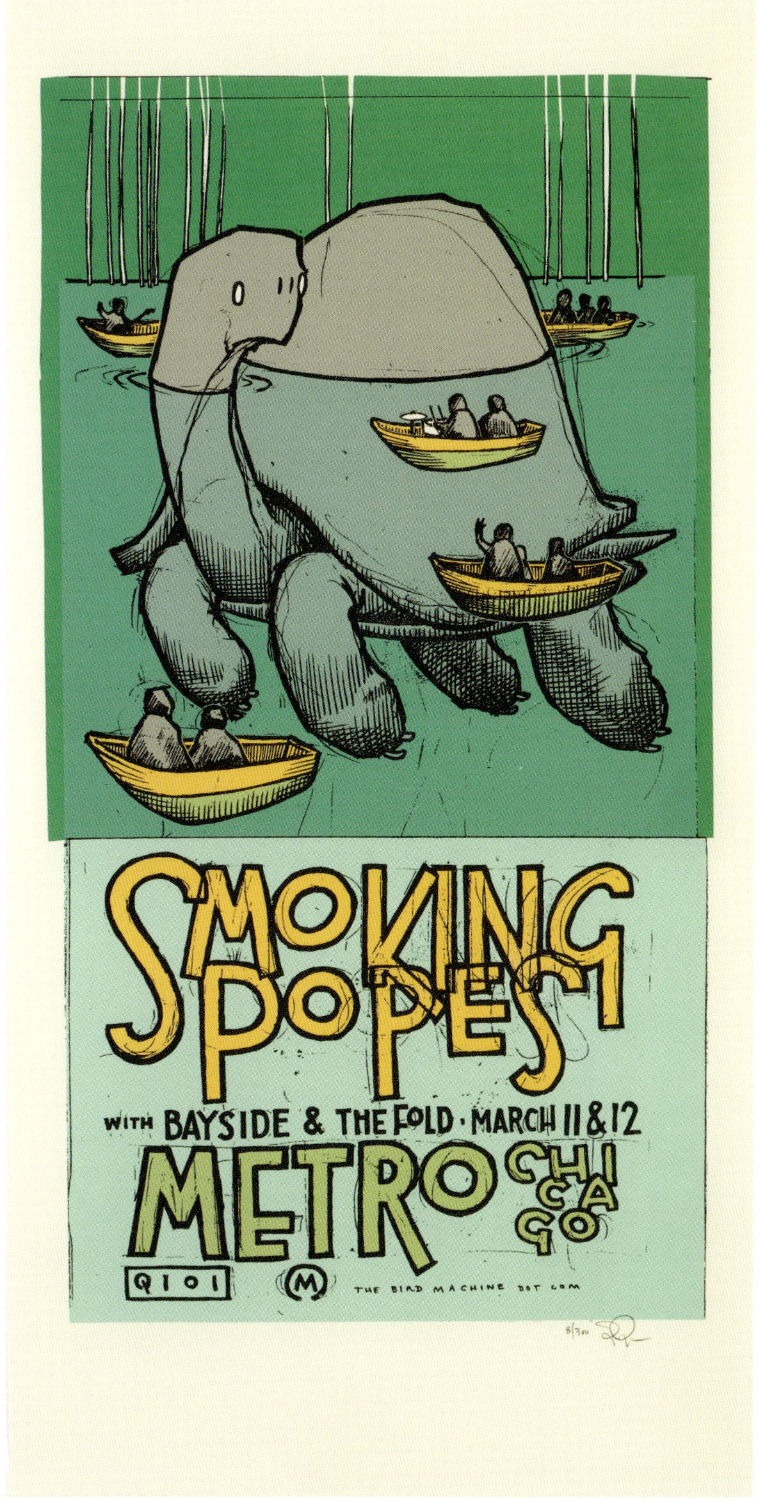

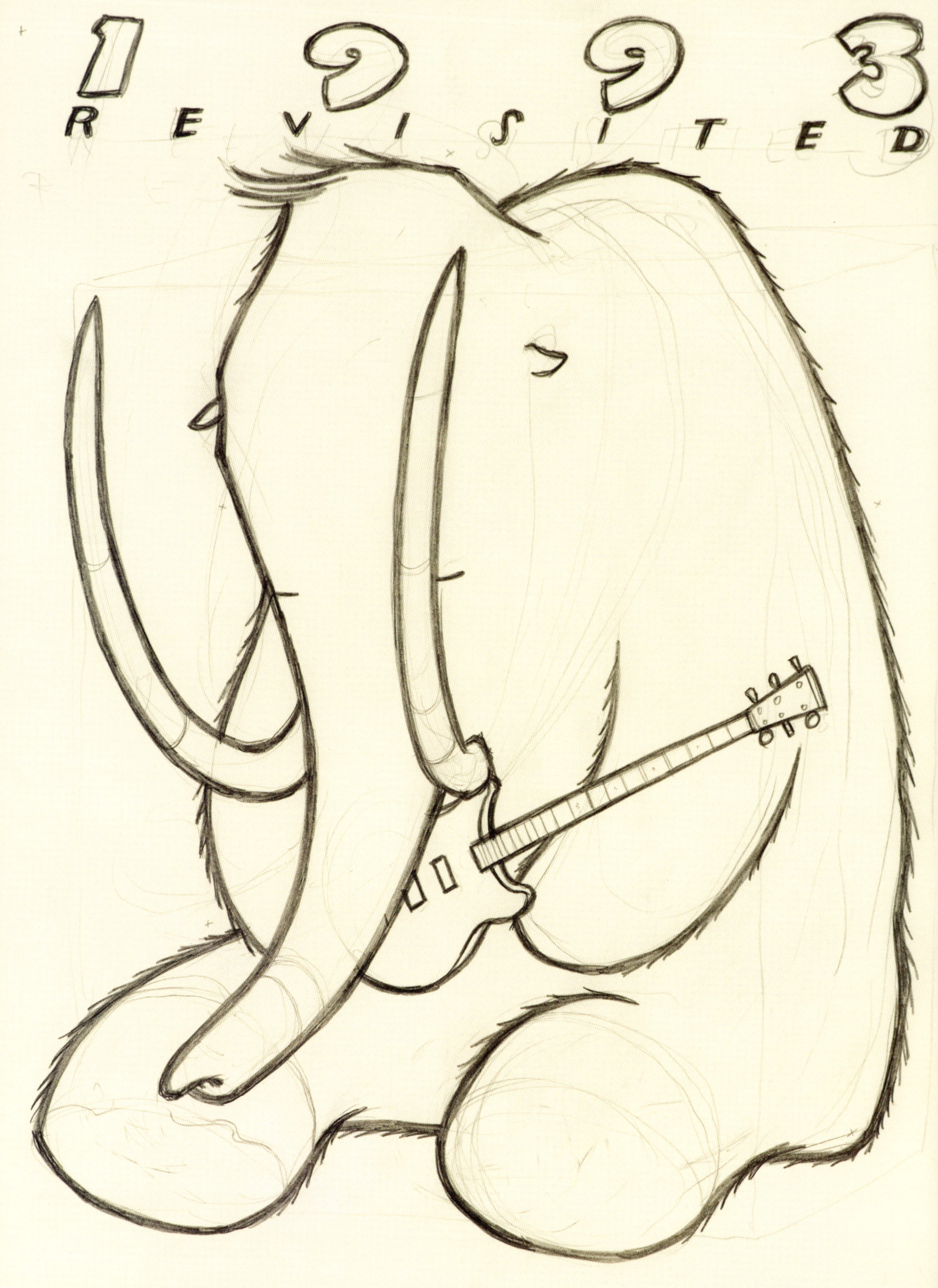
1993
REVISITED

1993 Revisited

2008

20 x 26 inches

6 screens

When I was in school in Urbana, Illinois, there was a vibrant music scene, which reached a sort of pinnacle in 1993 and '94. Most of these bands broke up or drifted apart, but in 2008, some folks decided to get a sampling of bands from that era back together, for "1993 Revisited." This mammoth is slowly thawing, and you know what happens when the ice is gone.

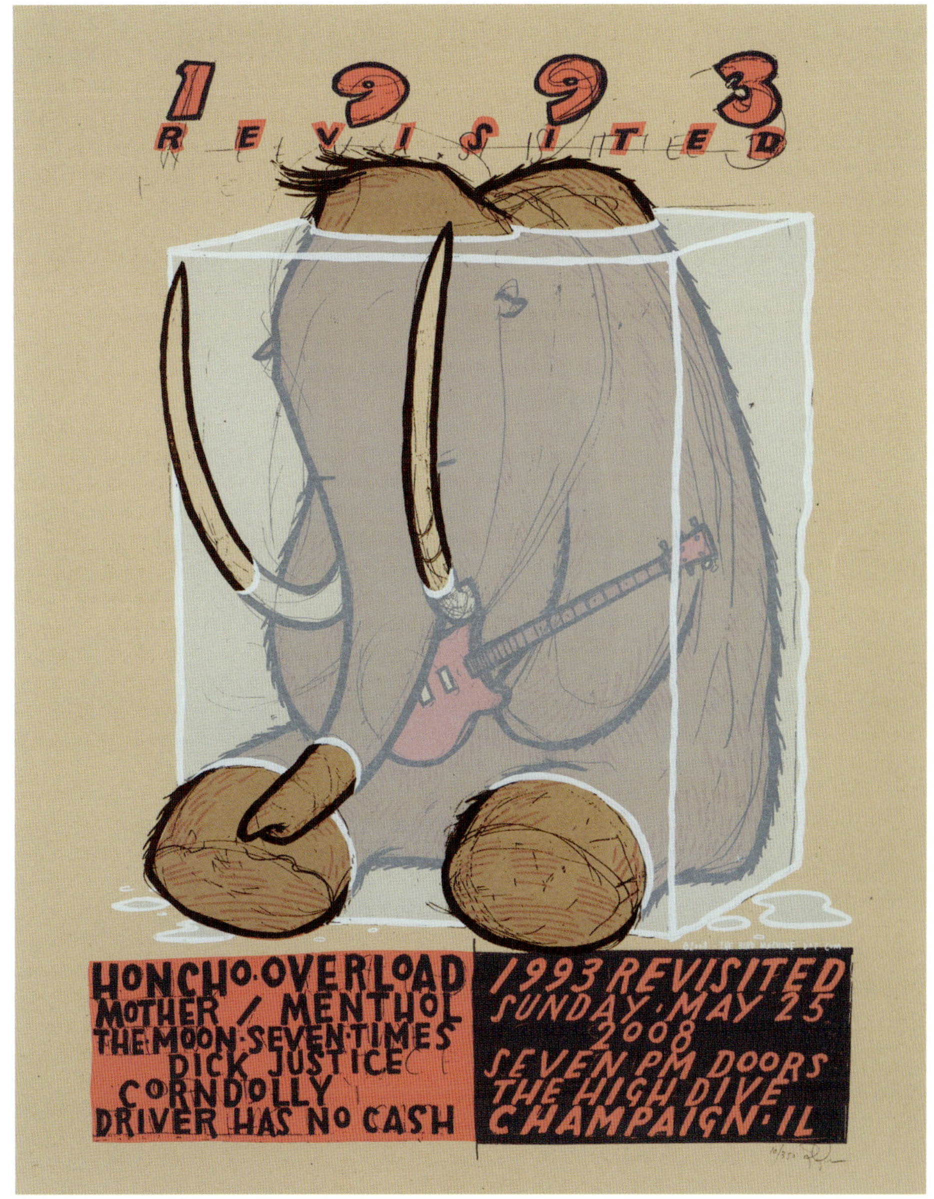

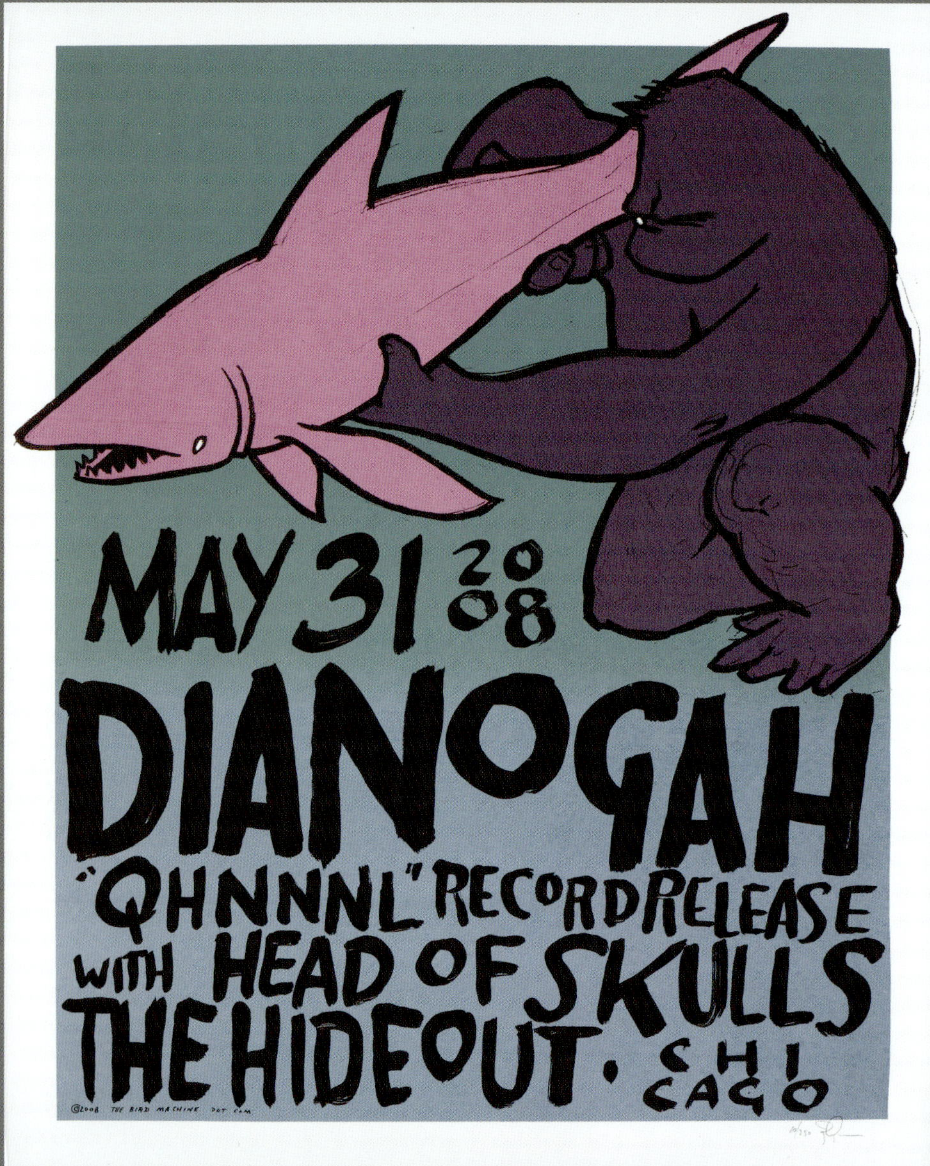

Dianogah (*Qhnnnl* Record Release Show)
2008
20 x 26 inches
3 screens

When my band, Dianogah, released our fourth album, *Qhnnnl*, I figured the most appropriate way to summarize the themes which ran through the songs would be by depictions of a shark being used as a rifle by a gorilla. I also drew the same shark being played like a guitar, by a bear, and the same shark being used to cut down a tree, by Abe Lincoln. These other images were used elsewhere.

Dianogah (Cave Bear)

2005

18 x 24 inches

4 screens

Dianogah has been compared to a sleepy old cave bear which only rarely comes out to stretch its back, claw some trees, and maybe do something in the woods.

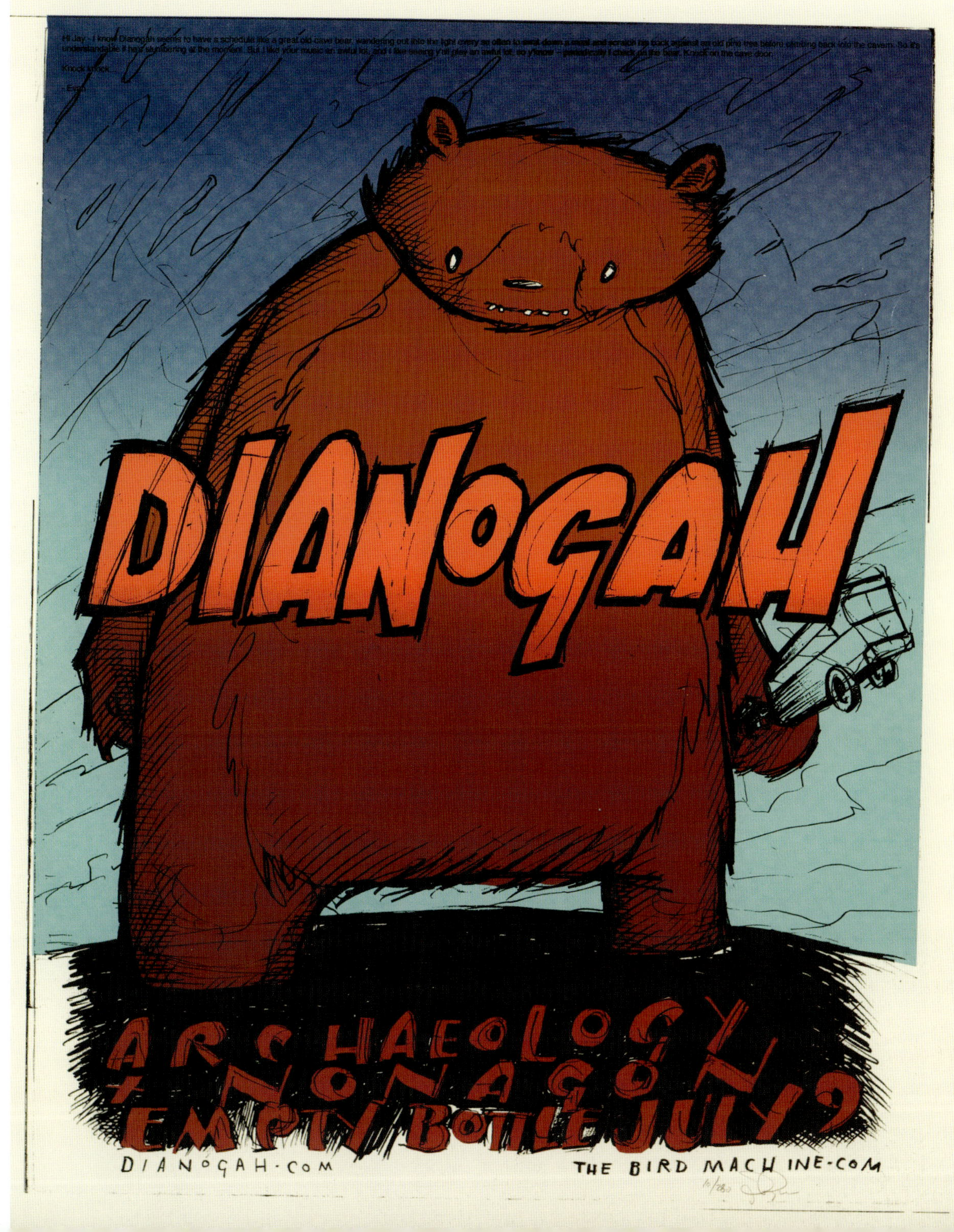

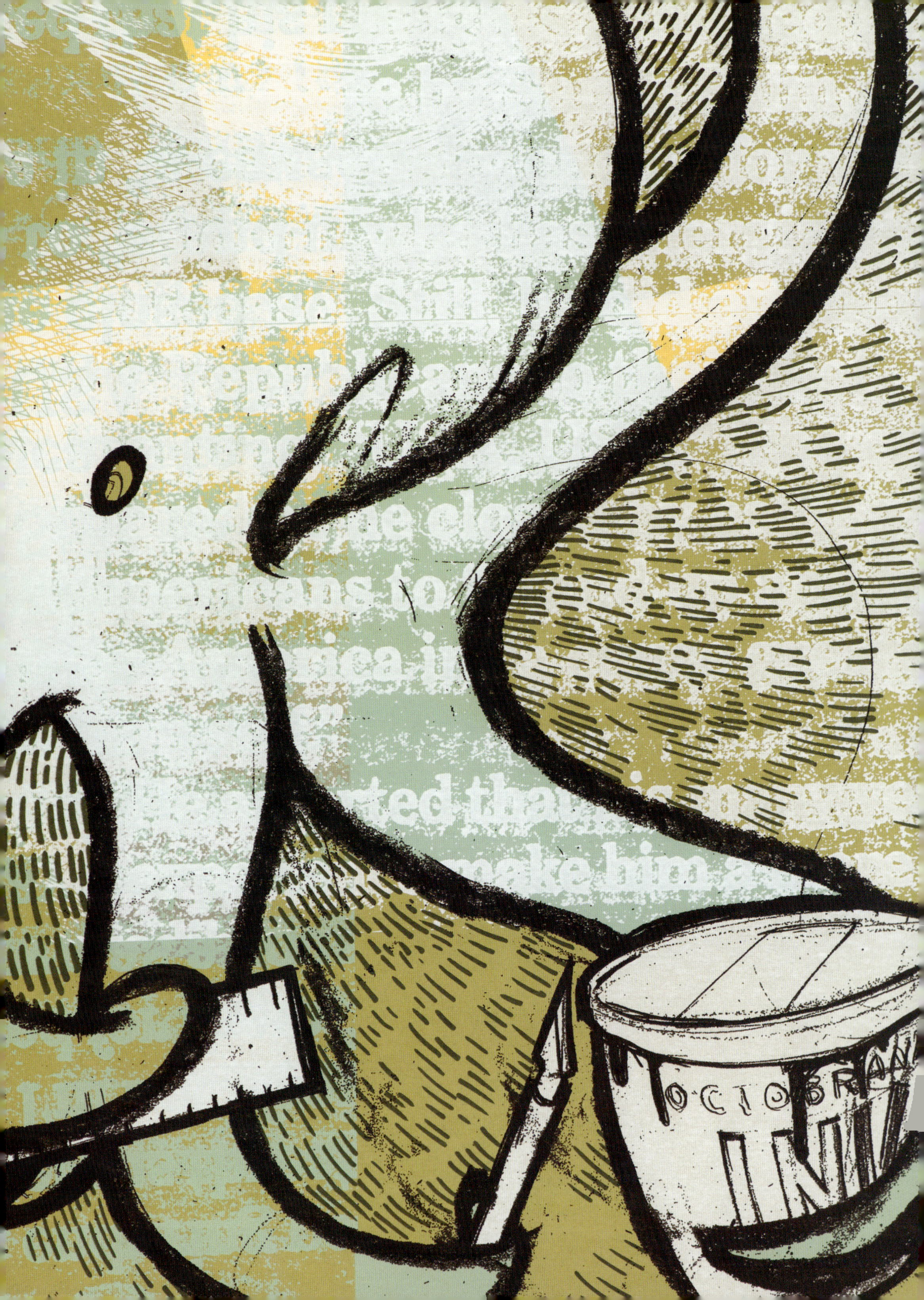

Interlocution
2008
20 x 26 inches
5 screens

This print show, organized by John Lysak and Laurie Godfrey at Edinboro University in Pennsylvania, included work from such upstarts as Oskar Kokoschka and Henri de Toulouse-Lautrec, as well as more established printmakers such as Jenny Schmid, Tom Huck, and Diana Sudyka. The ubiquitous Lithoctopus was depicted for his ability to represent most forms of printmaking.

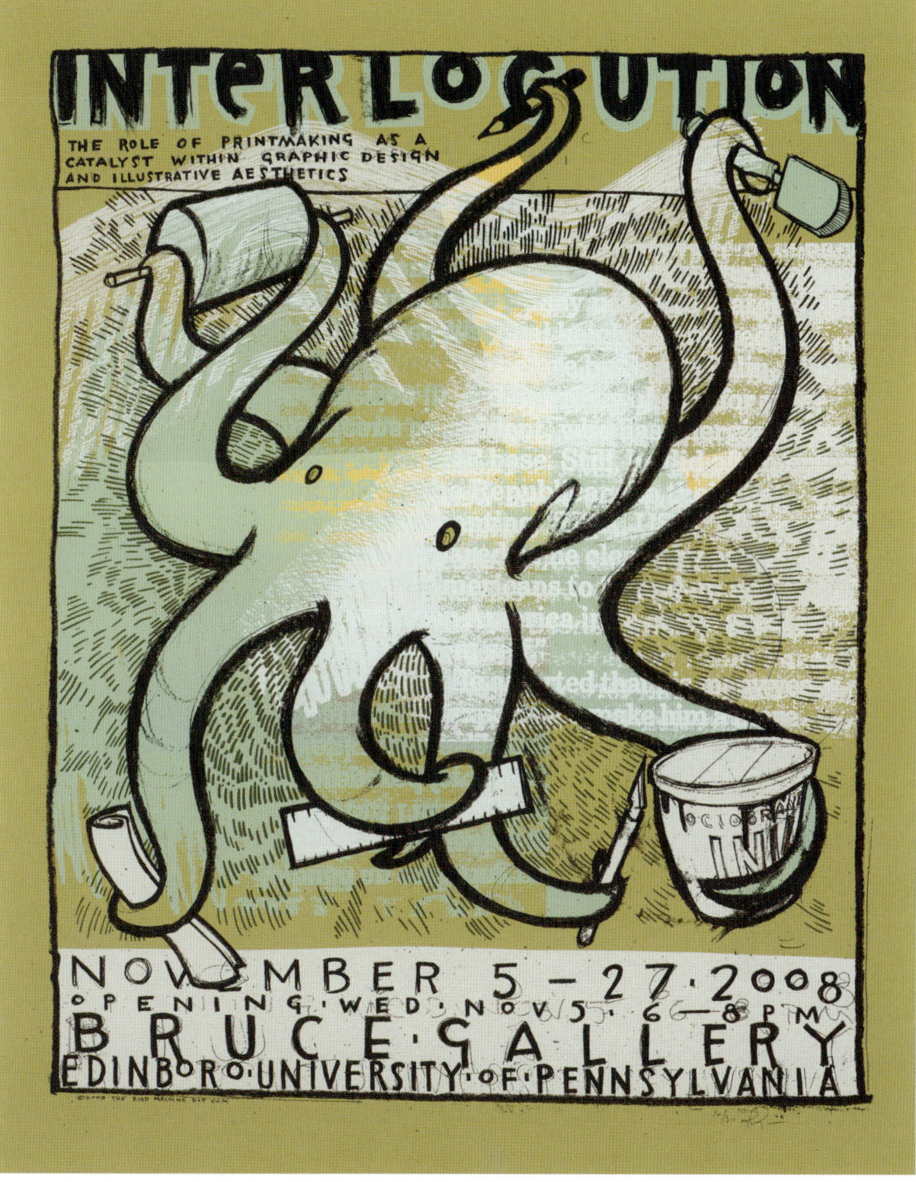

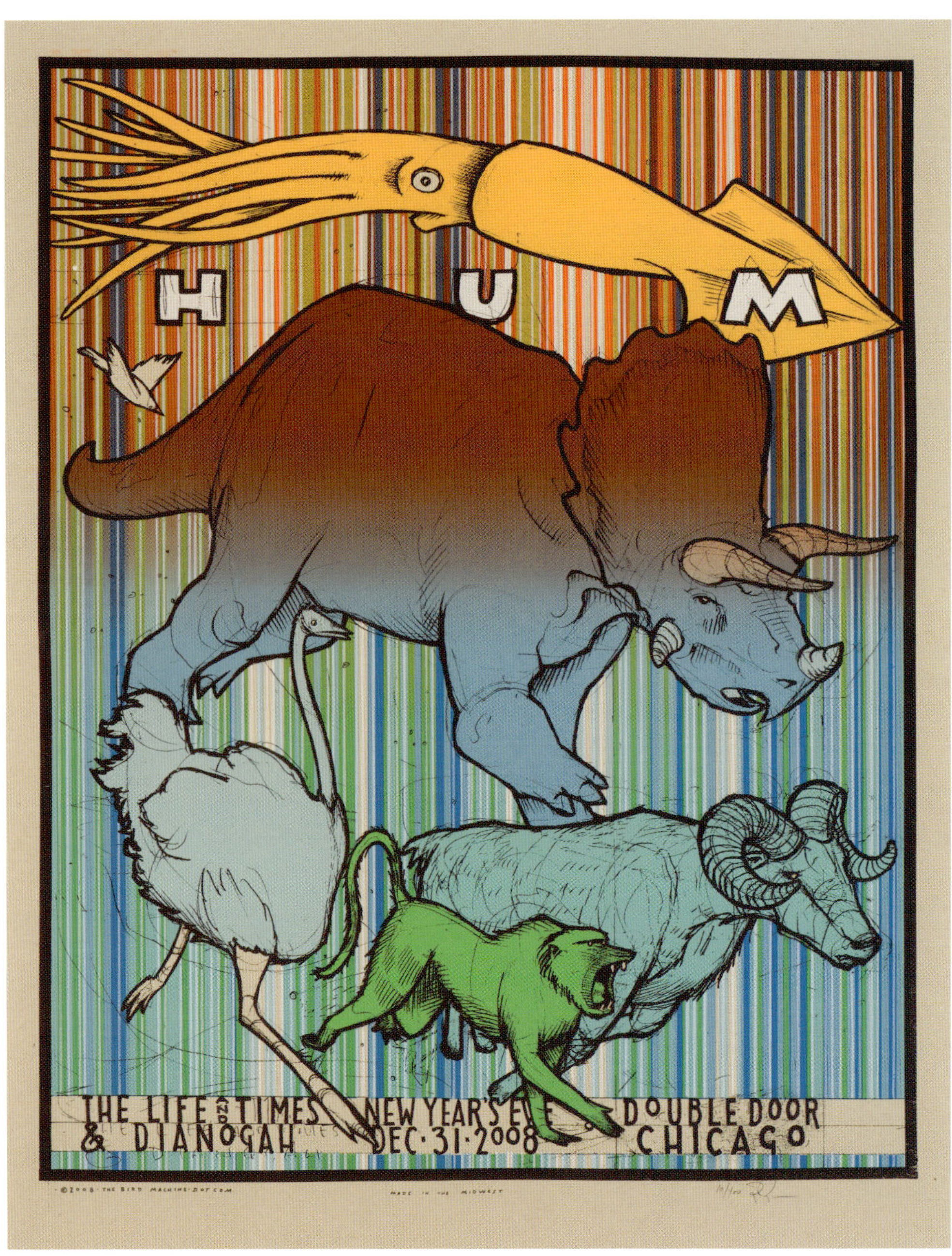

Hum New Year's Eve 2008
2008
20 x 26 inches
5 screens

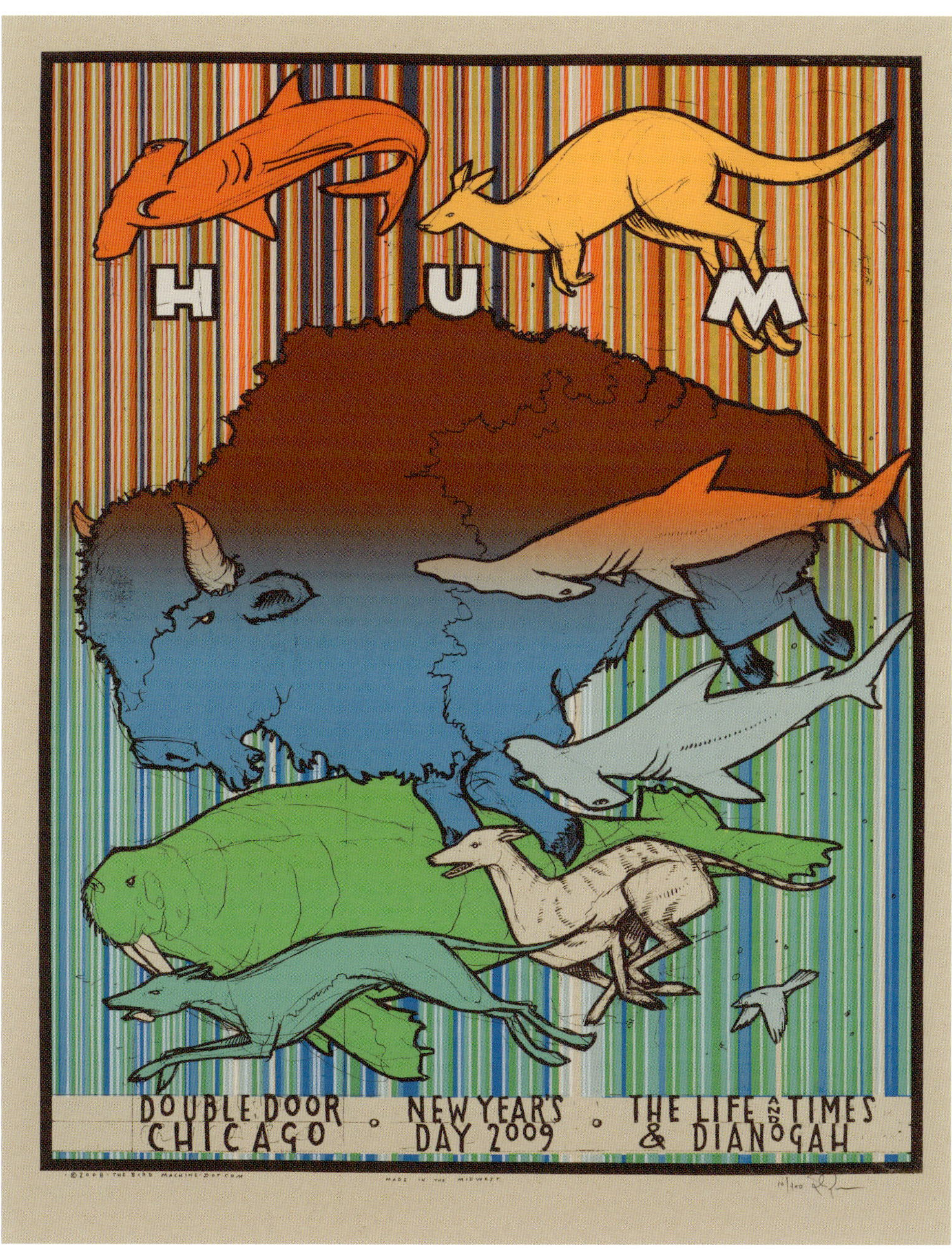

Hum New Year's Day 2009
2009
20 x 26 inches
5 screens

Hum has been a favorite band since they played at the Blind Pig when Diana and I went on our first date in 1992. They stopped playing together in 2000, but have reunited about every two years to play a couple shows. This diptych features one of the few documented cases of greyhounds running with hammerhead sharks, and also proves the theory of the rumored squid/baboon alliance.

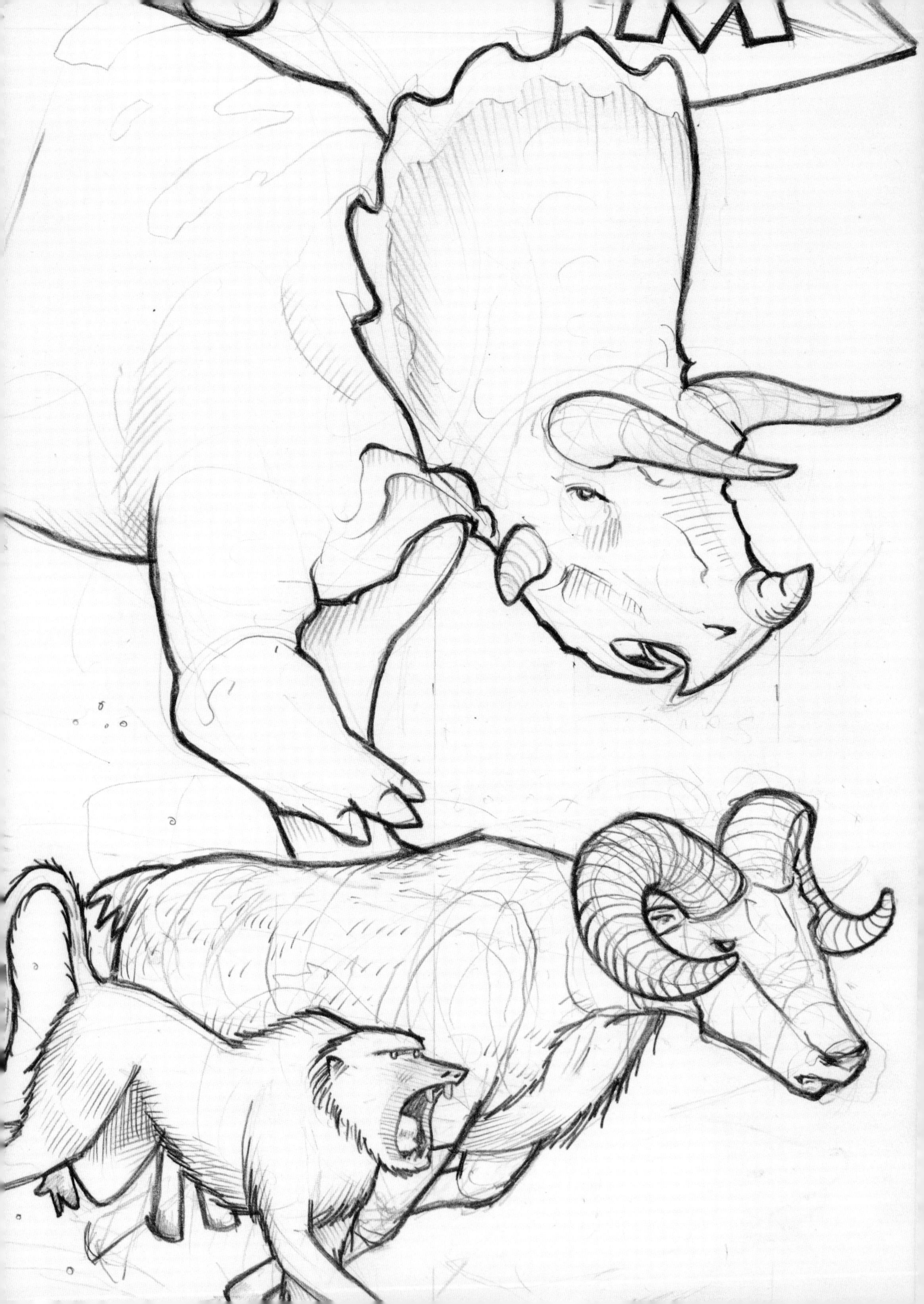

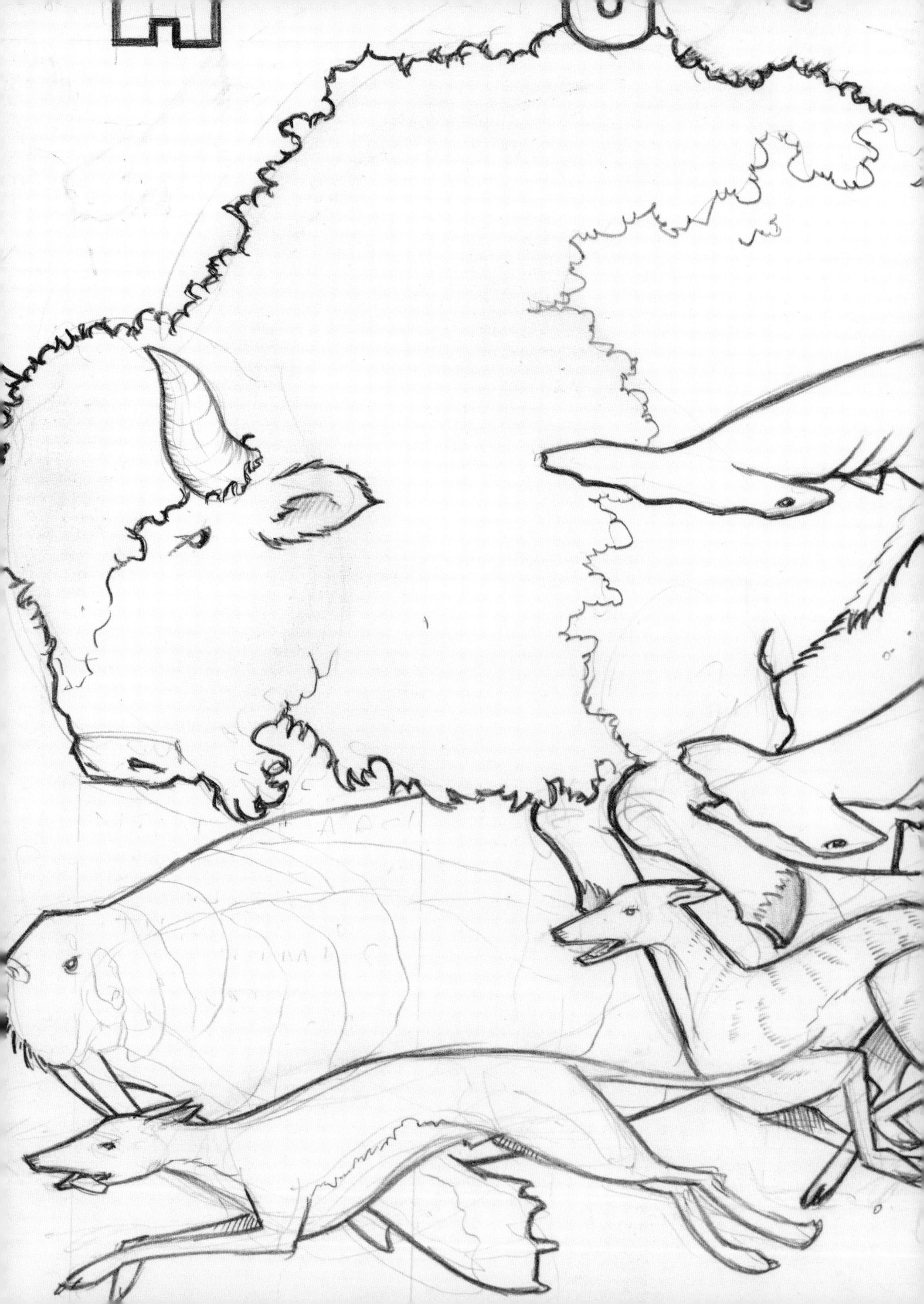

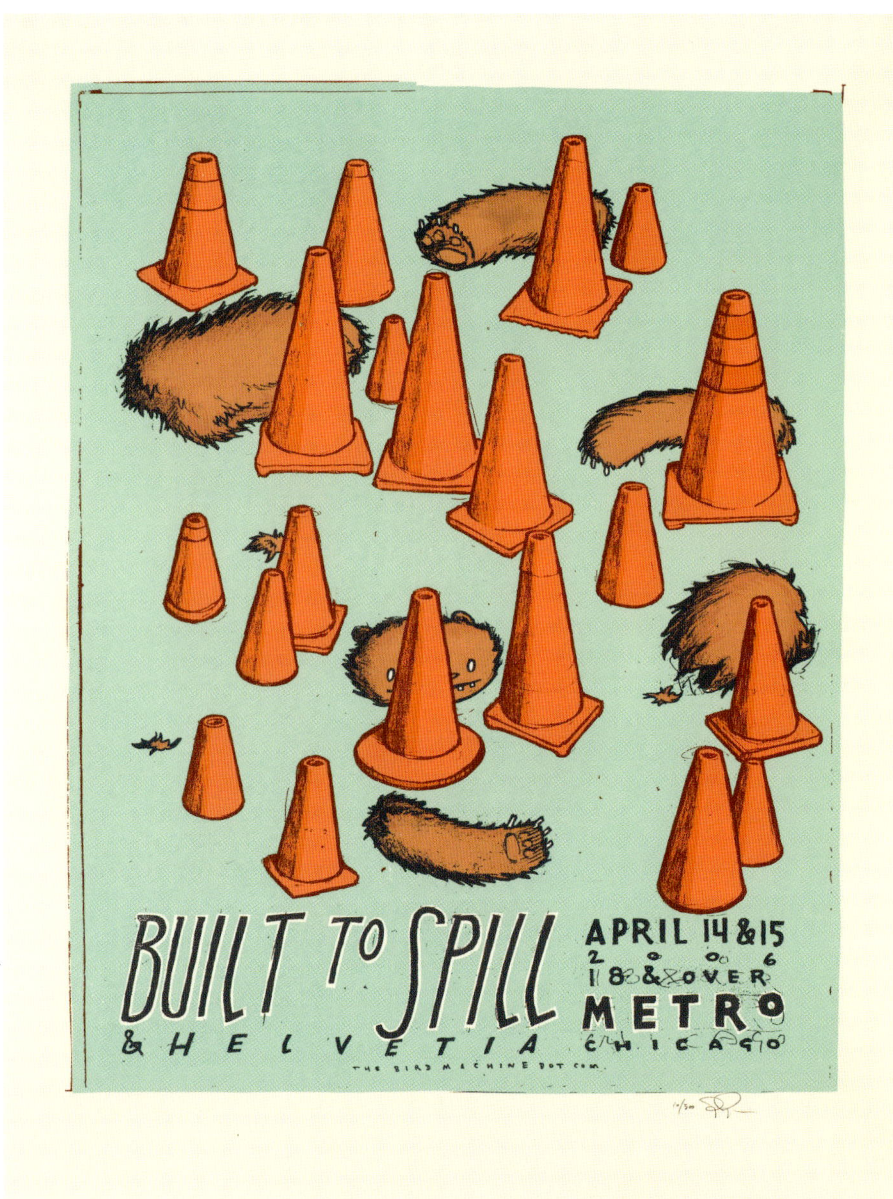

Built to Spill

2006

18 x 24 inches

5 screens

As you know, it is a well-documented fact that I only draw from real life. This poster was based on something I saw outside a Thai restaurant in Minneapolis on a bitterly cold night, about 1 in the morning, after speaking at the Fitzgerald Theater (home of *A Prairie Home Companion* radio show). We came upon a family of road cones waiting patiently to cross the street, just as a bear happened to stumble out from behind a nearby condo building, frozen and slow. The bear tipped, and shattered in the cold, and the road cones cautiously investigated.

Upon my return to Chicago, I was contacted by the nightclub Metro to make this poster, which I did, quickly. As soon as we finished, I learned that the tour was cancelled due to a basketball injury which singer Doug Martsch had suffered. I contacted the band to make sure it would be alright to release these prints into the world, despite the show's cancellation, and they approved.

Built to Spill
2006
18 x 24 inches
6 screens

When the tour was rescheduled, the bear took out his previously frozen frustrations on the cones. My friend Geoff Peveto of the Decoder Ring Design Concern suggested that the bear use a firetruck, but the bear couldn't get his paws on one in time for the poster, so he improvised.

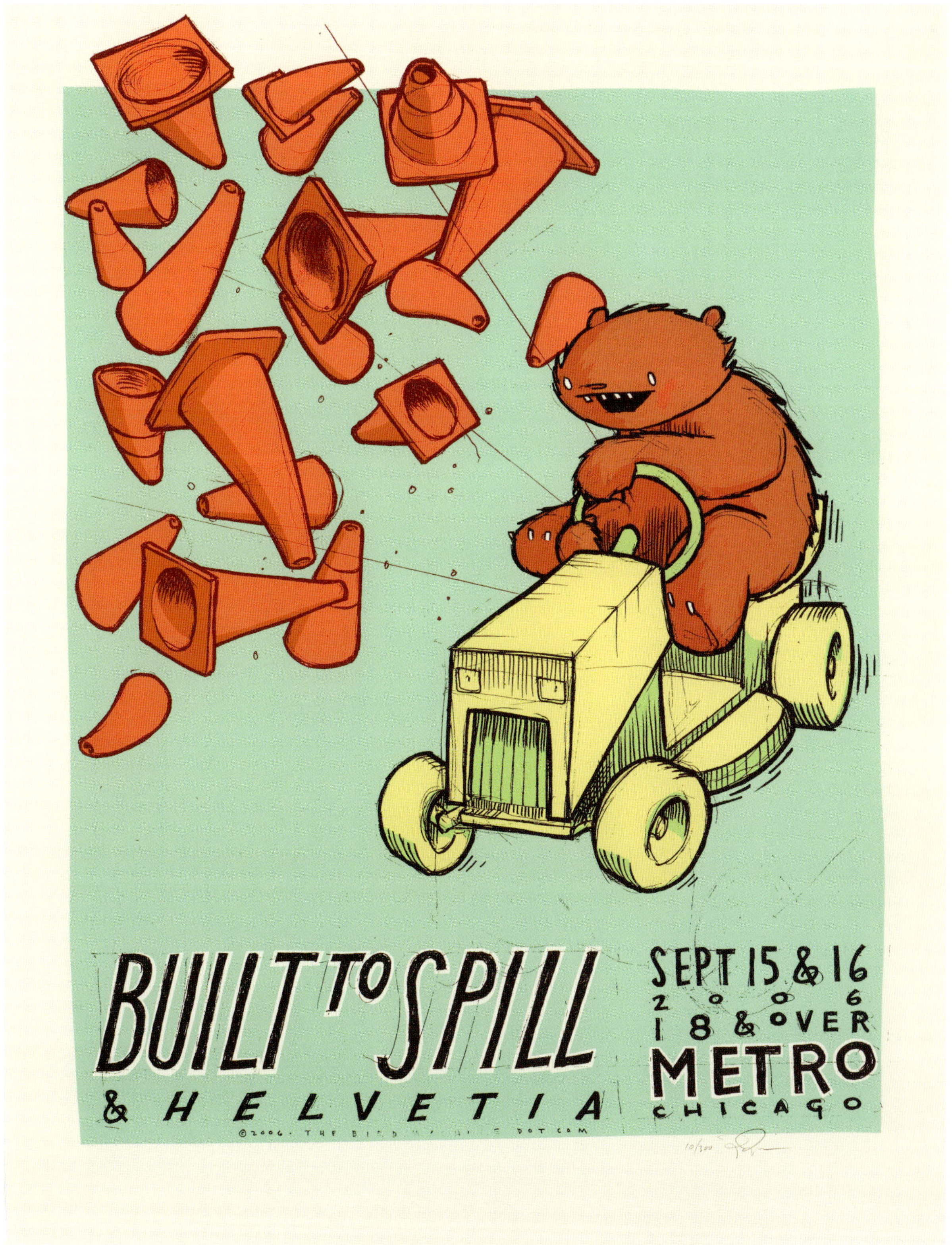

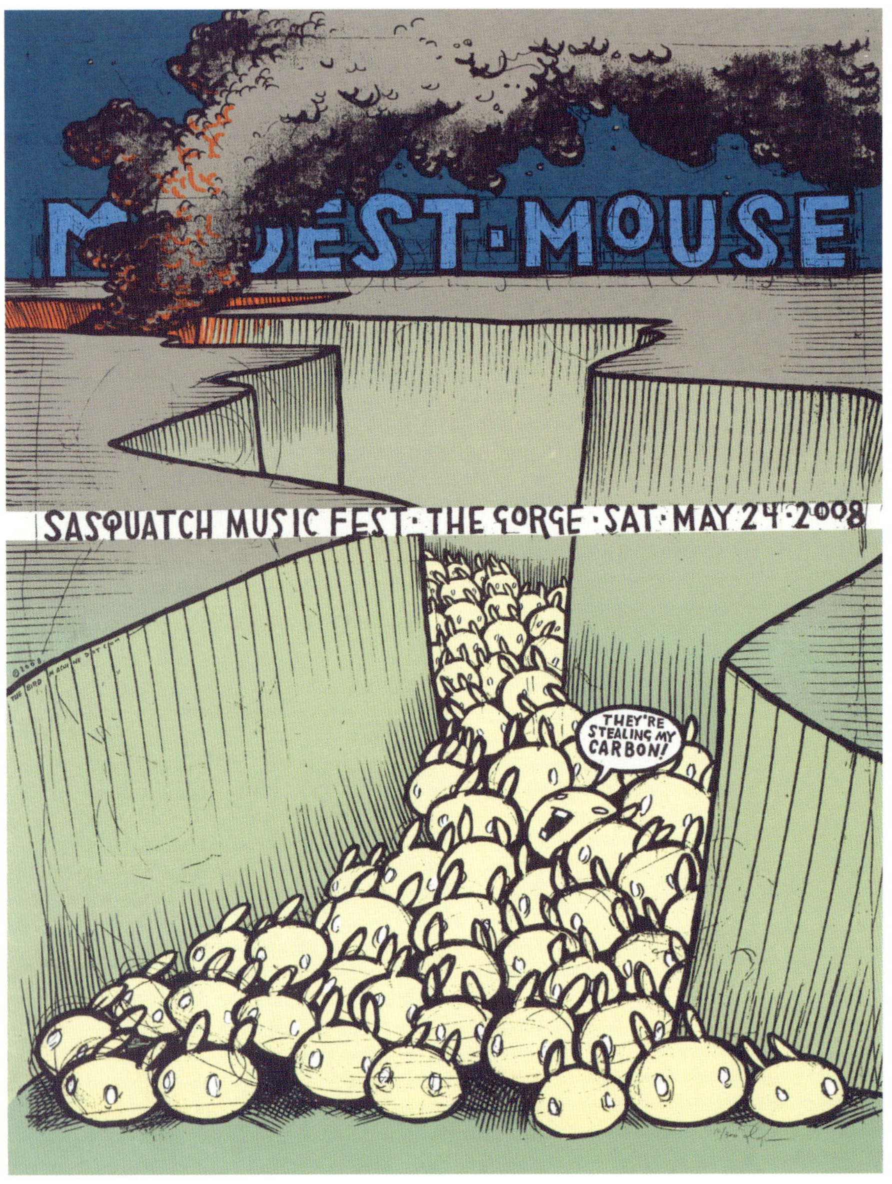

Modest Mouse

2008

18 x 24 inches

6 screens

"Some day you will die and somehow something's gonna steal your carbon."

Madison Exchange
2008
26 x 35 inches
8 screens

A Madison Exchange is a bike racing maneuver in which one rider "throws" a team member along the track, transferring all of his momentum to his partner. These animals and objects were caught moving in parallel, and were printed with grad student help at the University of Wisconsin.

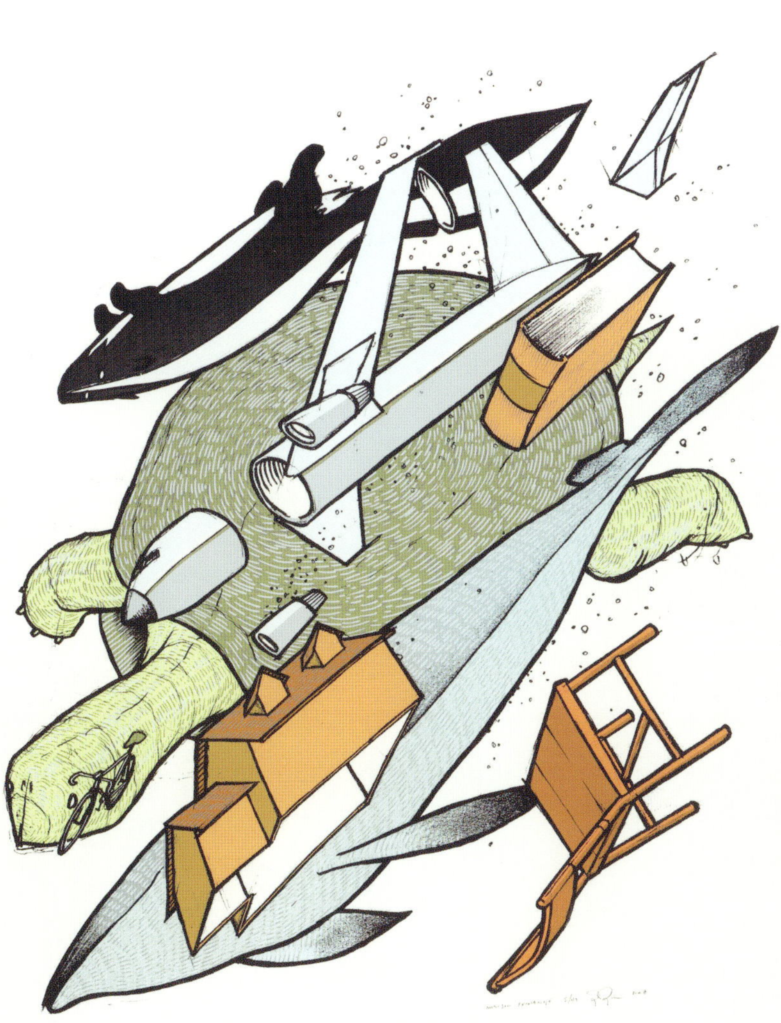

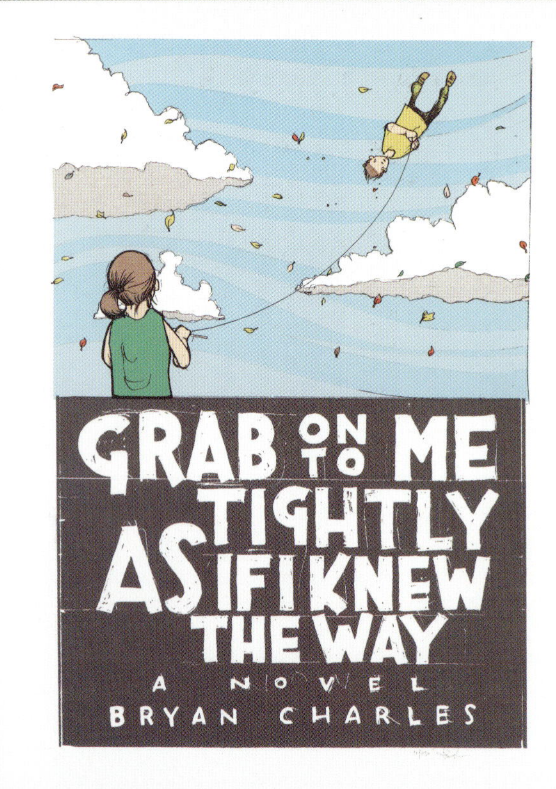

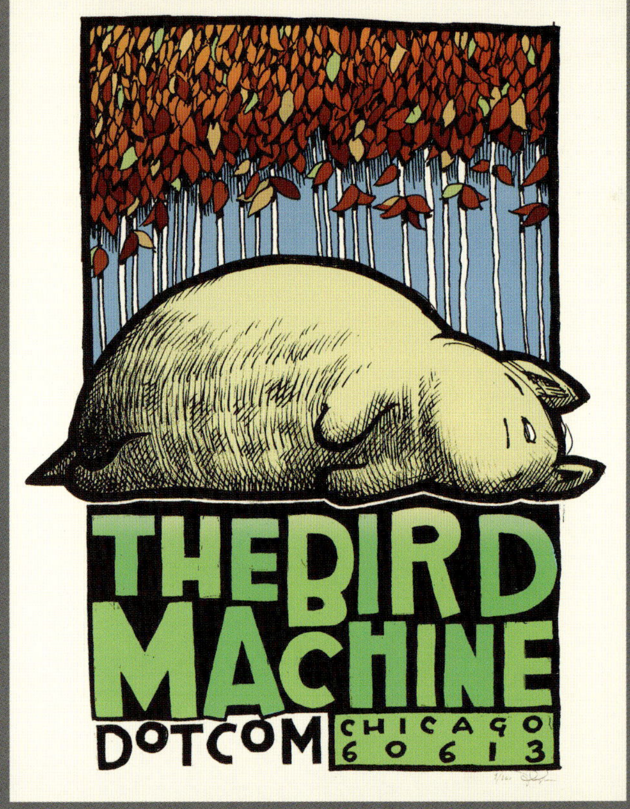

Grab On to Me Tightly as If I Knew the Way
2006
19 x 25 inches
9 screens

This print was made after the cover of Brian Charles' debut novel. I tried to summarize all of the teenage protagonist's relationships in one image. At 9 screens and 450 pieces, this was a big print job for us in 2006.

Sleeping in the Trees
2005
18 x 24 inches
6 screens

Our first and only self-promo print, to date. This little guy perfectly embodies what Steve Albini refers to as my "undifferentiated mammals."

Swimming Diplodocus

2007

8.5 x 28.5 inches

4 screens

The swimming diplodocus was submitted to a skateboard company as one of a group of deck designs, none of which were accepted. I thought he needed to get out in the world, so we made this print.

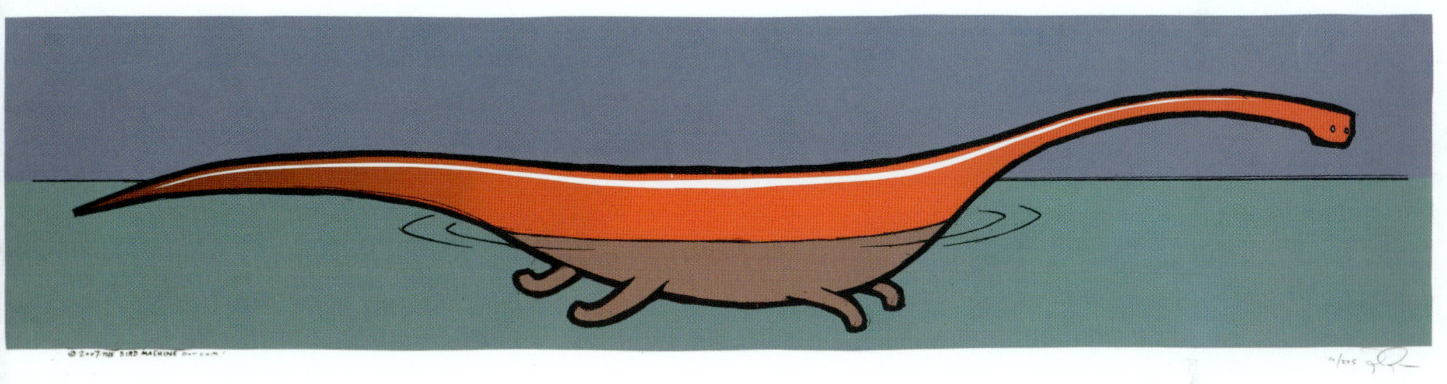

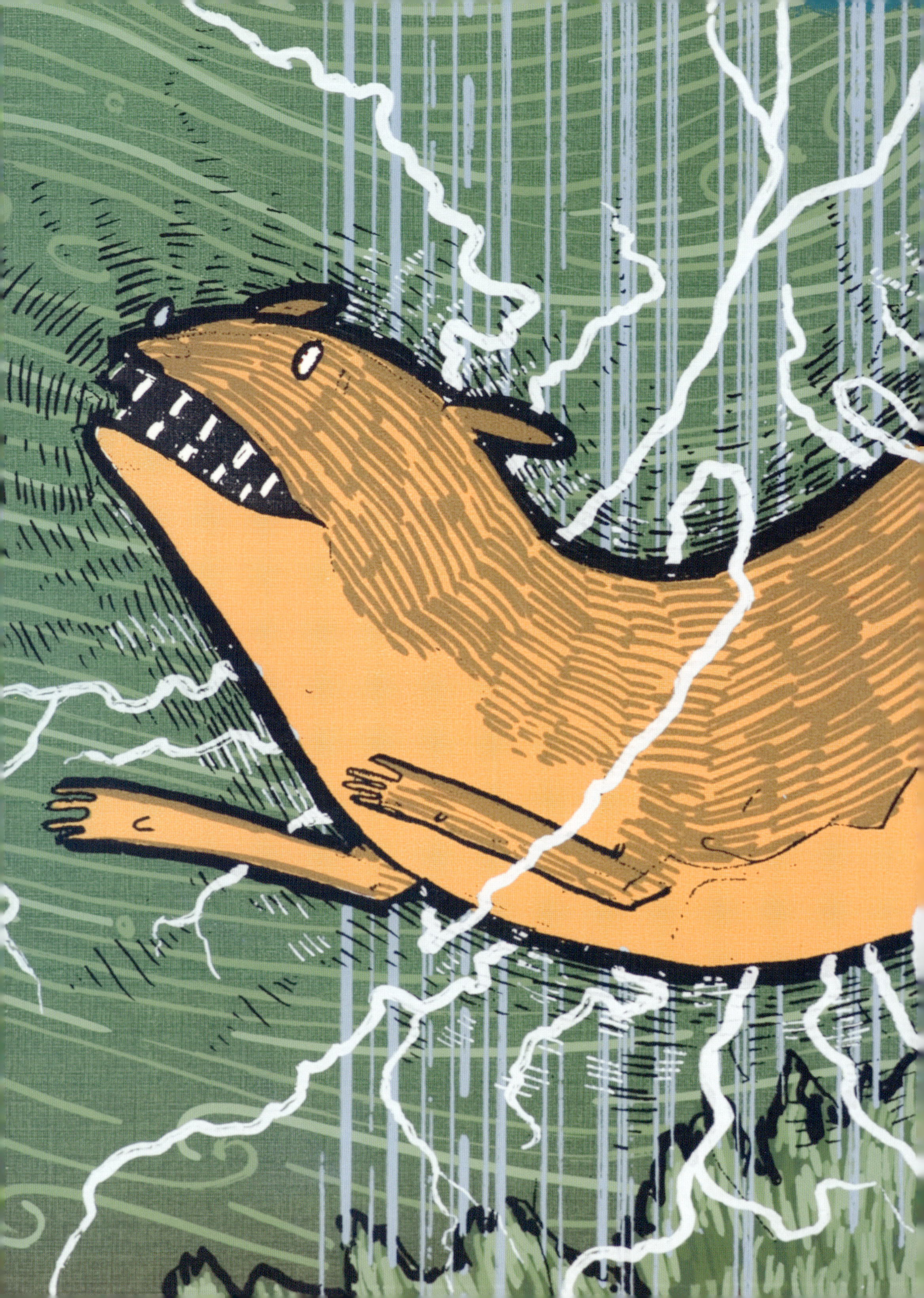

Thunderbeast (from *Beasts*)

2008

20 x 26 inches

11 screens

Jacob Covey, of Seattle's Fantagraphics Books, organized a volume, titled *Beasts*, consisting of dozens of illustrators each depicting a mythological animal. While the book contained everything from Bigfoot and the Loch Ness Monster to harpies and werewolves, I was assigned the Raiju, or Thunderbeast, from Japanese mythology. The Thunderbeast takes the form of a weasel or monkey, leaps from tree to tree in agitation during thunderstorms, and takes refuge in human bellybuttons at night, which is why the wary sleep facedown. I made one image for inclusion in the book, and made a second version, depicted here, as a screenprint when *Beasts* became a traveling gallery show.

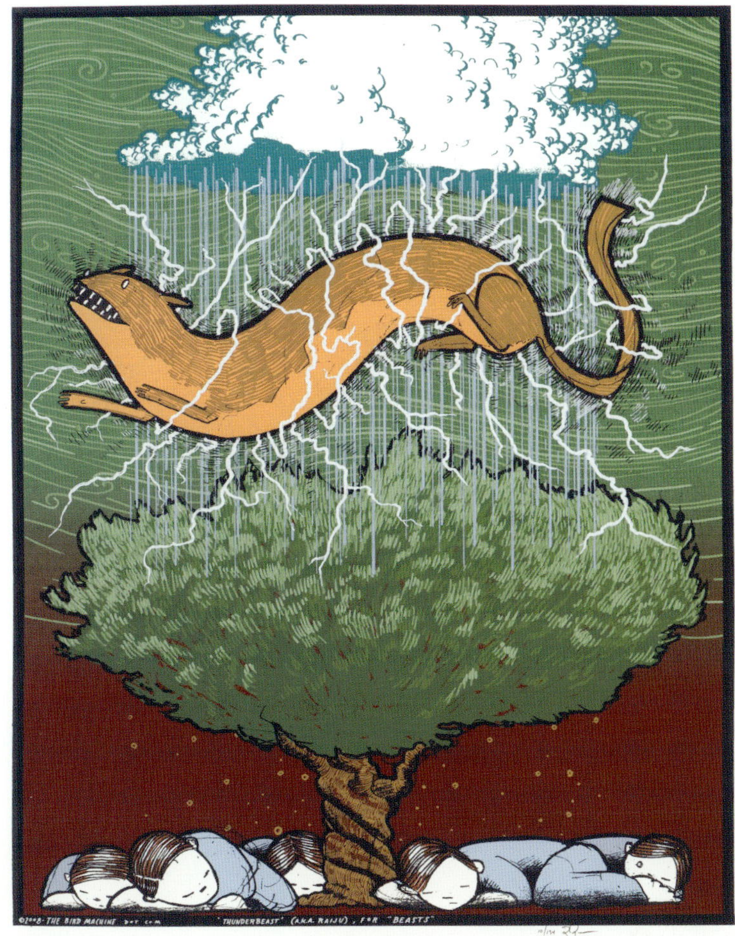

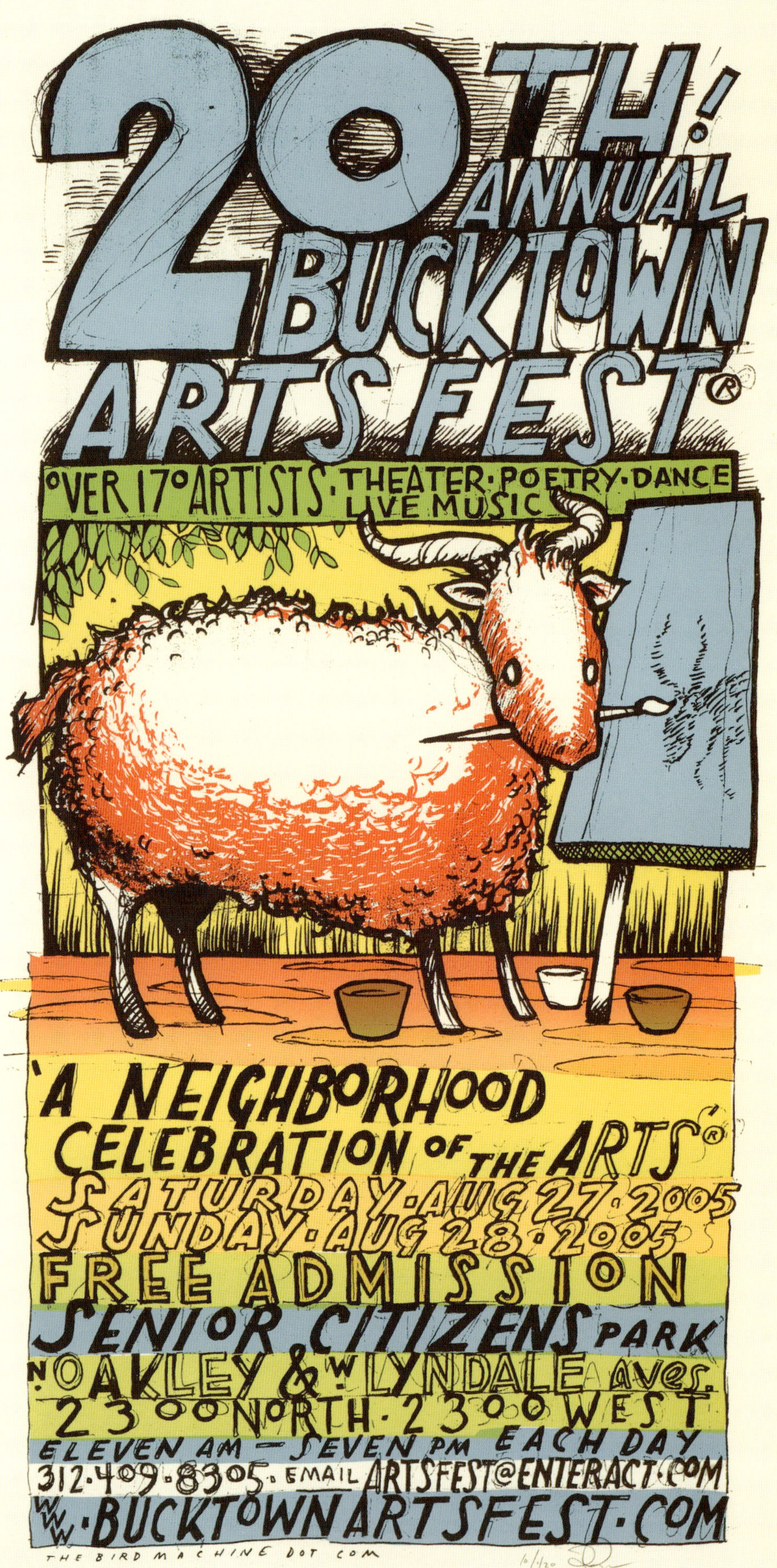
20TH!
ANNUAL
BUCKTOWN
ARTS FEST®
OVER 170 ARTISTS · THEATER · POETRY · DANCE
LIVE MUSIC
'A NEIGHBORHOOD
CELEBRATION OF THE ARTS'®
SATURDAY · AUG 27 · 2005
SUNDAY · AUG 28 · 2005
FREE ADMISSION
SENIOR CITIZENS PARK
N. OAKLEY & W. LYNDALE aves.
2300 NORTH · 2300 WEST
ELEVEN AM – SEVEN PM EACH DAY
312·409·8305 · EMAIL ARTSFEST@ENTERACT·COM
WWW·BUCKTOWNARTSFEST·COM
THE BIRD MACHINE DOT COM
10/120

20th Annual Bucktown Arts Fest

2005

12 x 24 inches

4 screens

Bucktown, a traditionally German neighborhood on Chicago's northwest side, had residents who used goat-drawn carts as late as the 1950s. This well-respected outdoor art fair gave me few guidelines for the print aside from the requirement that there be a goat.

Flatstock 9

2006

12 x 24 inches

4 screens

This print, used for the cover of this book, includes linework that is both positive and negative of the original drawing. Little dude is wondering wtf the poster-maker was thinking.

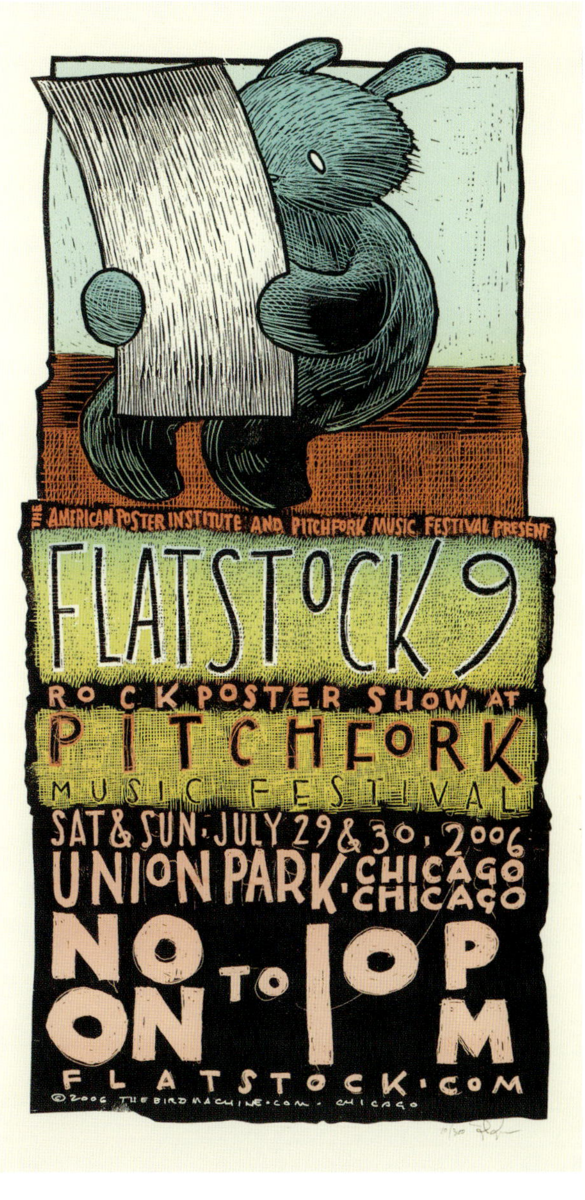

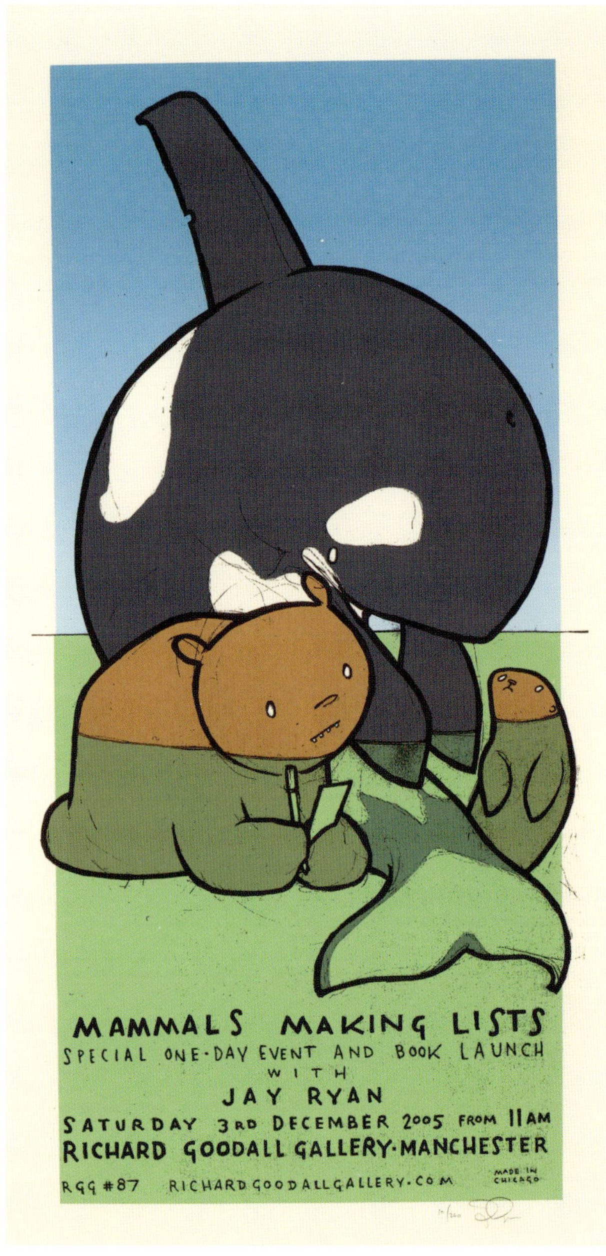

Mammals Making Lists
2005
12 x 24 inches
5 screens

I was encouraged to tie this show in to 2004's successful "Squirrels Taking Risks" show at the Richard Goodall Gallery in Manchester, so the titles establish a rhyming theme. This print was made soon after a round of interactions with orca whales in the San Juan Islands of Washington State. I literally carried my body weight's worth of my first book, *100 Posters / 134 Squirrels* books on the plane with me in my luggage to this show.

A Dozen Walrus
2008
8.5 x 28.5 inches
5 screens

No actual walrus were harmed in the making of this print, and yes, I looked it up: the plural for walrus is the same as the singular.

Cicada 17
2007
8.5 x 28.5 inches
7 screens

The last time that the 17-year cicadas of Brood 13 appeared in Chicago was the month that I graduated from high school in 1990. I was working a demolition/construction job over the summer before going to college, and loved being surrounded by such an enormous mass of huge but benign insects, buzzing away in the trees. Different broods of periodic cicadas return in different cycles, based on prime numbers of years, to avoid predators being able to depend on the massive influx of vulnerable prey. I spend my time making prints which announce that this or that band is coming to town, so I thought I'd make some posters to announce that these great little insects were on their way back in the summer of 2007. I hung these around Evanston, Illinois, near our house, but not everyone shared my enthusiasm for this event.

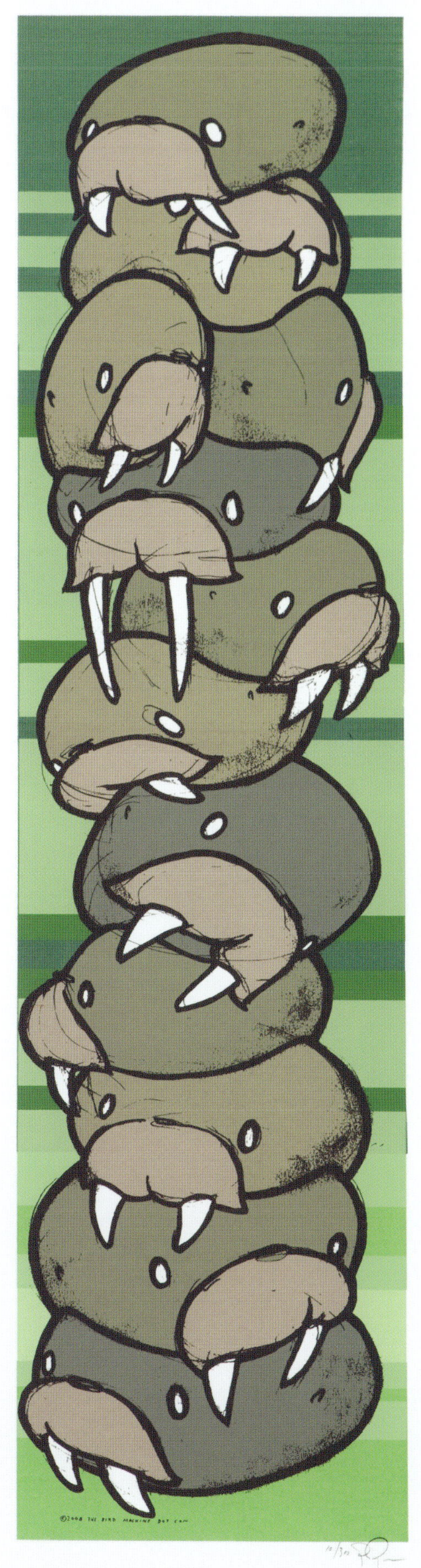

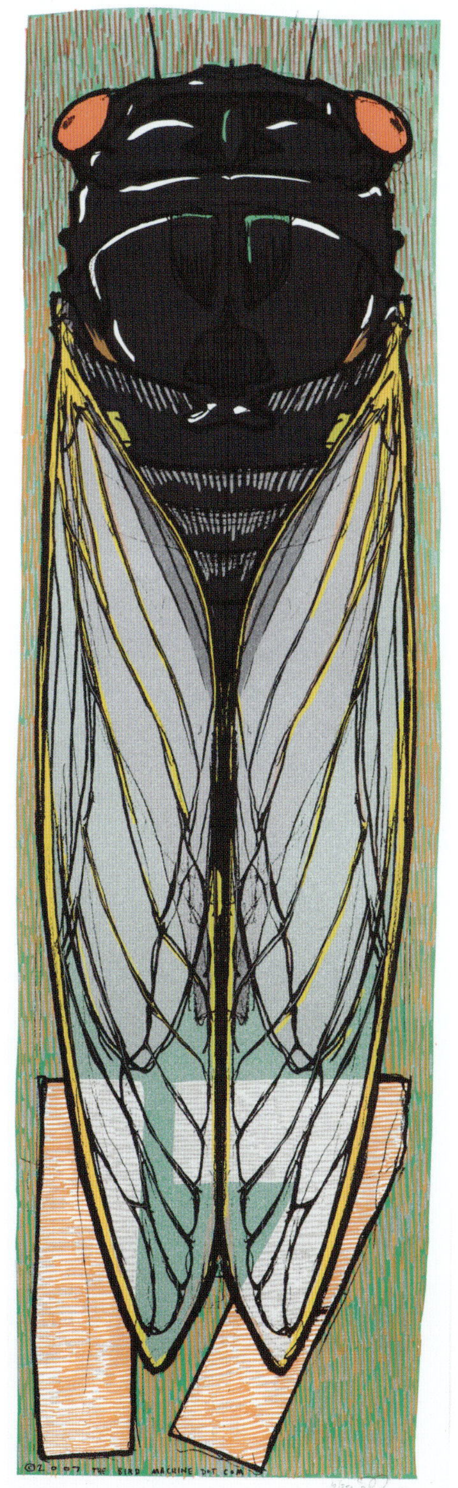

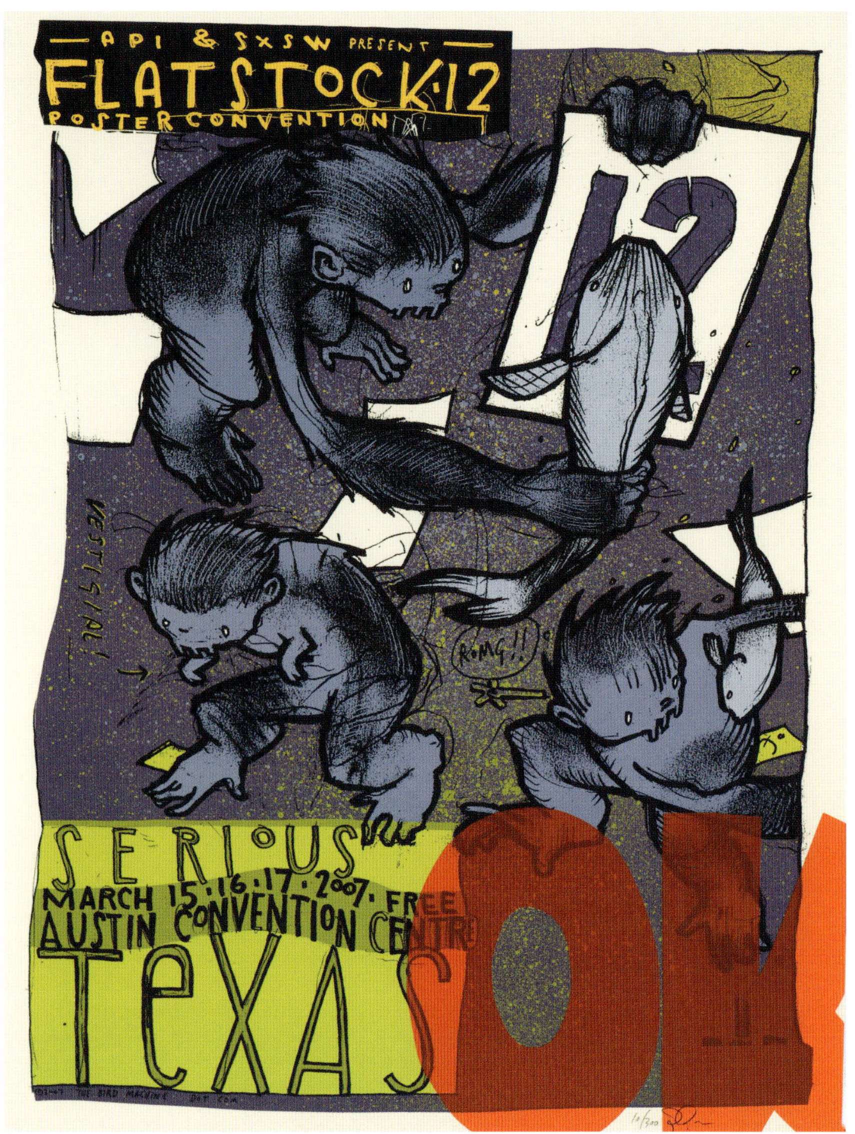

Flatstock 12

2007

18 x 24 inches

5 screens

I love my job: Spooky night monkey teaches fish to read numbers. Spooky night monkey has vestigial arms. Spooky night monkey has dropped a vintage Campagnolo "Pista" crankset and some Euros. As you can see, this poster has been rated "OK."

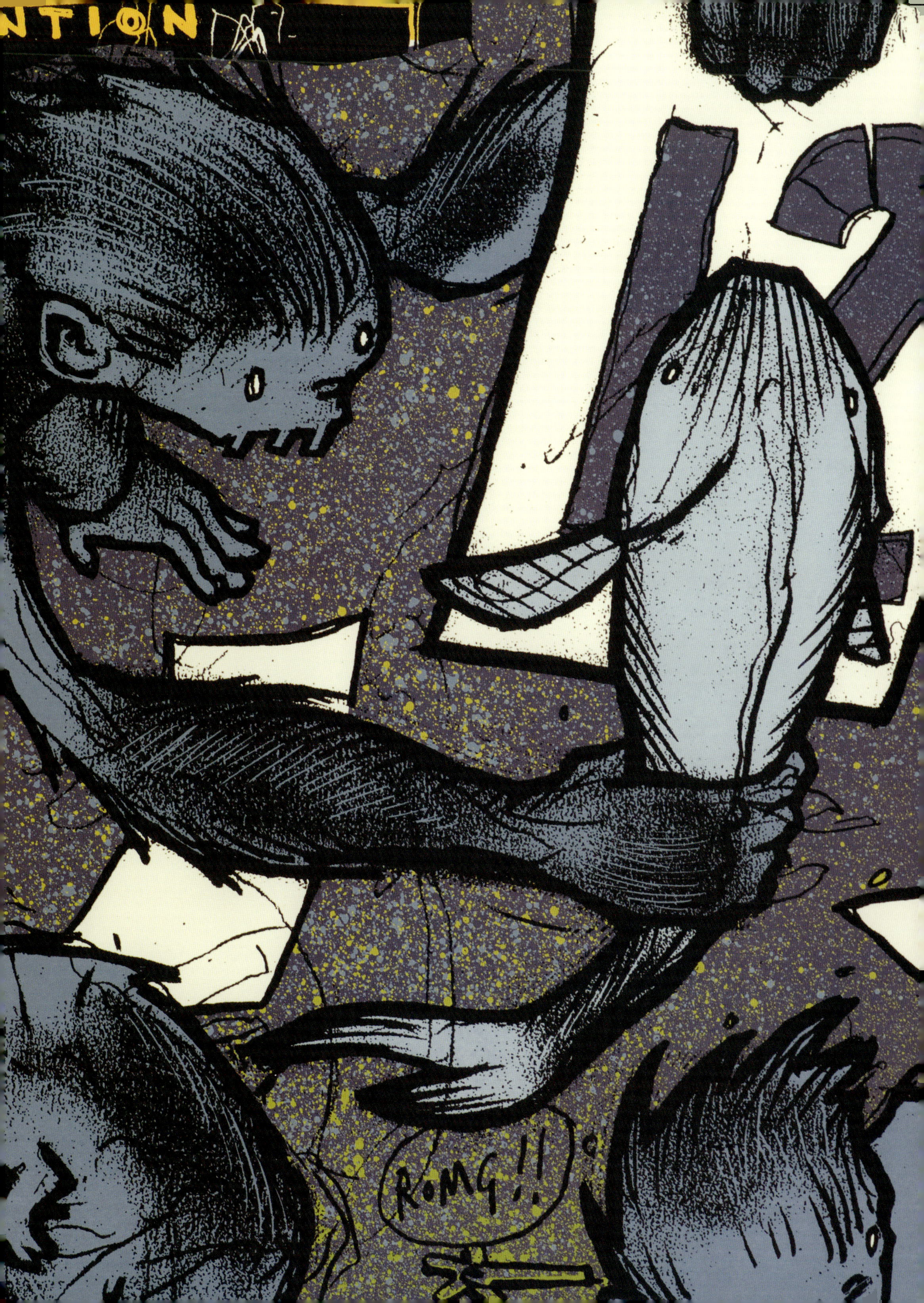
NTION
ROMG!!

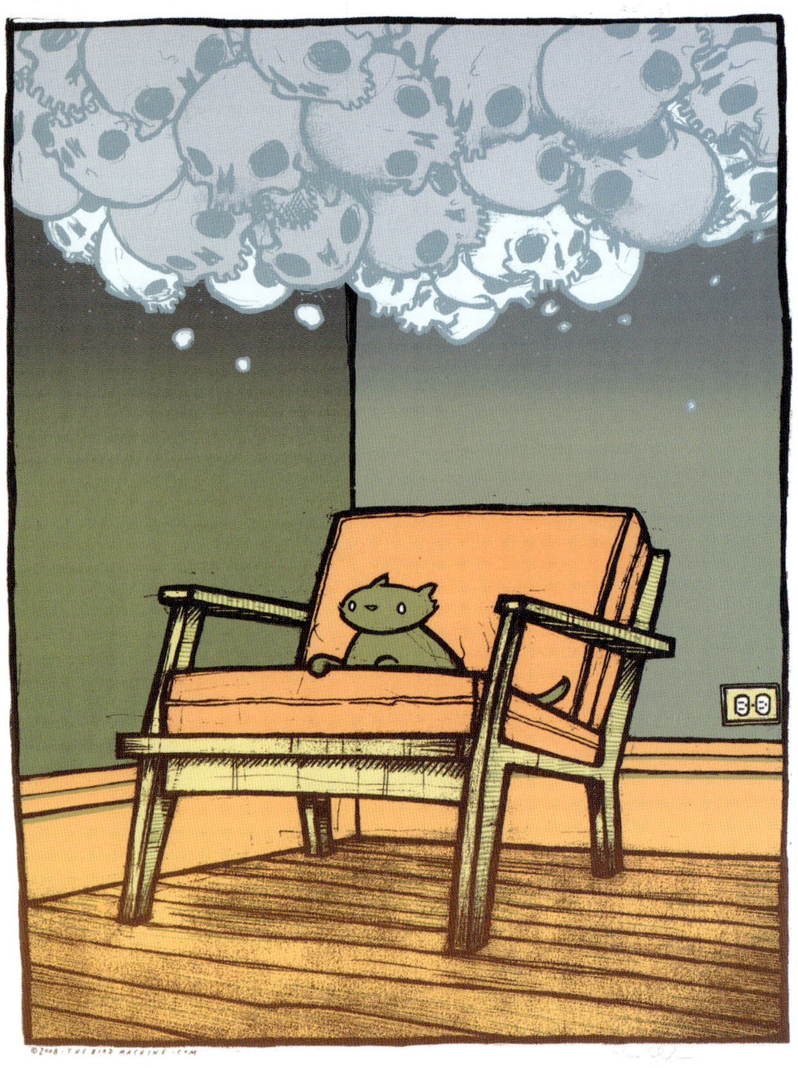

She Protects Us
2008
17.5 x 23 inches
7 screens

Akiko is a quiet, reserved little owl of a cat, whose main job at our house is apparently to warn us about bugs and spiders on the ceiling. Here she sits, in my grandmother's chair, defending us from hovering doom.

Running with Scissors
2006
17.5 x 23 inches
4 screens

Two things I remember vividly from my childhood: 1) being warned repeatedly about carrying scissors point-up, and 2) running into the dining room while wearing socks, which usually resulted in a hard wipe-out.

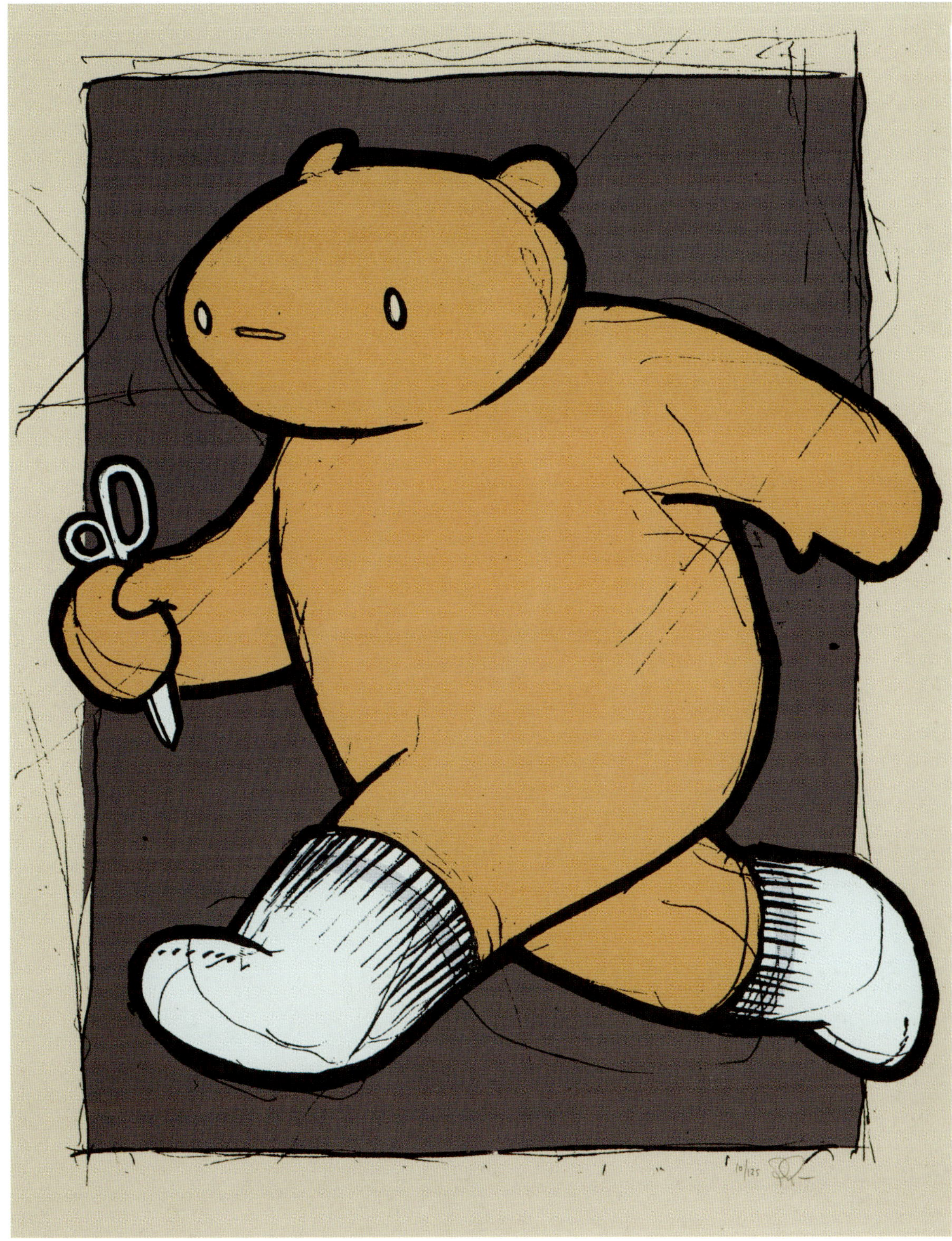

Objects In and Out of Water

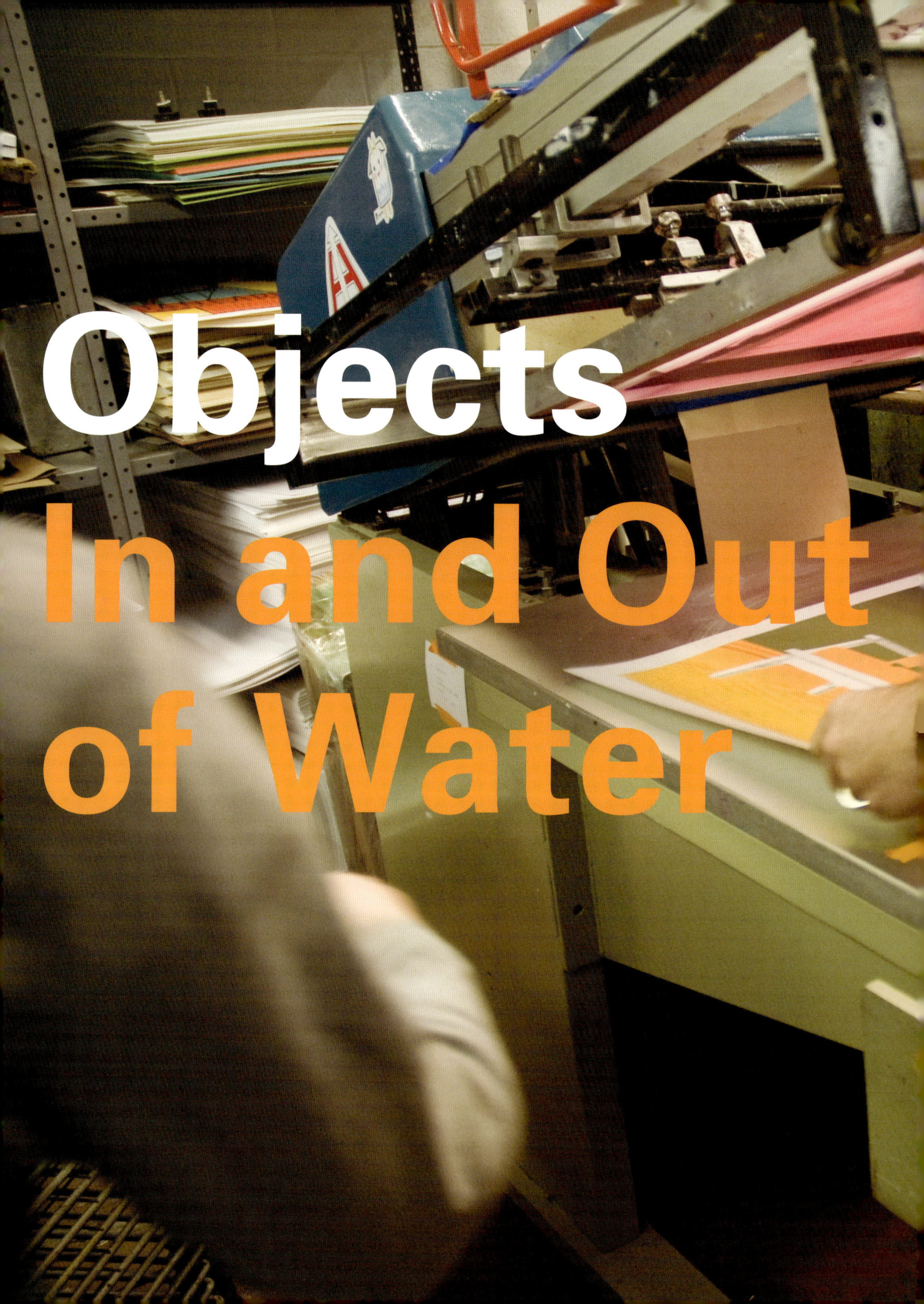

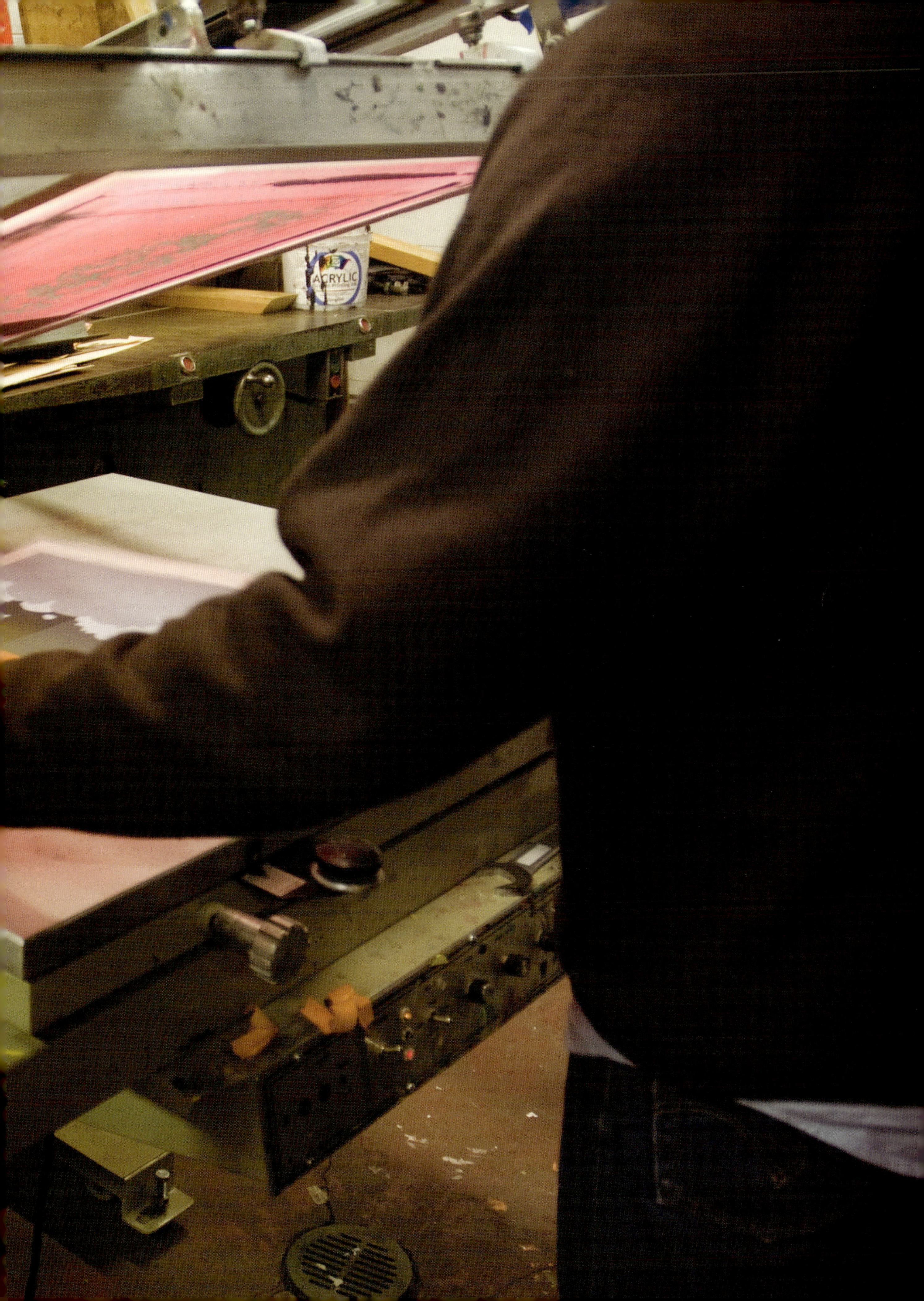
ACRYLIC

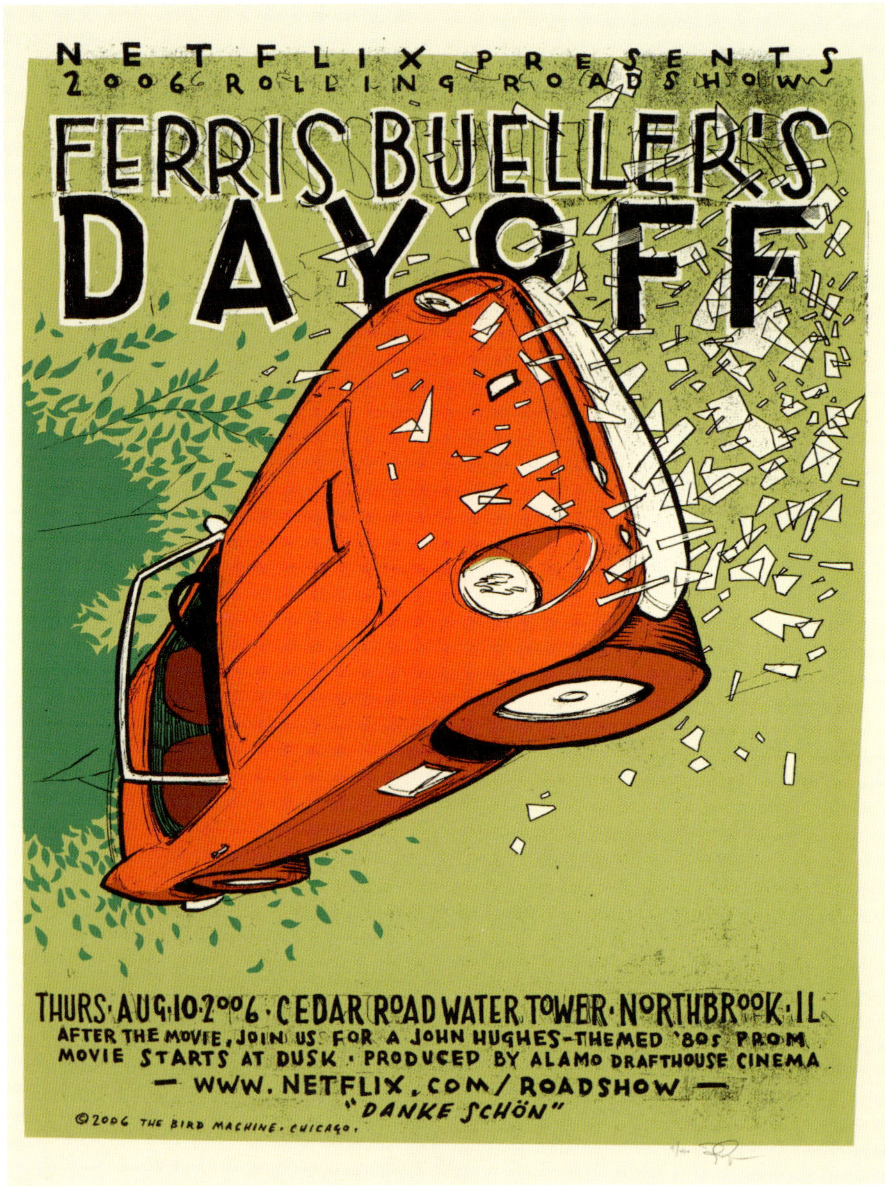

Ferris Bueller's Day Off

2006

18 x 24 inches

4 screens

While I was growing up in the (smaller, more rural) suburbs of Chicago in the mid-'80s, John Hughes' movies seemed to perfectly embody my confusion about the limited musical spectrum which was available to me, versus the awareness that there was a more vibrant teenage popular culture happening somewhere else. For this screening, I didn't want to draw Matthew Broderick's face, so the moment when Cameron's dad's Ferrari goes out the window seemed like the penultimate plot point, and a good one to depict in this print.

A Christmas Story

2007

18 x 24 inches

4 screens

The Bumpus Family Dogs ruin the Christmas dinner. Fa-ra-ra-ra-ra, Ra-ra, Ra-ra. This movie is filled with potential poster images, but these dogs seem less obvious and still easily recognizable.

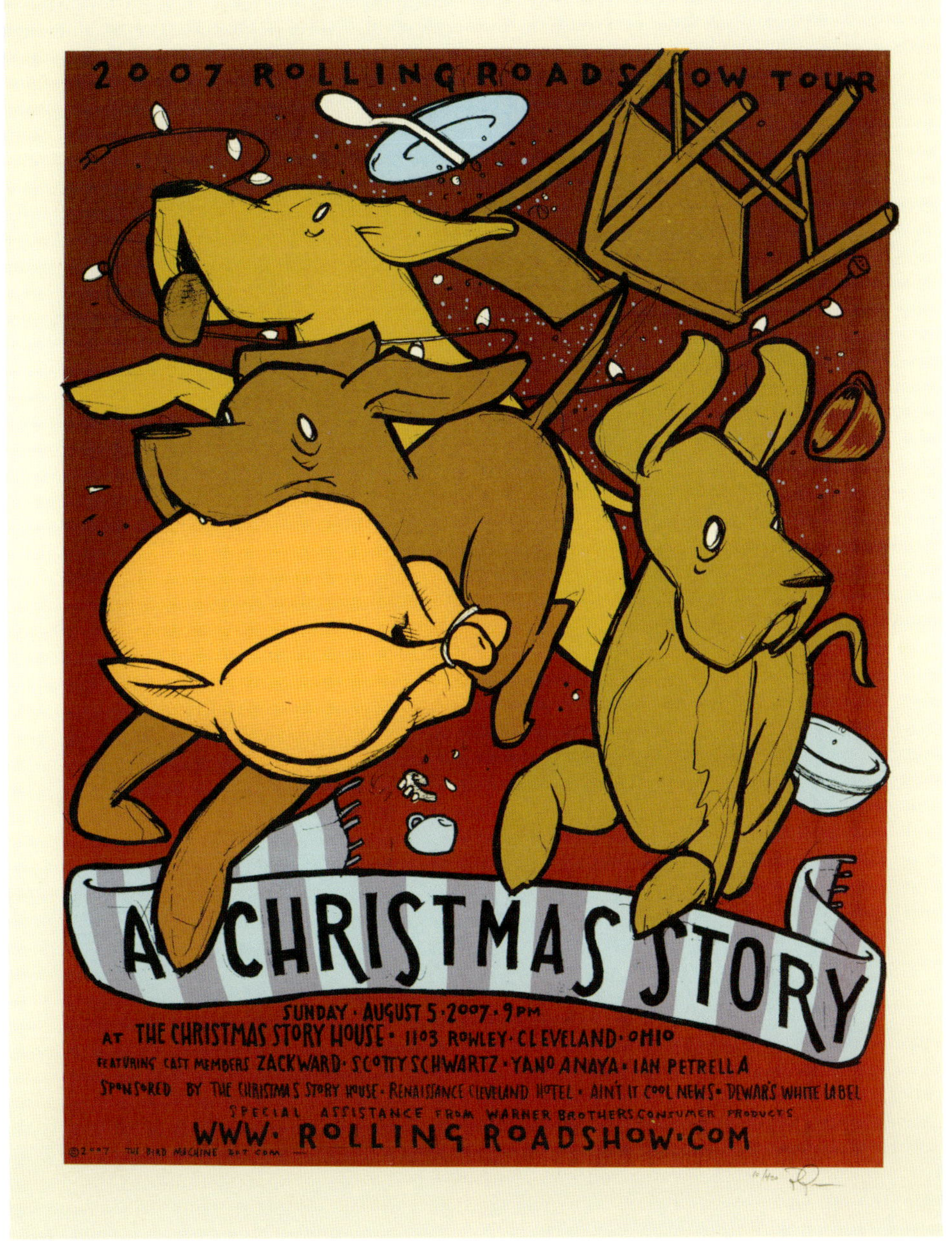

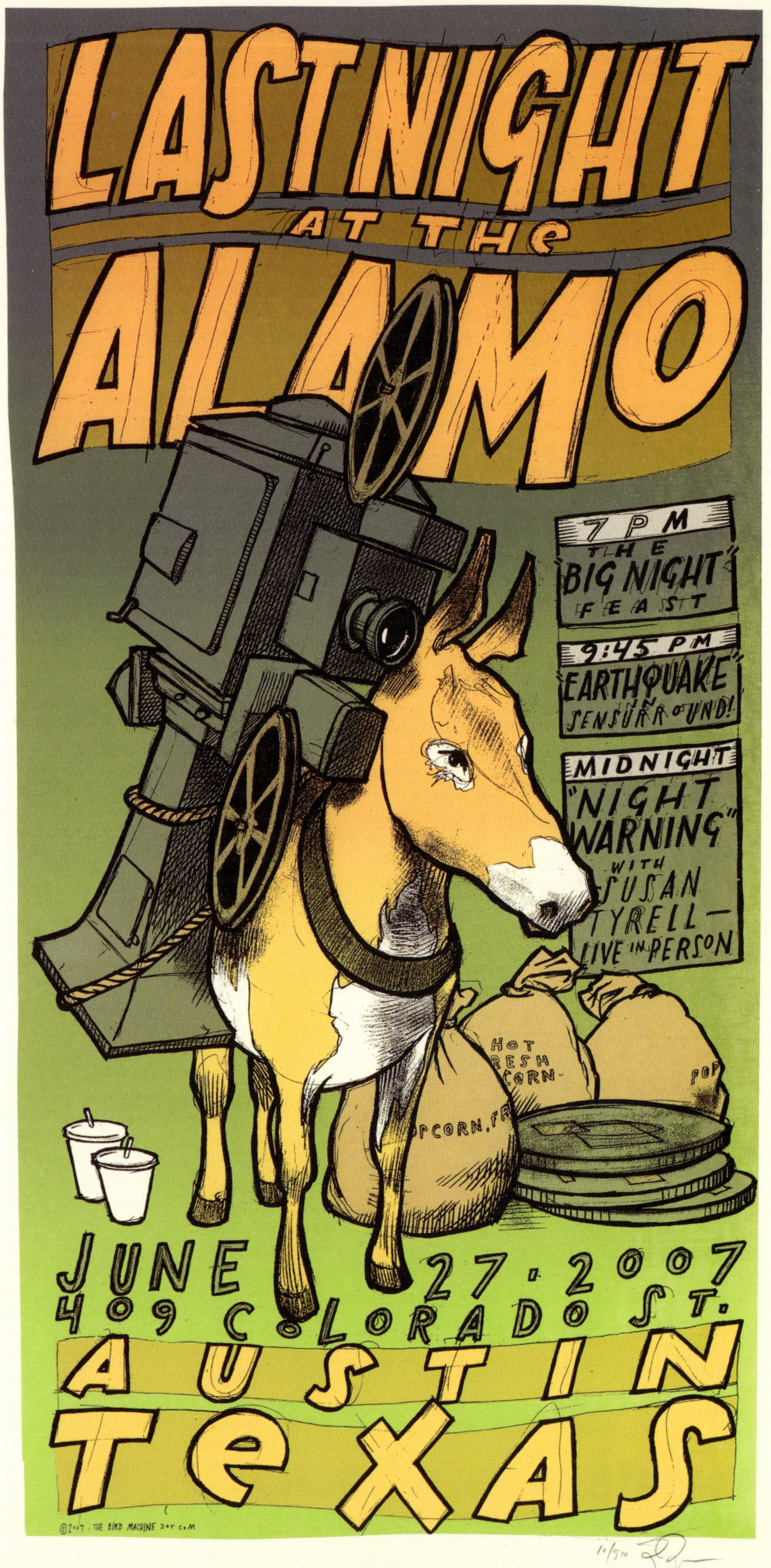

LAST NIGHT
AT THE
ALAMO
7 PM
THE "BIG NIGHT" FEAST
9:45 PM
"EARTHQUAKE" IN SENSURROUND!
MIDNIGHT
"NIGHT WARNING" WITH SUSAN TYRELL — LIVE IN PERSON
HOT FRESH CORN
POPCORN
JUNE 27 · 2007
409 COLORADO ST.
AUSTIN
TEXAS
©2007 · THE BIRD MACHINE DOT COM

Last Night at the Alamo

2007

12 x 24 inches

4 screens

This unusual movie theater in Austin shows classic films, and organizes the "Rolling Roadshow" series of screenings around the country. They were moving venues from their old Colorado Street location, so here we have their moving burro, loaded with the awesome old projector they use, the hot popcorn, and some drinks—all set to go.

2001: A Space Odyssey

2008

26 x 40 inches

6 screens

The opportunity to make a poster for the screening of one of my all-time favorite movies made me step back to reconsider my process: I used a ruler for drawing the pod and the monolith, and included computer-generated type in the image, which seemed appropriate given the film's theme of human/computer relations.

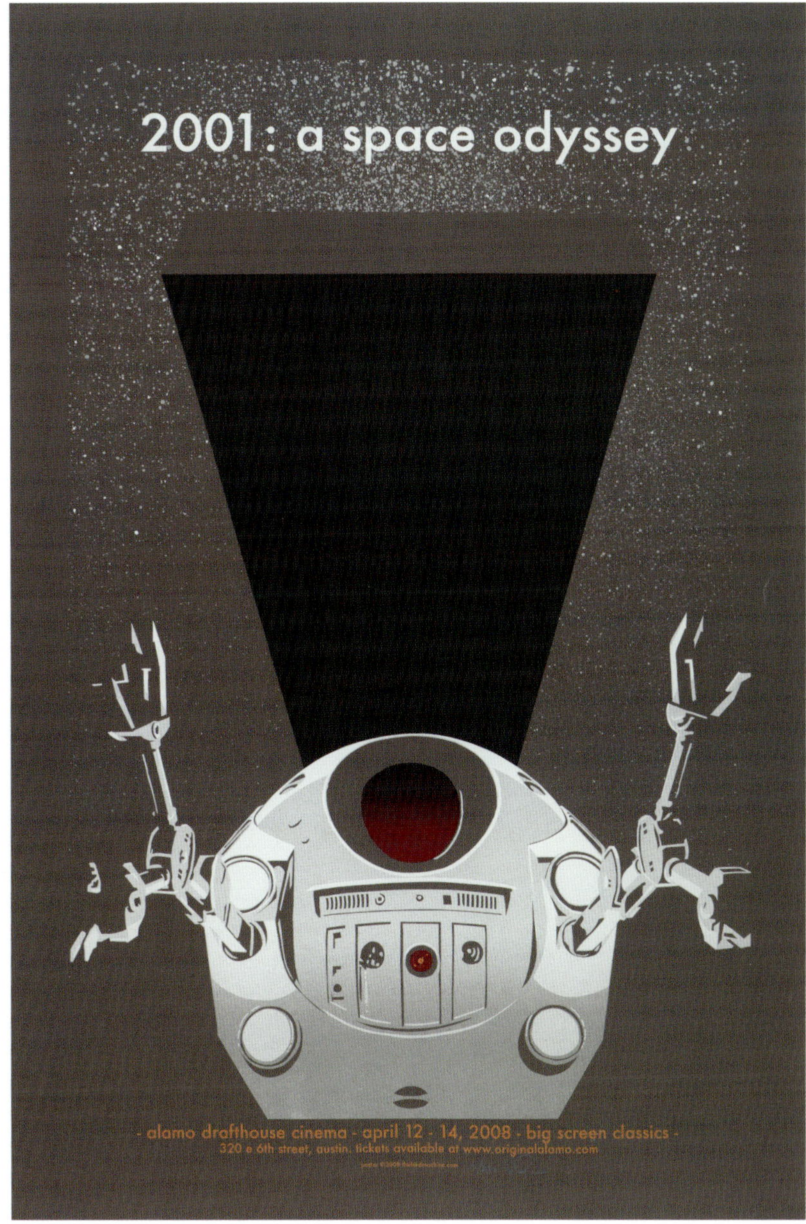

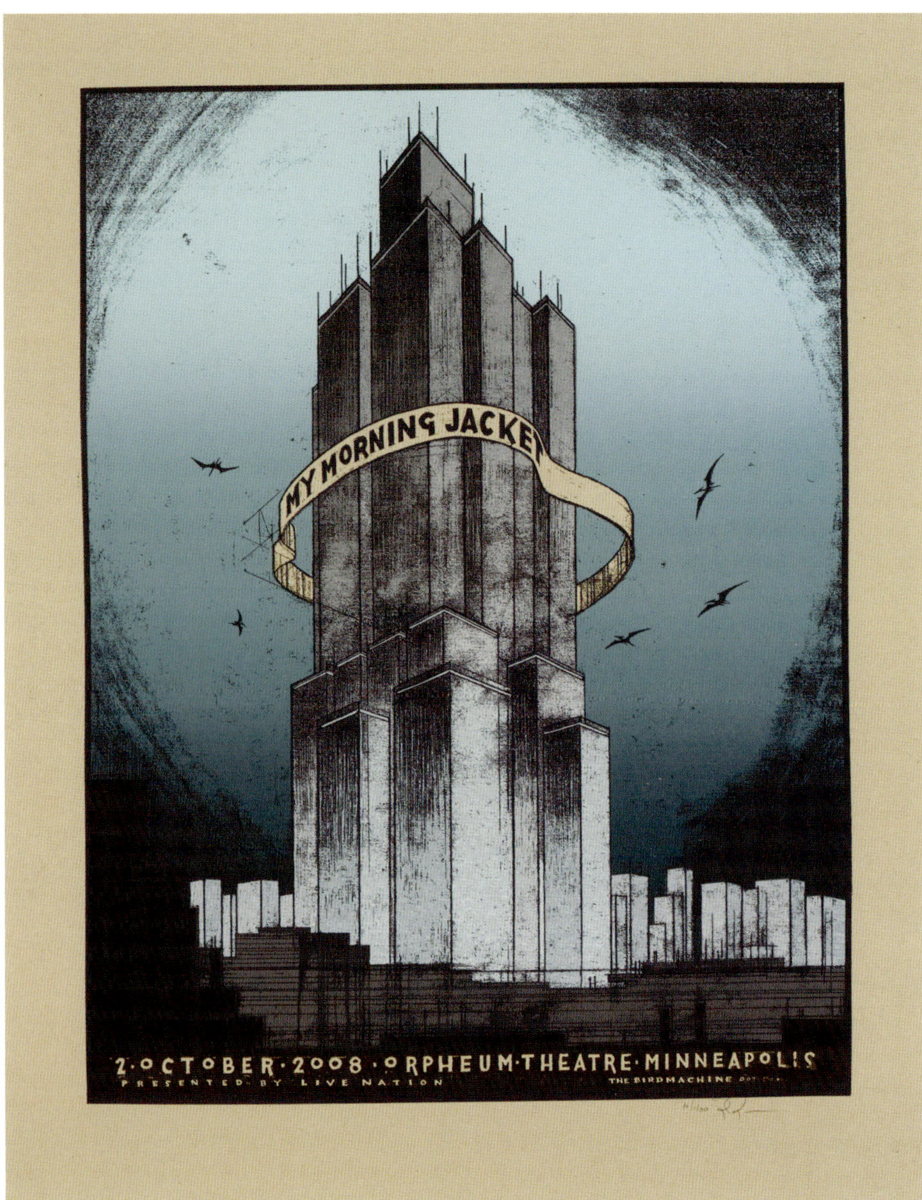

My Morning Jacket (Minneapolis)
2008
20 x 26 inches
6 screens

Dwell magazine had an article on architectural draftsman Hugh Ferriss, which inspired me to pull out the old rulers and take a stab at his dramatic renderings. The pterodactyls which are included were not directly inspired by Mr. Ferriss' work.

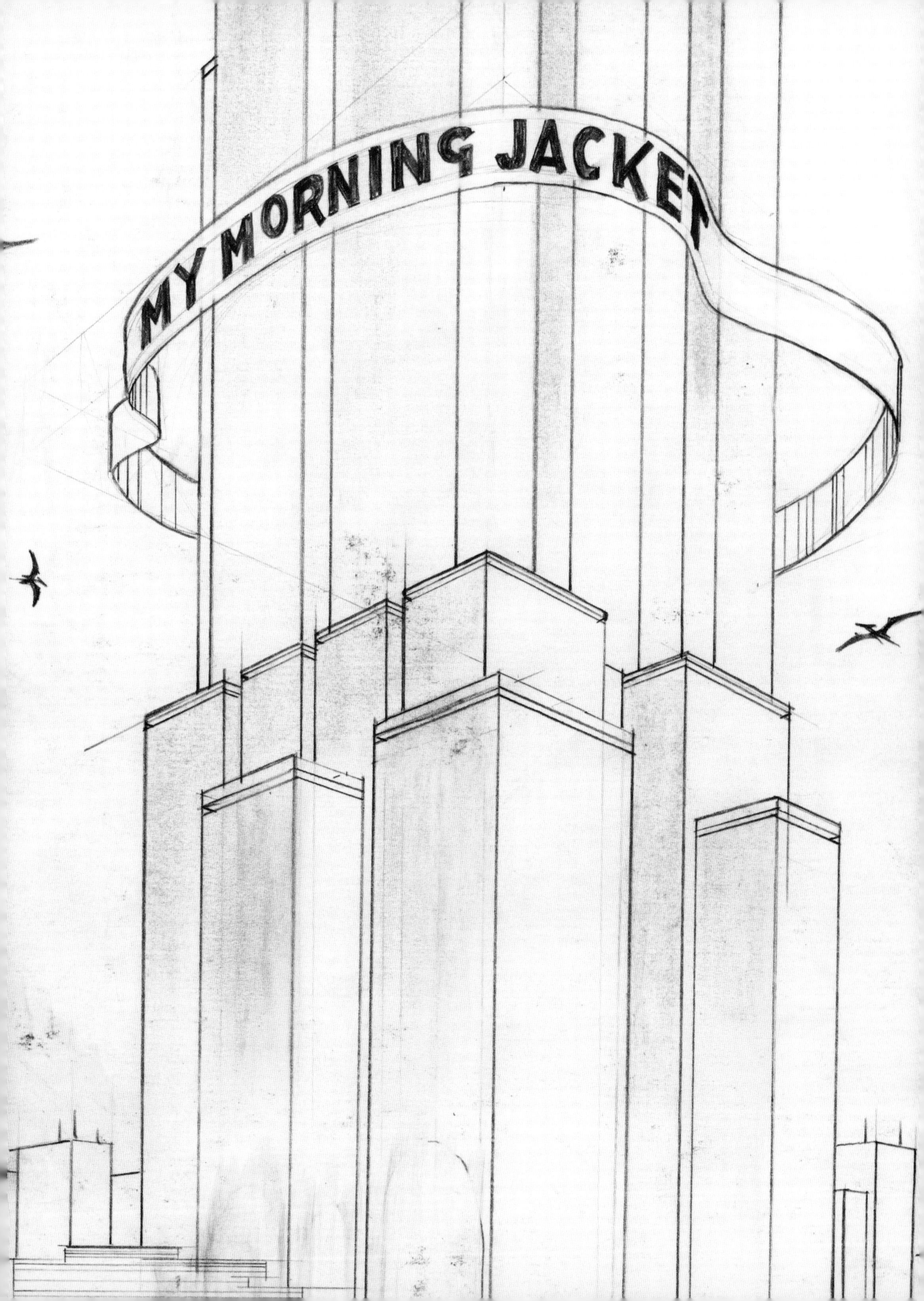
MY MORNING JACKET

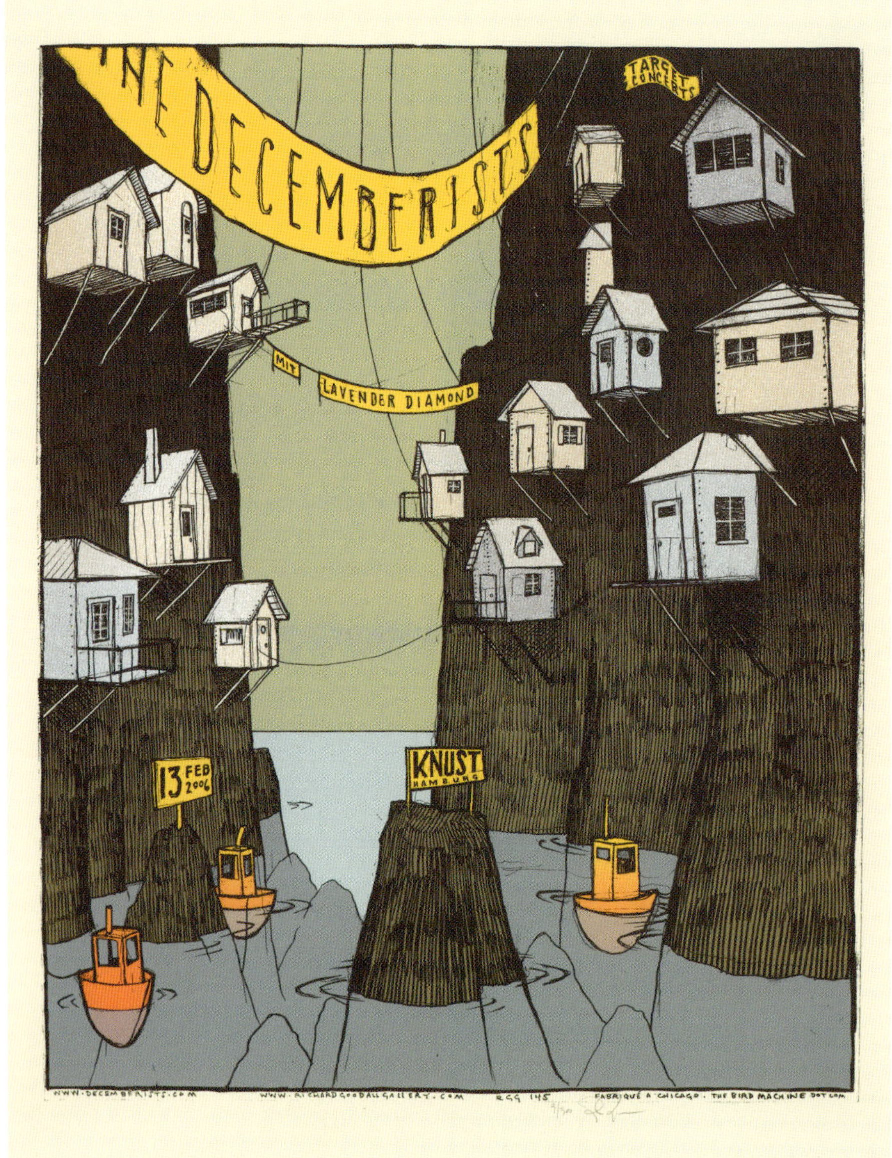

The Decemberists
2006
18 x 24 inches
5 screens

I don't know what the song is specifically about, but this print is based on the Decemberists' "Sons & Daughters," with aluminum-clad houses built on the water. One of the three major typos I've ever (so far) put in a print—this was printed in 2006, but is for a show in 2007.

Flatstock 10

2006

12 x 24 inches

4 screens

I've always been interested in houses and buildings, as projects to be built or rebuilt, as spaces people occupy and decorate, as places to park one's bicycle. As I try to do with each Flatstock poster, this house is home to all sorts of Gigposters-community inside jokes, as well as a school of fish, and Seth the greyhound peeking from the fourth-floor window. This print was made while our actual house was being re-sided, so I was particularly attentive to the siding.

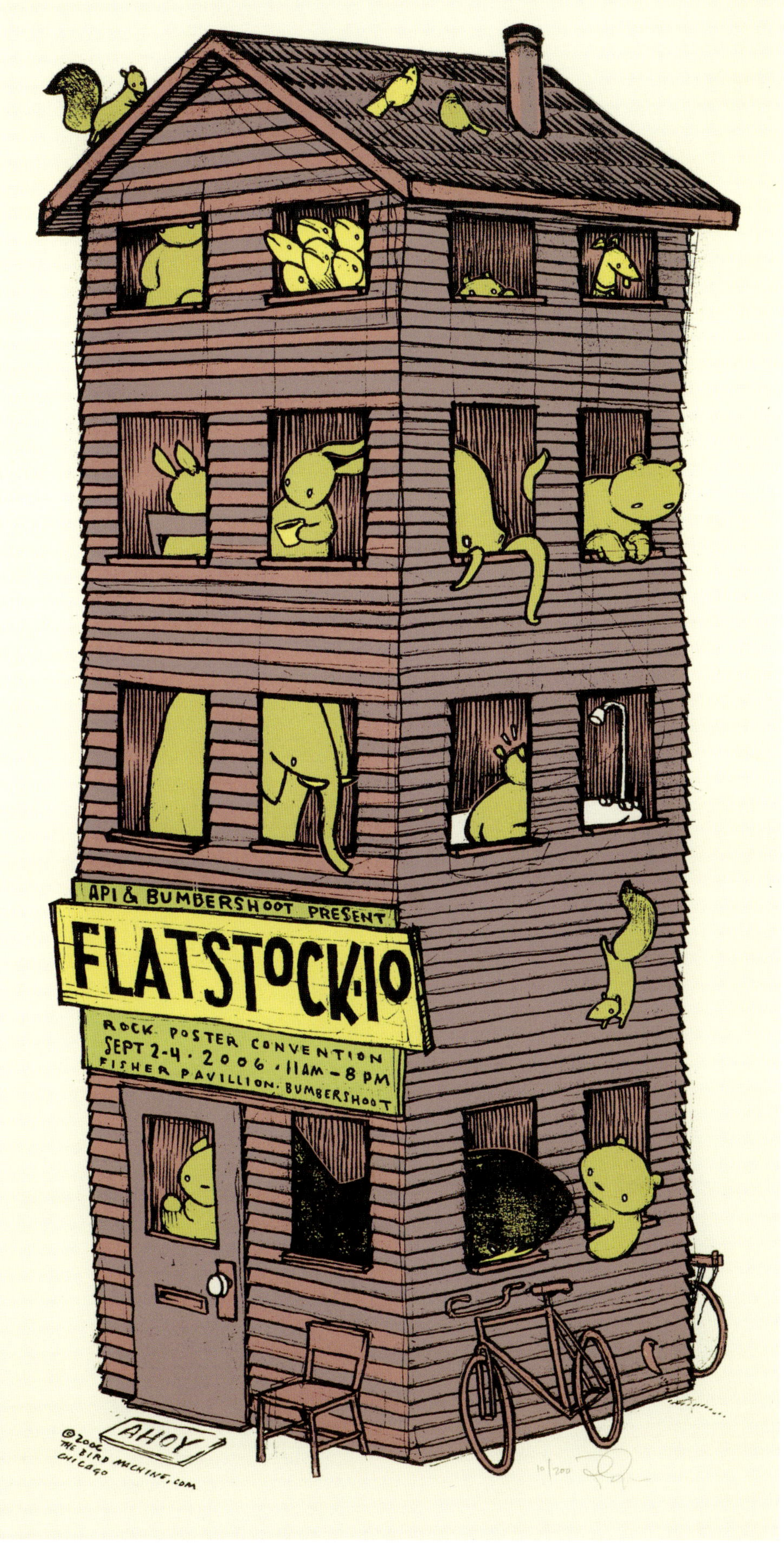

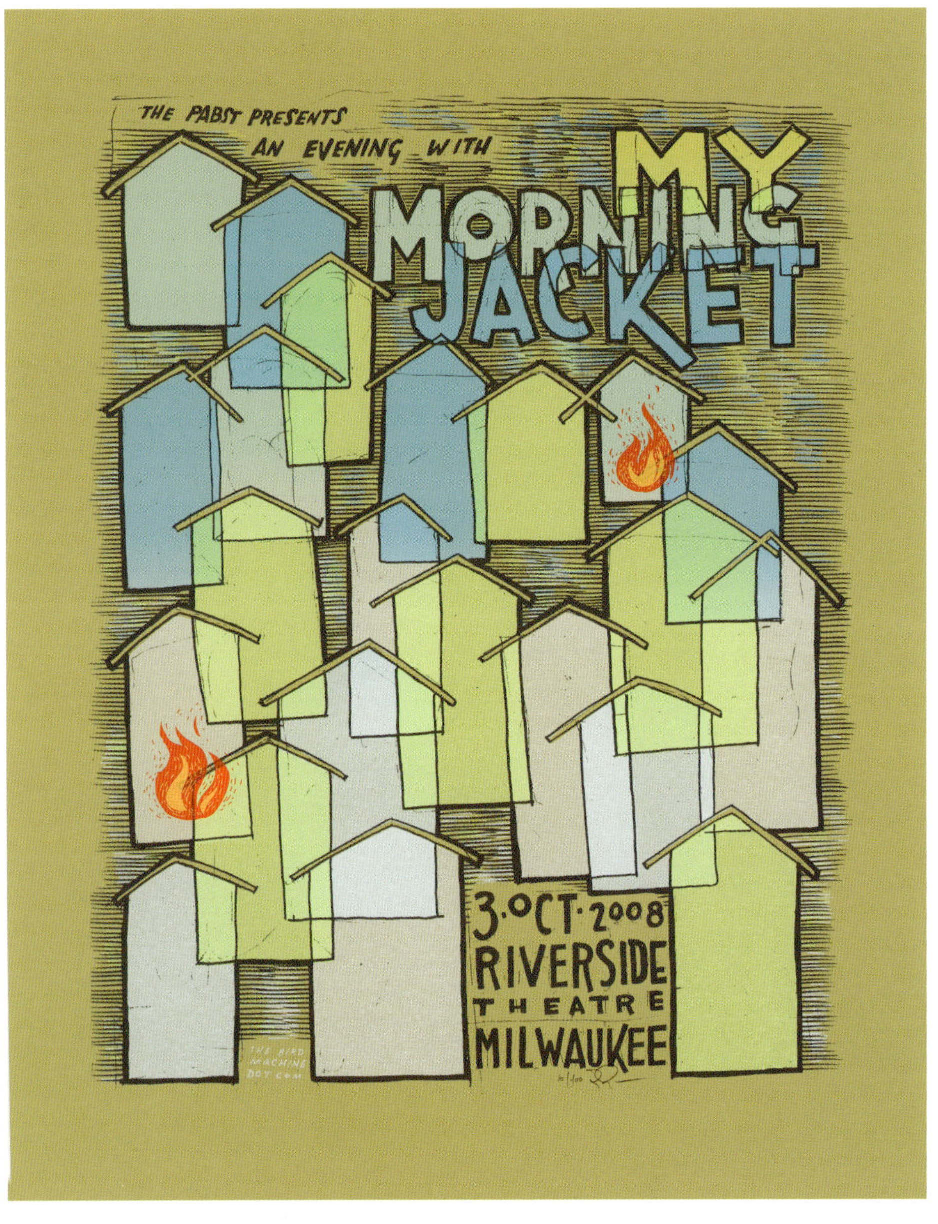

My Morning Jacket (Milwaukee)

2008

20 x 26 inches

6 screens

Two houses in this town are on fire, or two people in this town are aching for one another.

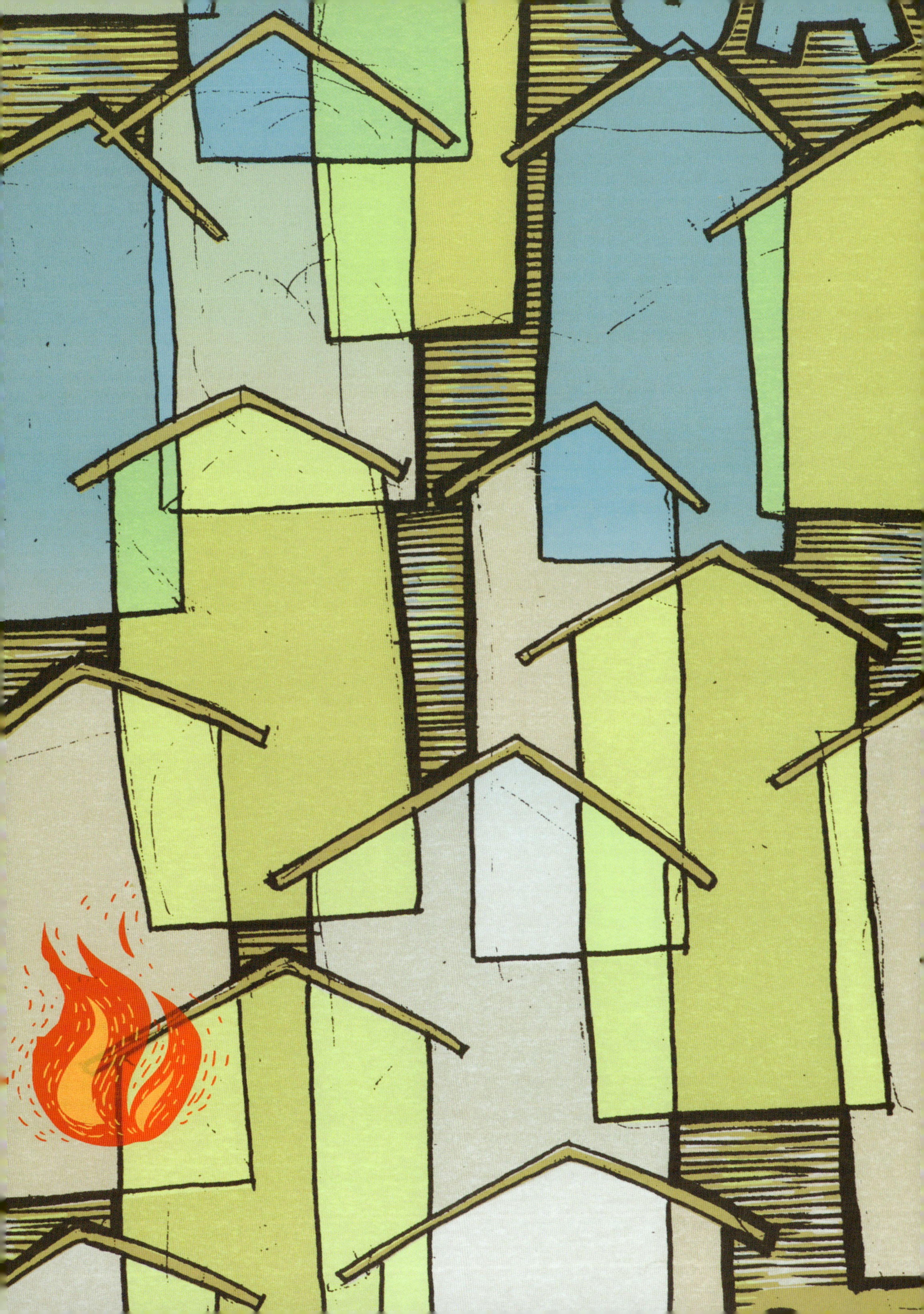

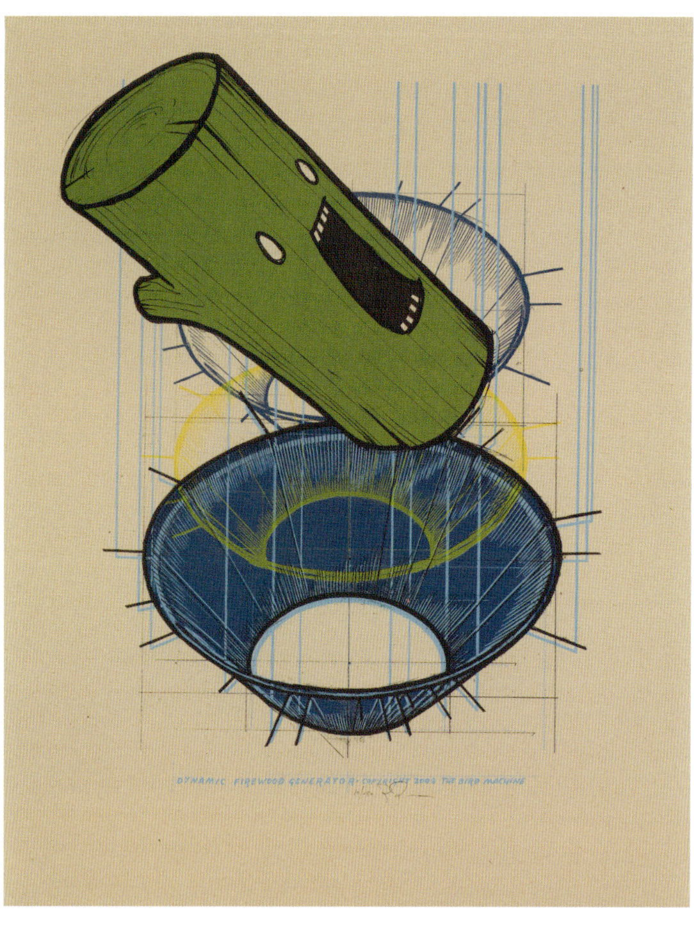

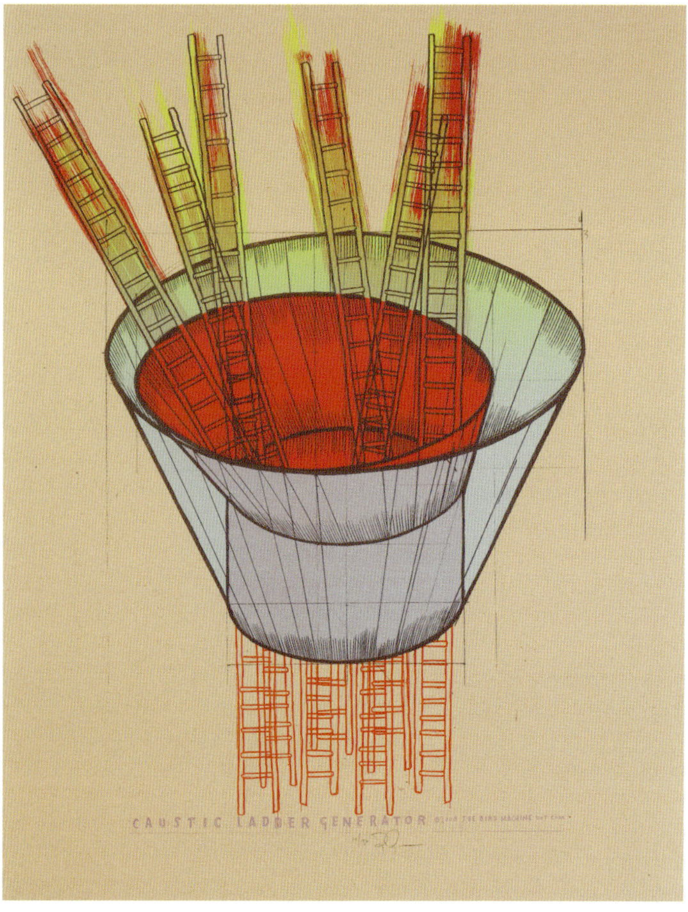

Dynamic Firewood Generator
2008
20 x 26 inches
4 screens

Online, I saw an image of an indoor velodrome, which appeared to have been assembled in a gallery space. The circular ramp was made of two-by-fours and plywood, built more like a half-pipe than a traditional quarter-mile indoor bike track. I started drawing my own version of the steep and tight little track, but in lieu of bikes racing around inside, I drew 25 dolphin ghosts being released from what soon appeared to be a mechanism of some sort. This diagram proved useful for building the machine that would produce dolphin ghosts, which many people mistakenly believe to come from dolphins. My next step was to change the machine slightly, four more times, to produce, respectively: ampersands, dynamic firewood, good canned food, and caustic ladders, which are normally hard to come by.

Caustic Ladder Generator
2008
20 x 26 inches
3 screens

Dolphin Ghost Generator
2008
20 x 26 inches
8 screens

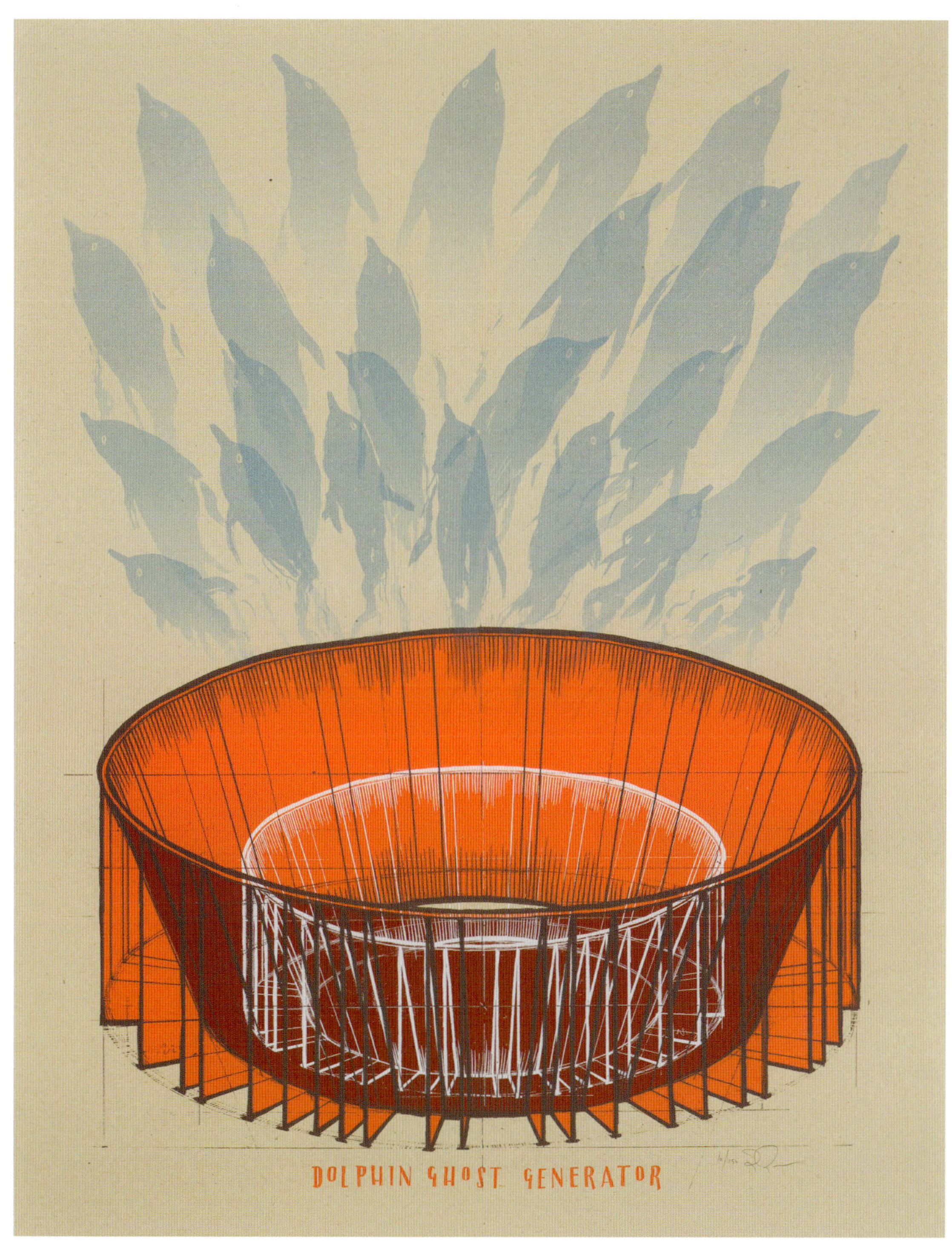
DOLPHIN GHOST GENERATOR

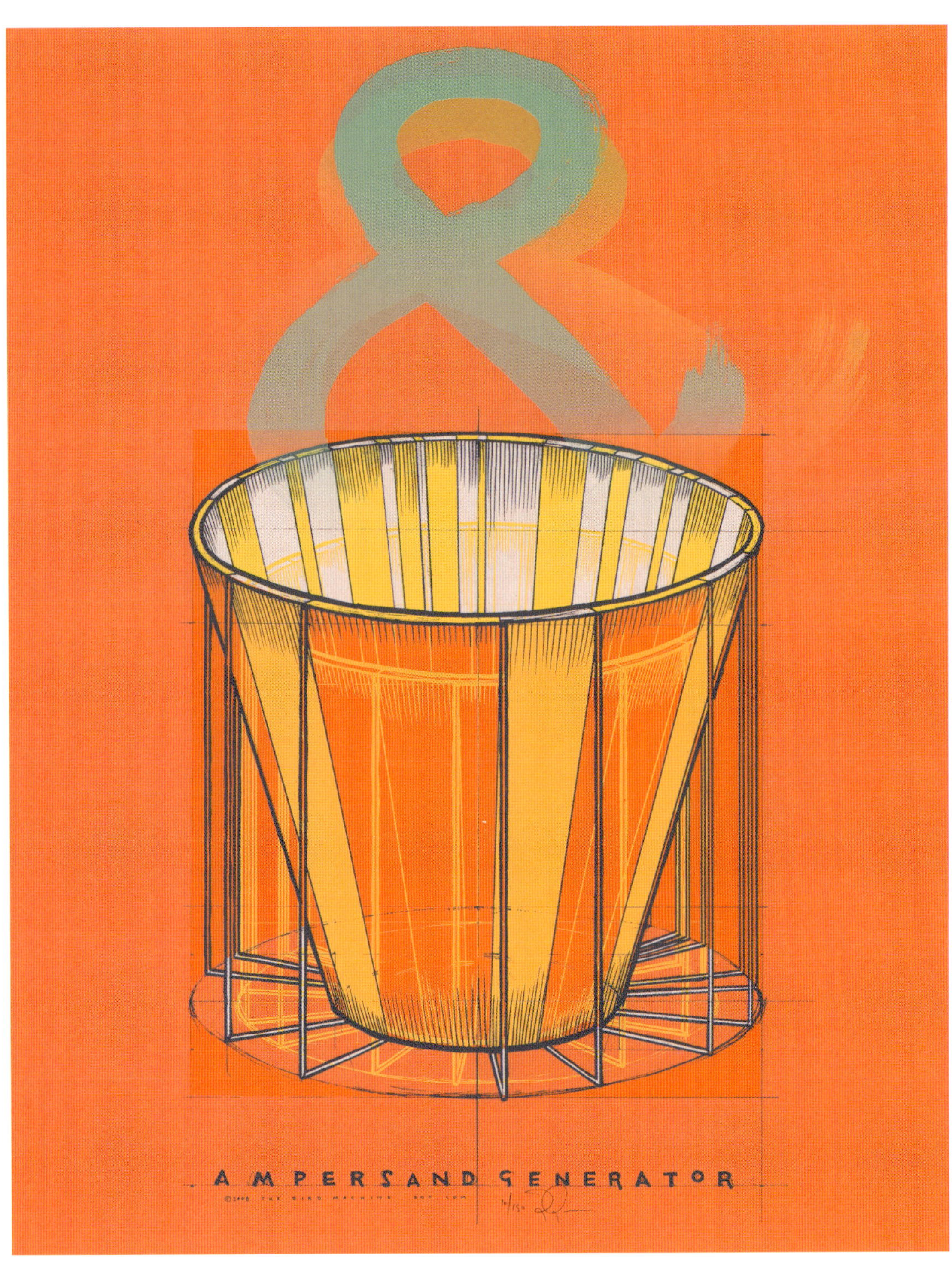
AMPERSAND GENERATOR

Ampersand Generator
2008
20 x 26 inches
6 screens

Good Canned Food Generator
2008
20 x 26 inches
4 screens

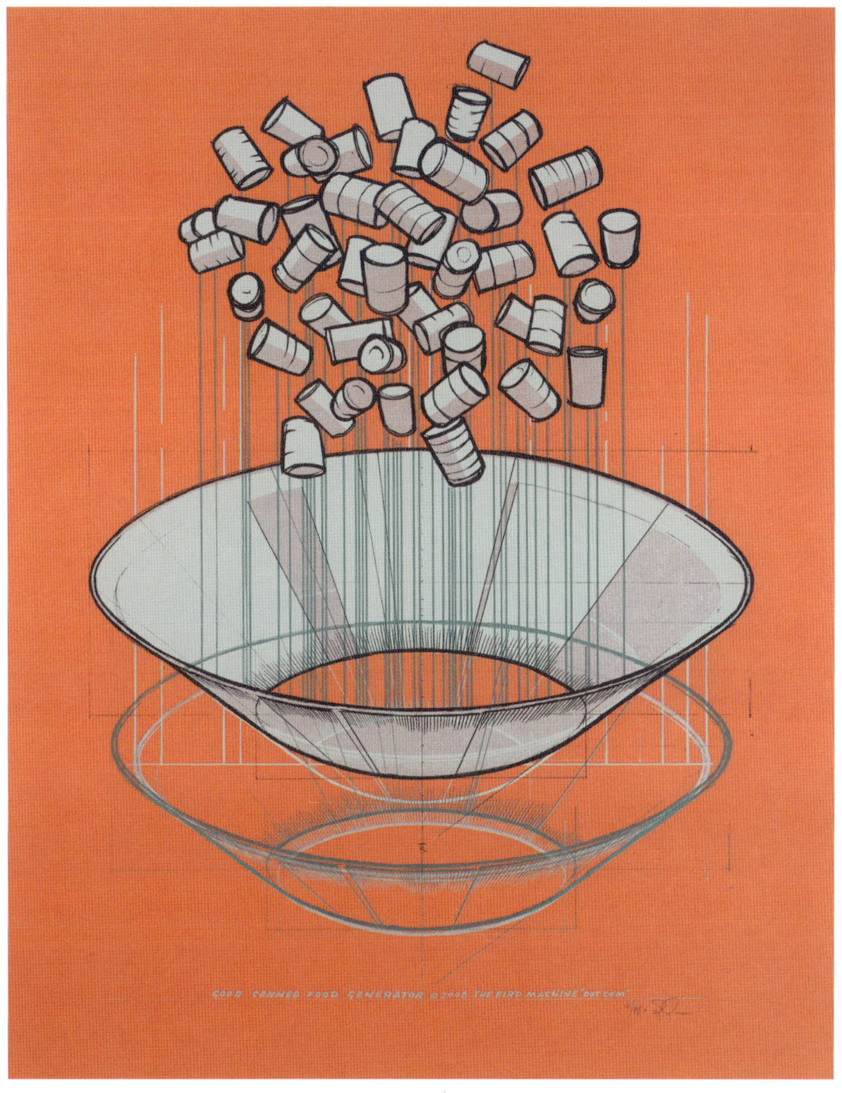

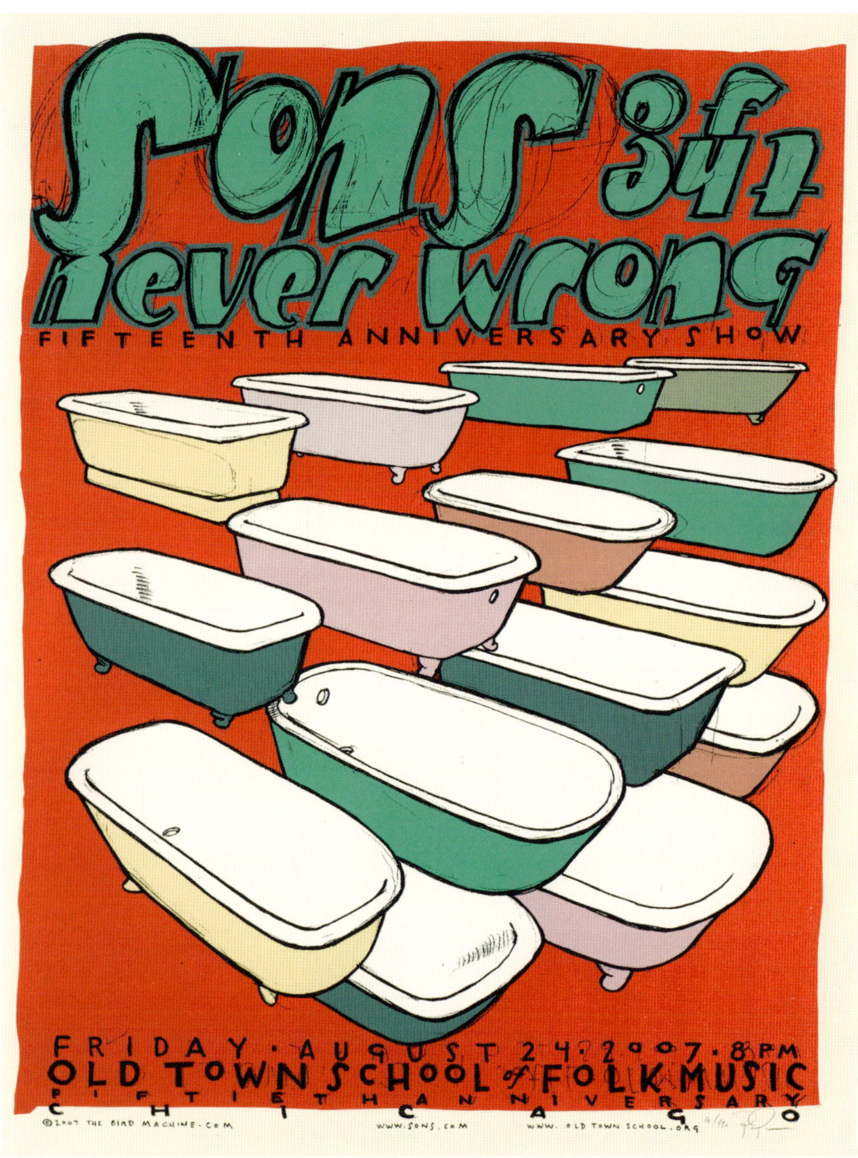

Sons of the Never Wrong

2007

18 x 24 inches

5 screens

I bicycled out of a snowstorm and into the town of Guffey, Colorado (population 20), where there is a yard inhabited by many old clawfoot tubs of various bathroomy colors. These tubs came to mind when the Sons of the Never Wrong commissioned a print for their band's fifteenth anniversary. Sue, Deb, and Bruce had good humor about connecting the tubs to their band: "all washed up" and "down the drain" were two of the themes they retroactively suggested.

Illinois State Cyclocross Championship 2007

2007

20 x 26 inches

4 screens

Cyclocross is typically regarded as a messy winter sport, with riders quickly dismounting from their knobby-tired road bikes to surmount stairs or other obstacles strewn along the twisting courses.

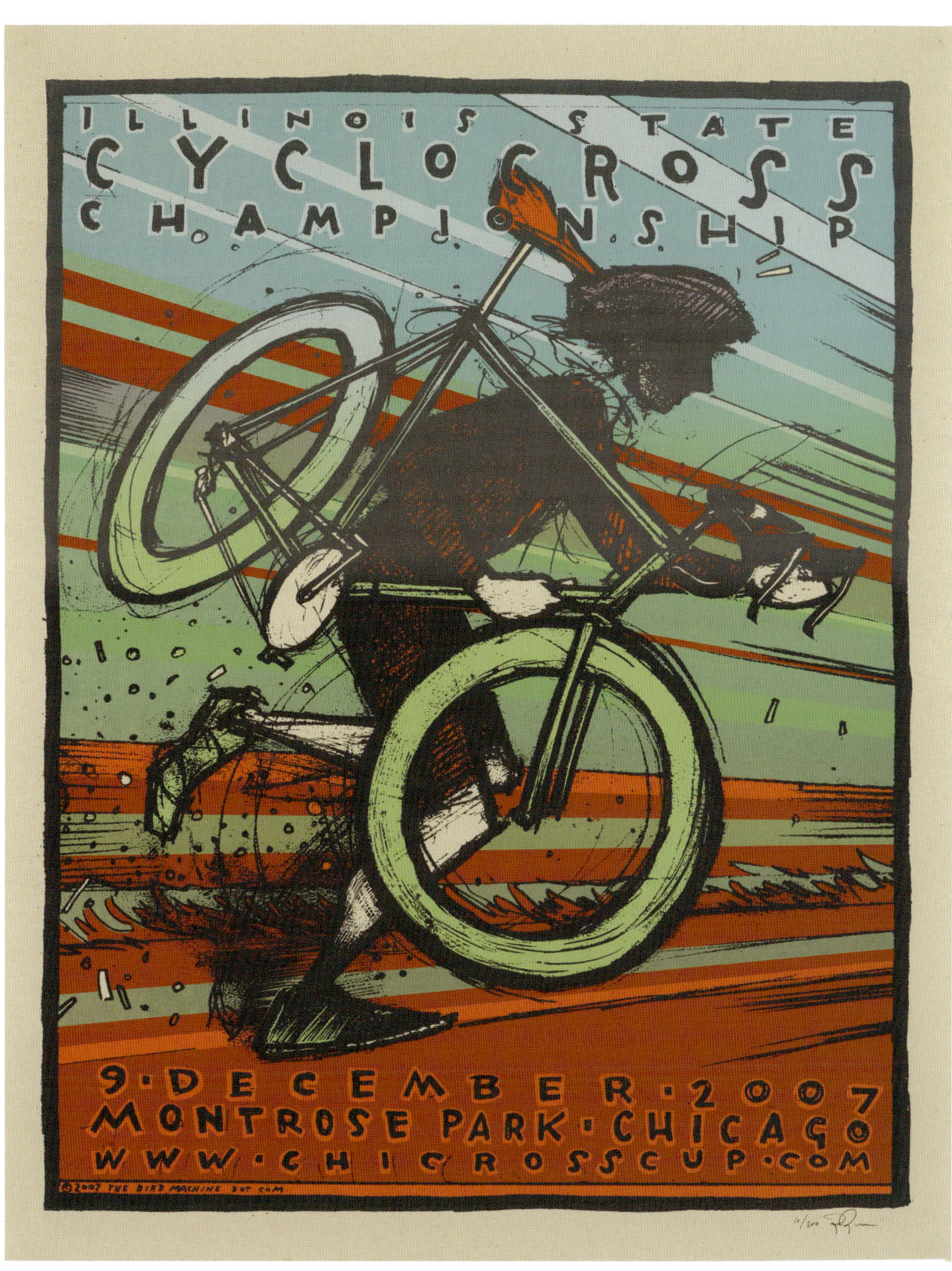
ILLINOIS STATE
CYCLOCROSS
CHAMPIONSHIP
9·DECEMBER·2007
MONTROSE PARK·CHICAGO
WWW·CHICROSSCUP·COM
©2007 THE BIRD MACHINE DOT COM

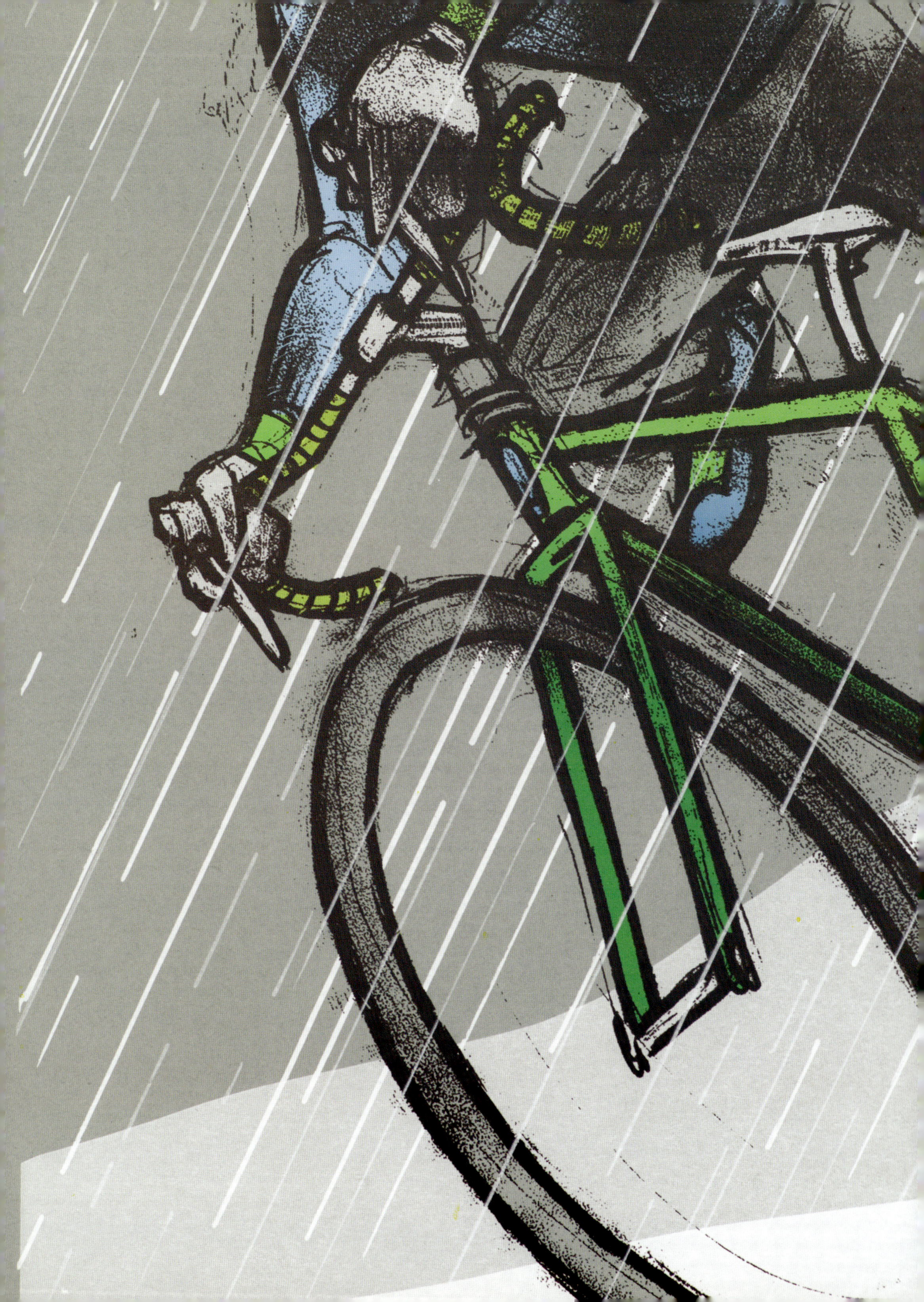

Illinois State Cyclocross Championship 2008
2008
20 x 26 inches
6 screens

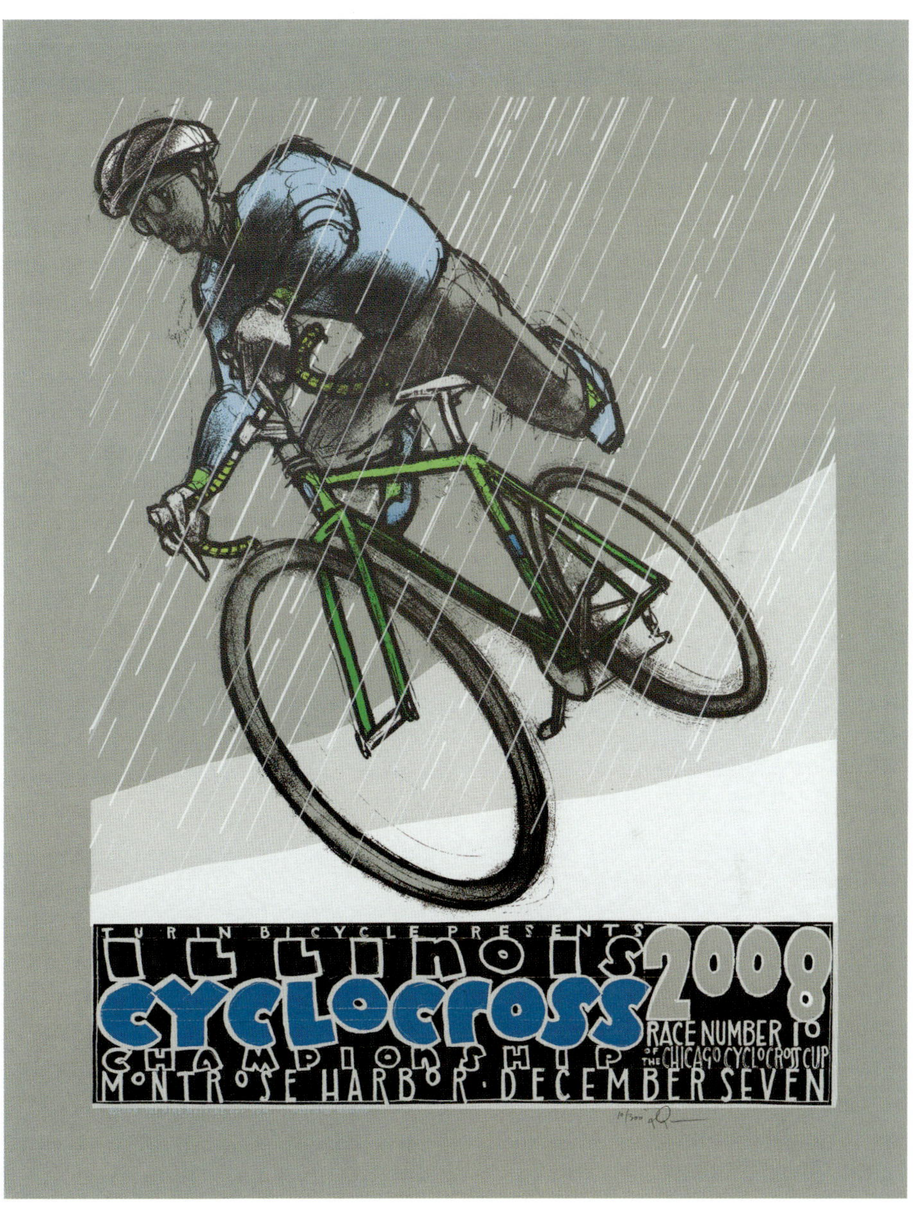

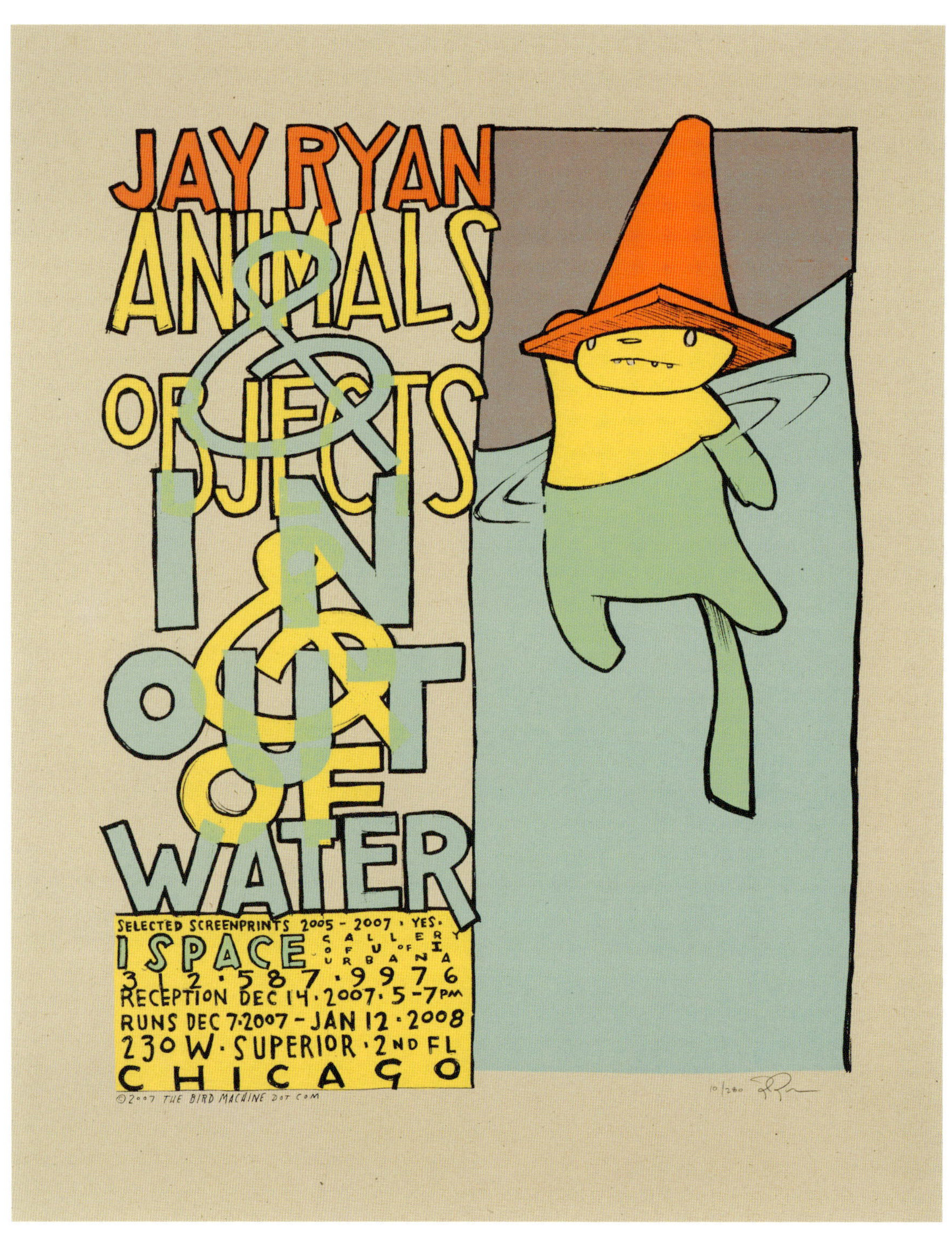
JAY RYAN
ANIMALS
&
OBJECTS
IN
&
OUT
OF
WATER
SELECTED SCREENPRINTS 2005 - 2007 · YES·
I SPACE
GALLERY OF U OF I URBANA
312·587·9976
RECEPTION DEC 14·2007·5-7PM
RUNS DEC 7·2007 - JAN 12·2008
230 W·SUPERIOR·2ND FL
CHICAGO
©2007 THE BIRD MACHINE DOT COM
10/280

Animals & Objects In & Out of Water (#1, I Space)
2007
20 x 26 inches
4 screens

Animals & Objects In & Out of Water (#2, Krannert Art Museum)
2008
20 x 26 inches
4 screens

I liked the accuracy of the title of the *100 Posters / 134 Squirrels* book, which was released in 2005. While trying to summarize the work I had done since then, I noticed some themes, and used them to name a show of my work which hung at the I Space Gallery in Chicago, before moving to the Krannert Art Museum in Urbana. I felt the title also translated to this book, obviously.

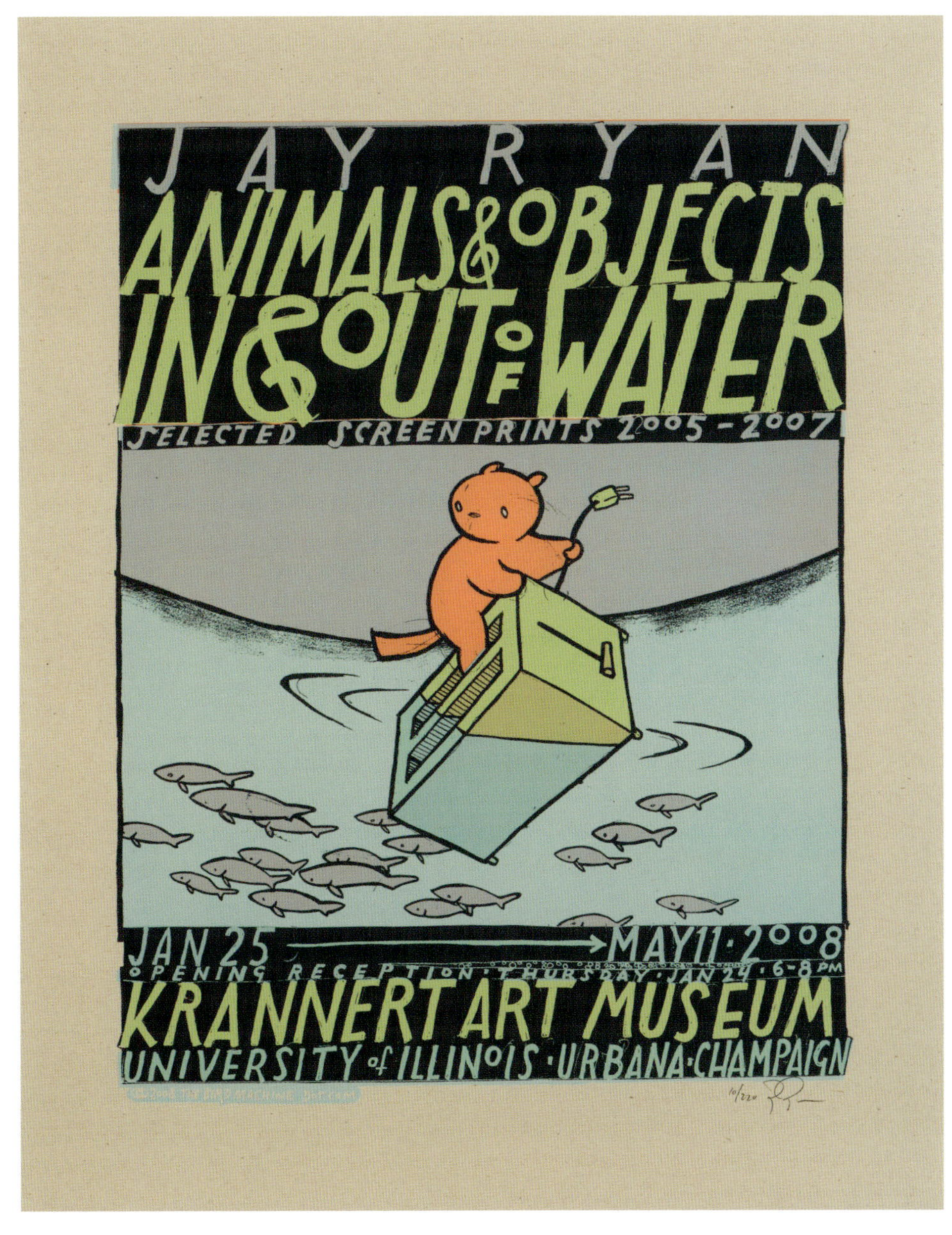

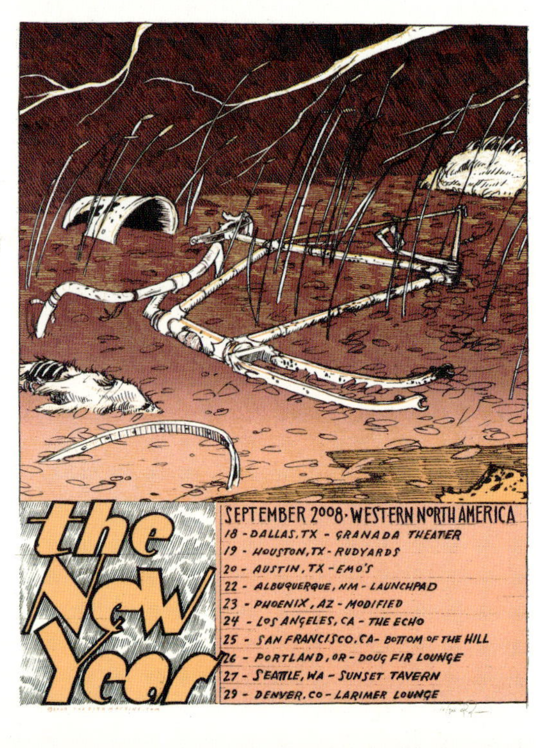
the New Year
SEPTEMBER 2008 · WESTERN NORTH AMERICA
18 - DALLAS, TX - GRANADA THEATER
19 - HOUSTON, TX - RUDYARDS
20 - AUSTIN, TX - EMO'S
22 - ALBUQUERQUE, NM - LAUNCHPAD
23 - PHOENIX, AZ - MODIFIED
24 - LOS ANGELES, CA - THE ECHO
25 - SAN FRANCISCO, CA - BOTTOM OF THE HILL
26 - PORTLAND, OR - DOUG FIR LOUNGE
27 - SEATTLE, WA - SUNSET TAVERN
29 - DENVER, CO - LARIMER LOUNGE

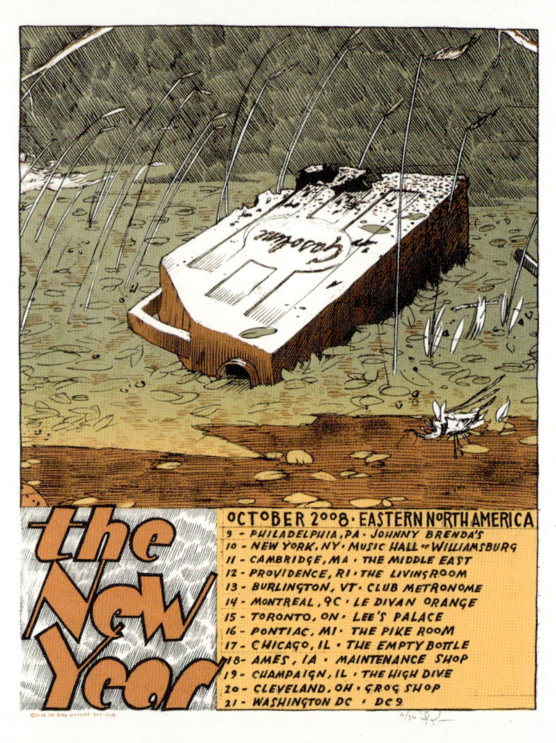
the New Year
OCTOBER 2008 · EASTERN NORTH AMERICA
9 - PHILADELPHIA, PA · JOHNNY BRENDA'S
10 - NEW YORK, NY · MUSIC HALL OF WILLIAMSBURG
11 - CAMBRIDGE, MA · THE MIDDLE EAST
12 - PROVIDENCE, RI · THE LIVINGROOM
13 - BURLINGTON, VT · CLUB METRONOME
14 - MONTREAL, QC · LE DIVAN ORANGE
15 - TORONTO, ON · LEE'S PALACE
16 - PONTIAC, MI · THE PIKE ROOM
17 - CHICAGO, IL · THE EMPTY BOTTLE
18 - AMES, IA · MAINTENANCE SHOP
19 - CHAMPAIGN, IL · THE HIGH DIVE
20 - CLEVELAND, OH · GROG SHOP
21 - WASHINGTON DC · DC9

The New Year (West Coast)
2008
20 x 26 inches
3 screens

The New Year (East Coast)
2008
20 x 26 inches
3 screens

The New Year, generally from Texas, write beautiful songs about decay and disintegration. Listening to the New Year's three albums while reading Cormac McCarthy's *The Road* gave me a unique bout of quiet introversion in 2008.

The New Year (Europe)
2008
20 x 26 inches
3 screens

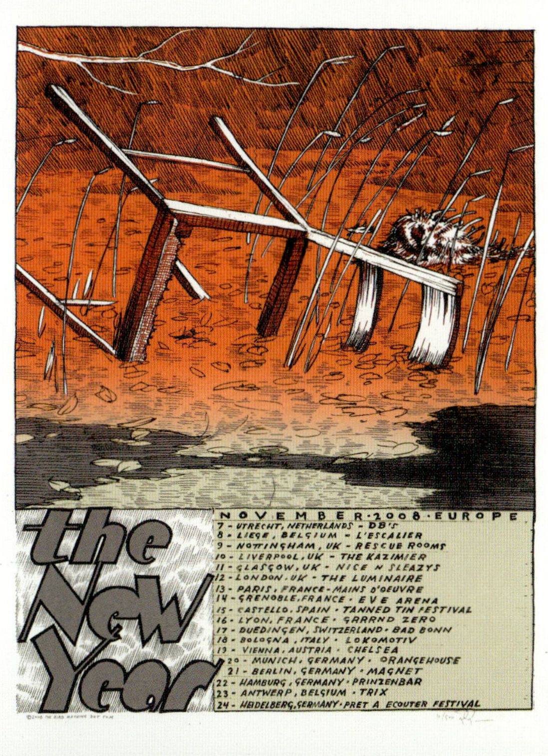

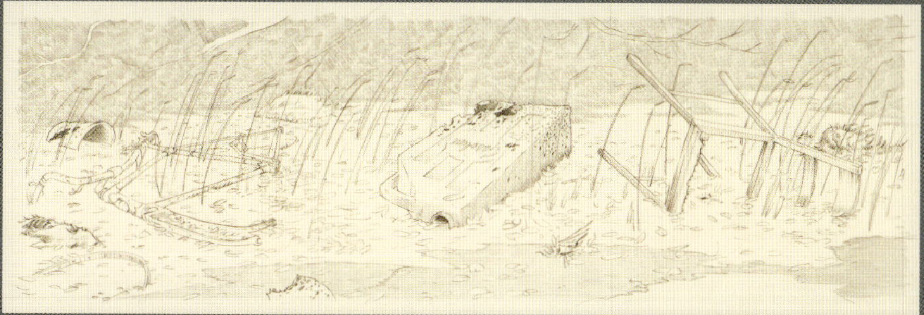

The Swell Season (Green)
2008
20 x 26 inches
3 screens

The Swell Season (Red)
2008
20 x 26 inches
3 screens

The Swell Season is a band which is rooted in the film *Once*, from 2007. These three prints are based on the two main characters and various inanimate elements from the film.

The Swell Season (Blue)
2008
20 x 26 inches
3 screens

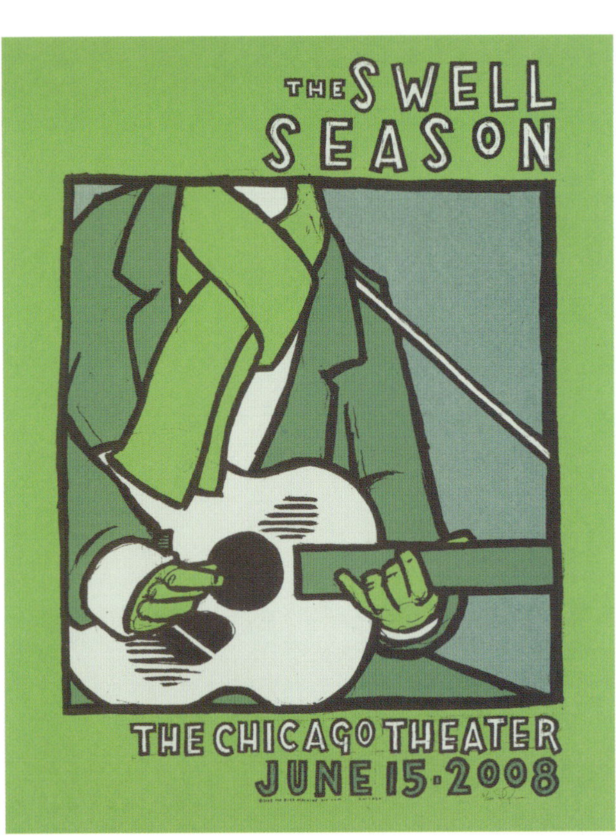

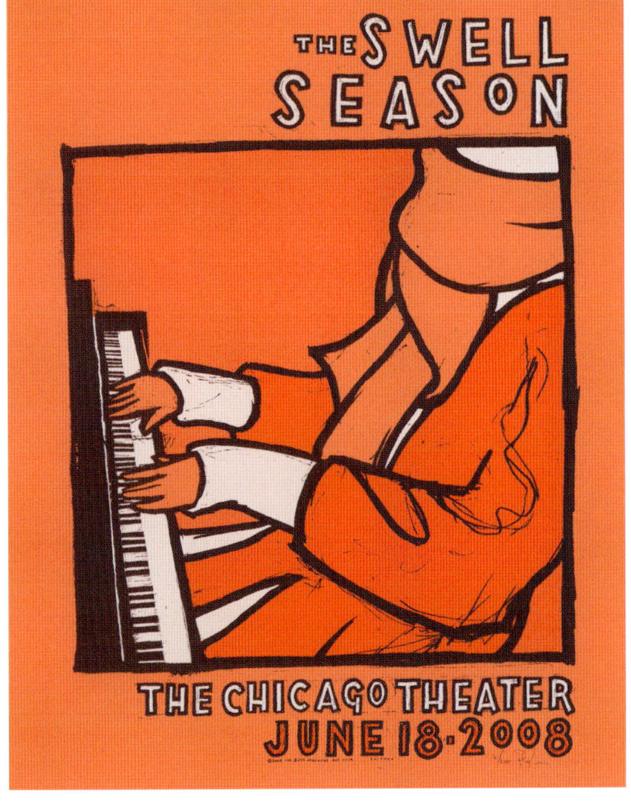

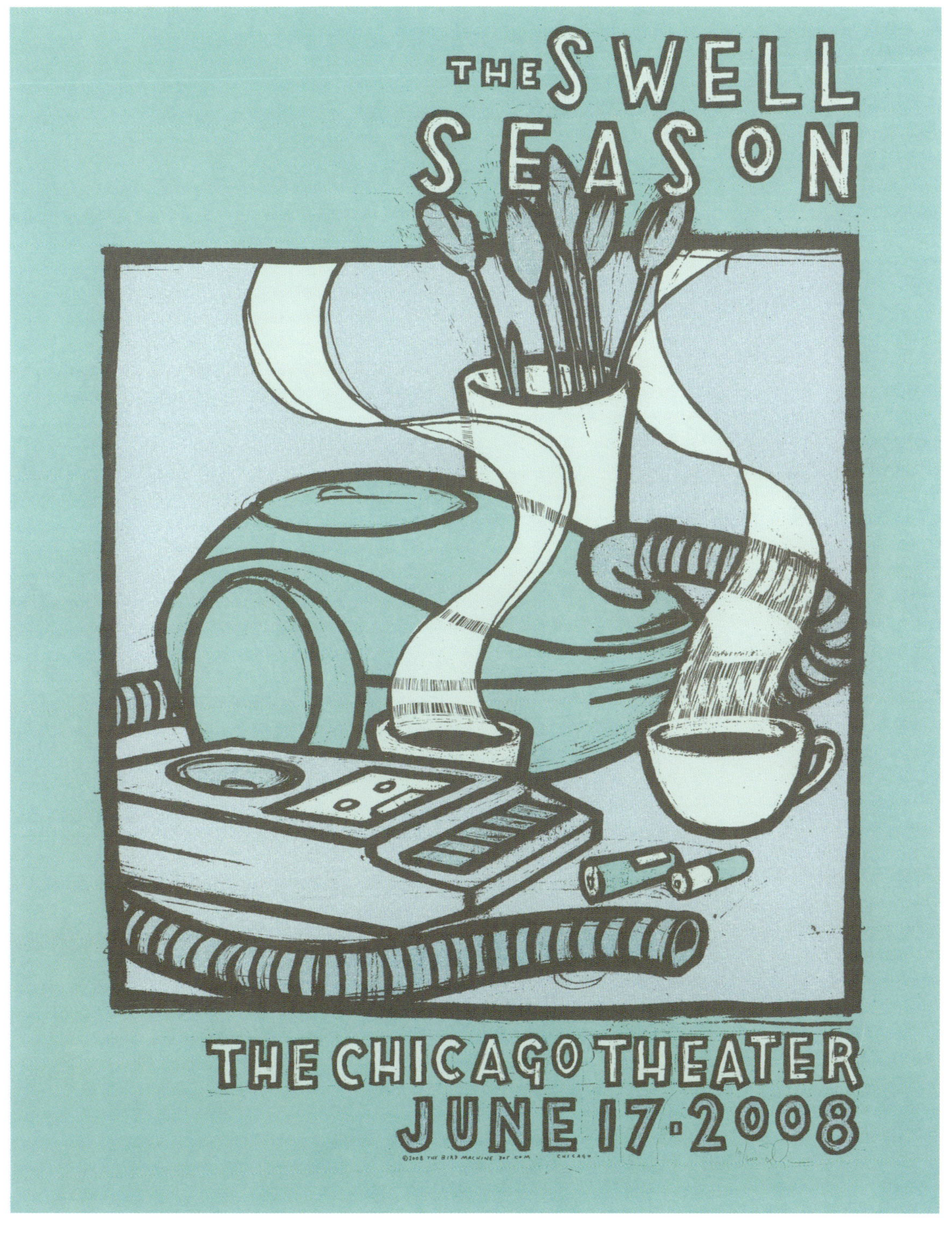
THE SWELL SEASON
THE CHICAGO THEATER
JUNE 17·2008
©2008 THE BIRD MACHINE DOT COM · CHICAGO

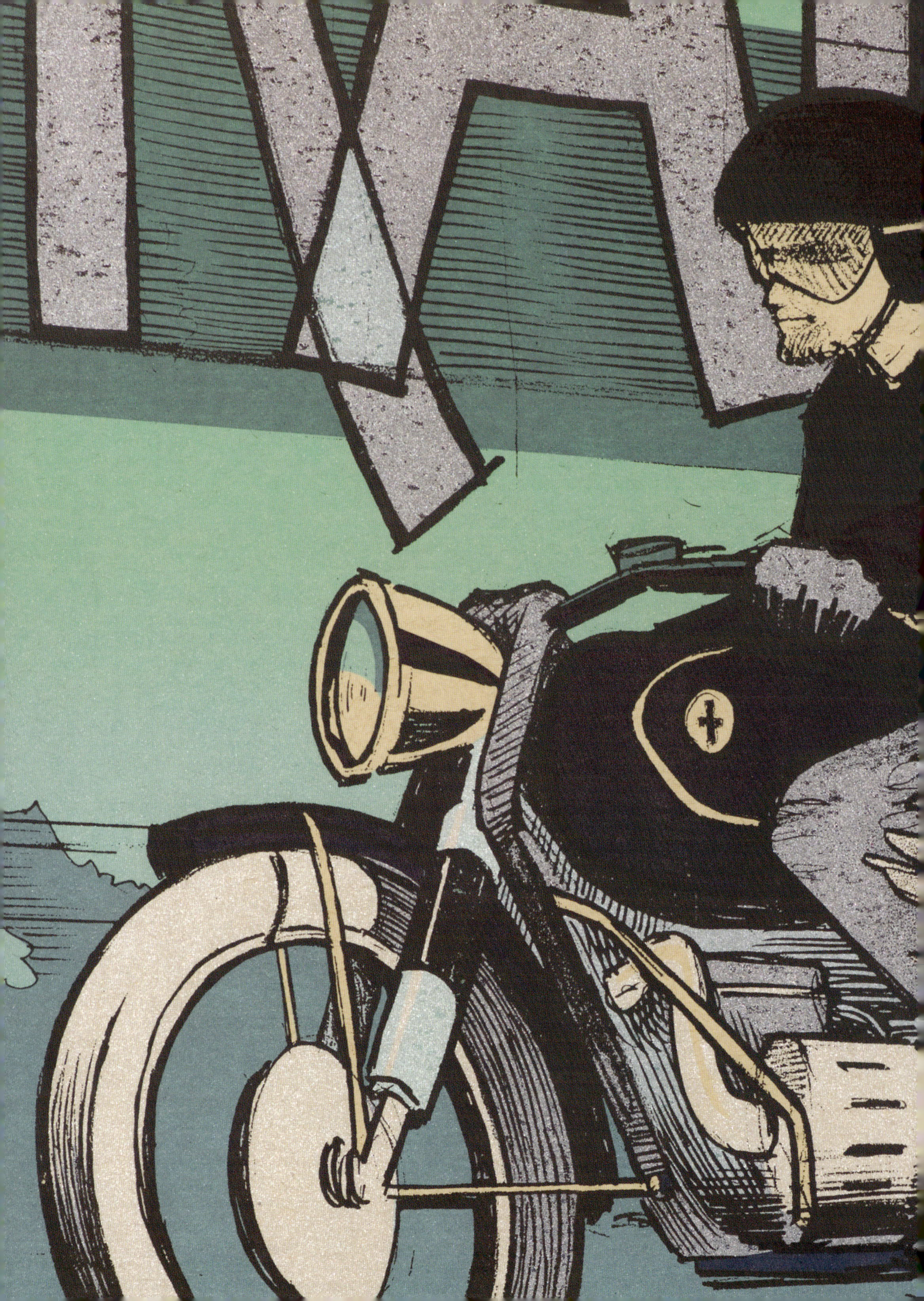

The Frames
2007
20 x 26 inches
5 screens

Radiohead wrote a song called "High and Dry", which includes the line, "Flying on your motorcycle, watching all the ground beneath you drop." The Frames wrote one called "Song for Someone," which lyrically referred to the Radiohead song. The Frames were involved in the movie *Once*, featuring a motorcycle, which is why this poster has a young couple flying on a motorcycle.

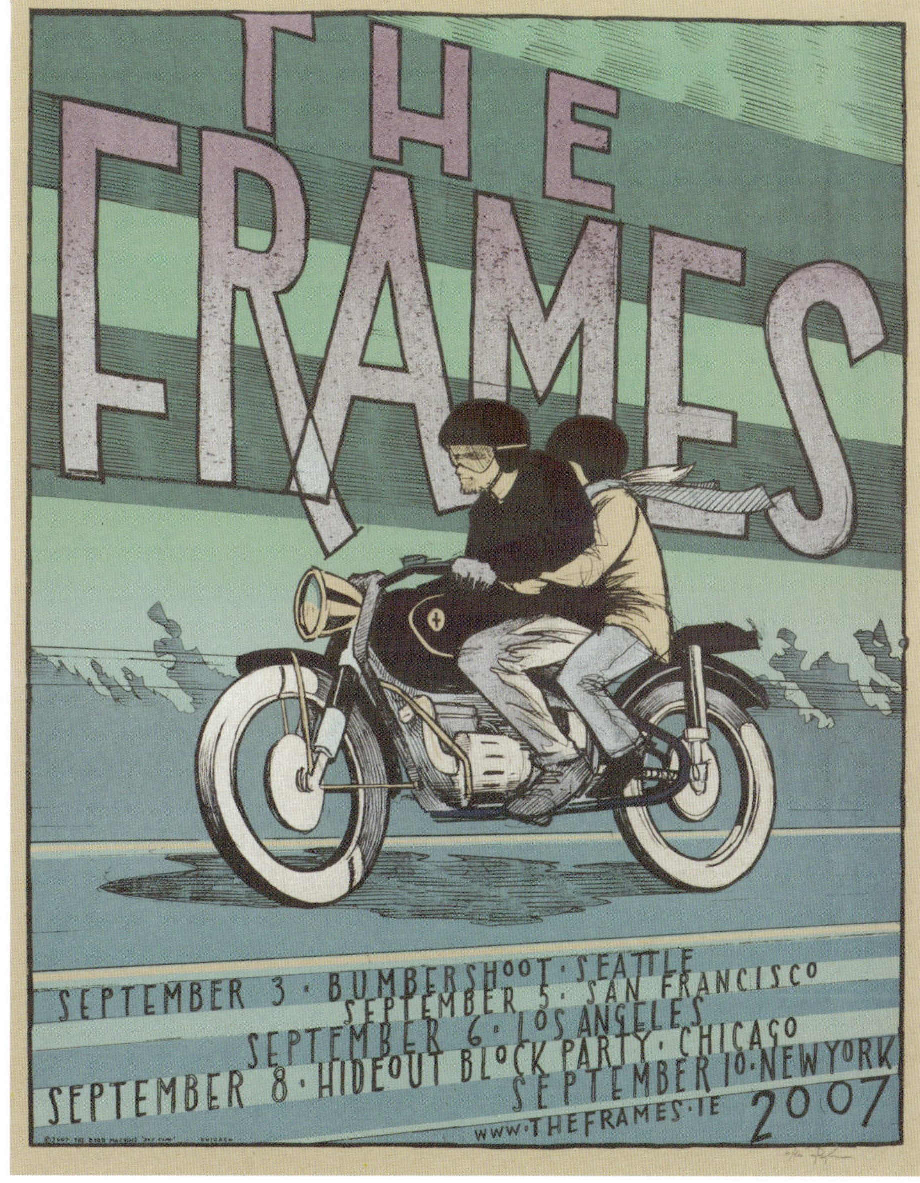

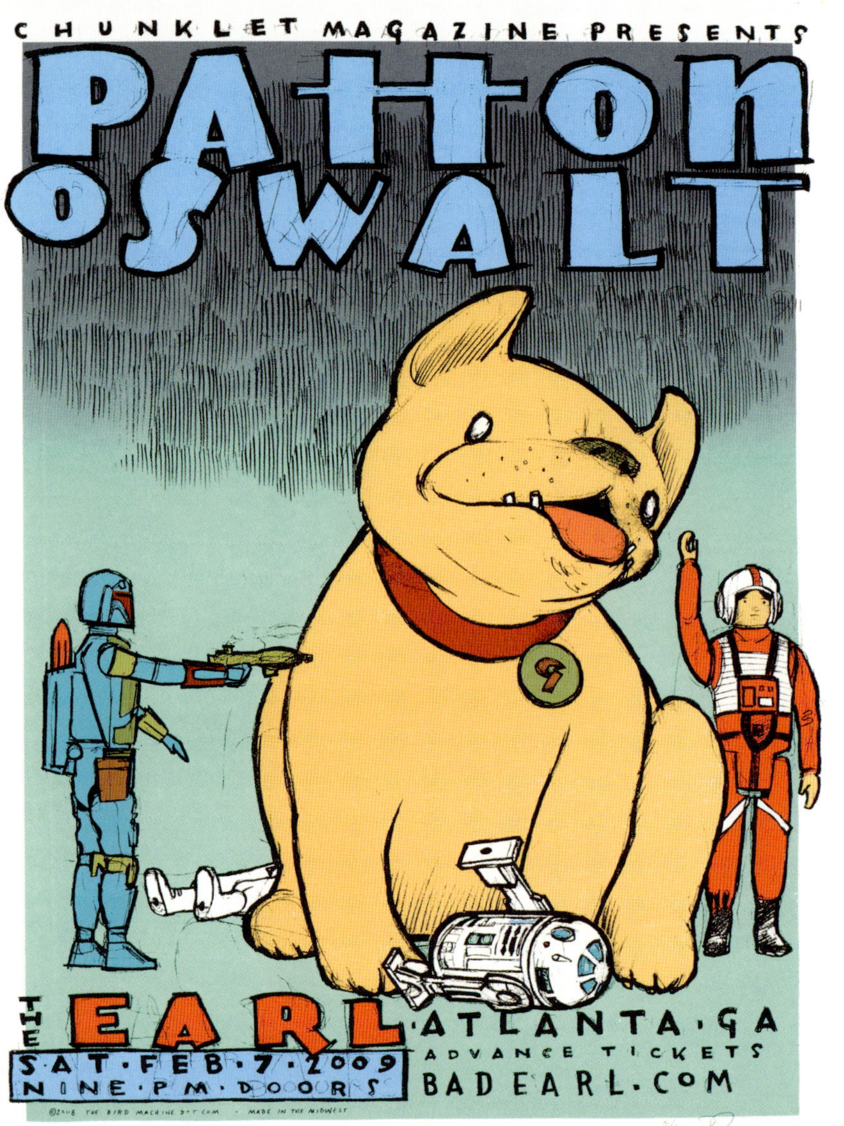

Patton Oswalt (Atlanta)
2008
17.5 x 23 inches
5 screens

Patton Oswalt (Athens)
2008
17.5 x 23 inches
5 screens

Patton Oswalt is one of the funniest and most foul comics working today, and my friends and I are his perfect target audience. He spends a lot of time with his French bulldog, Grumpus, and I'm gonna guess that he has at least a few vintage *Star Wars* toys in his house.

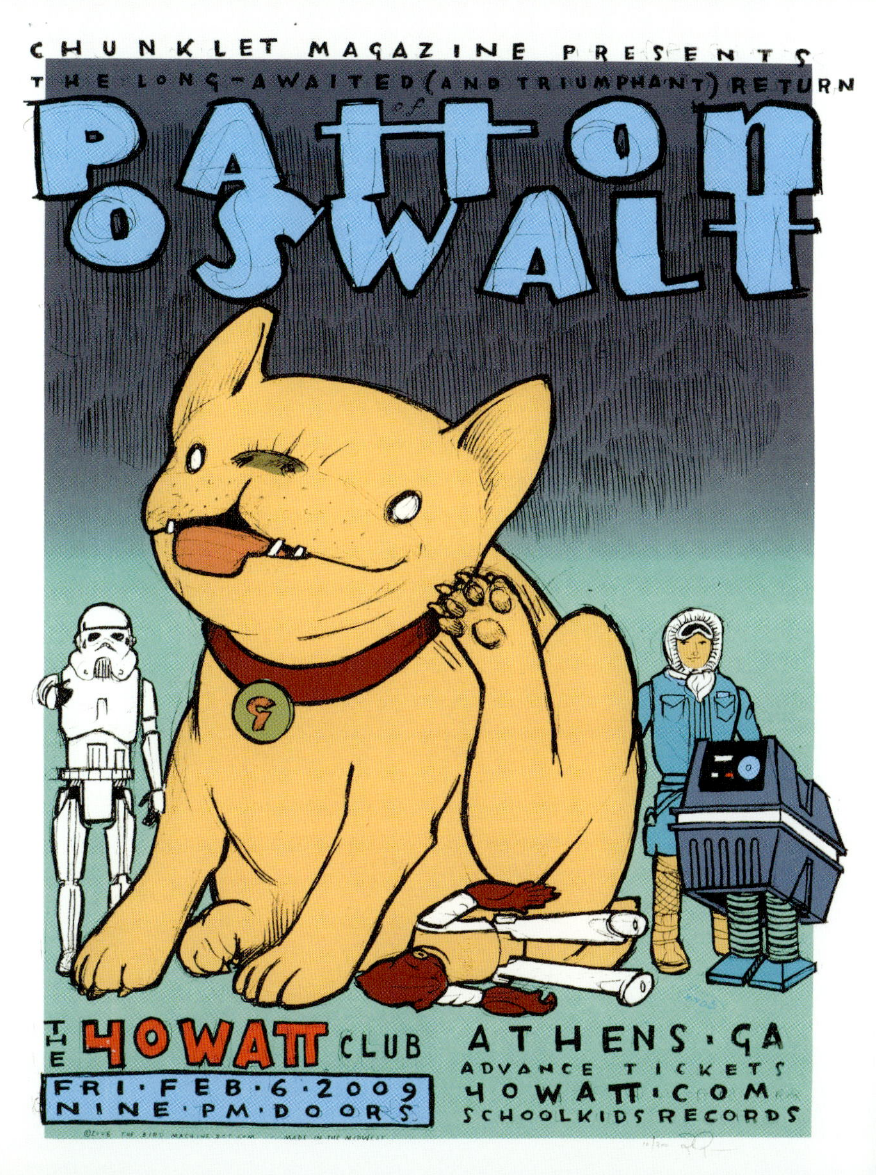

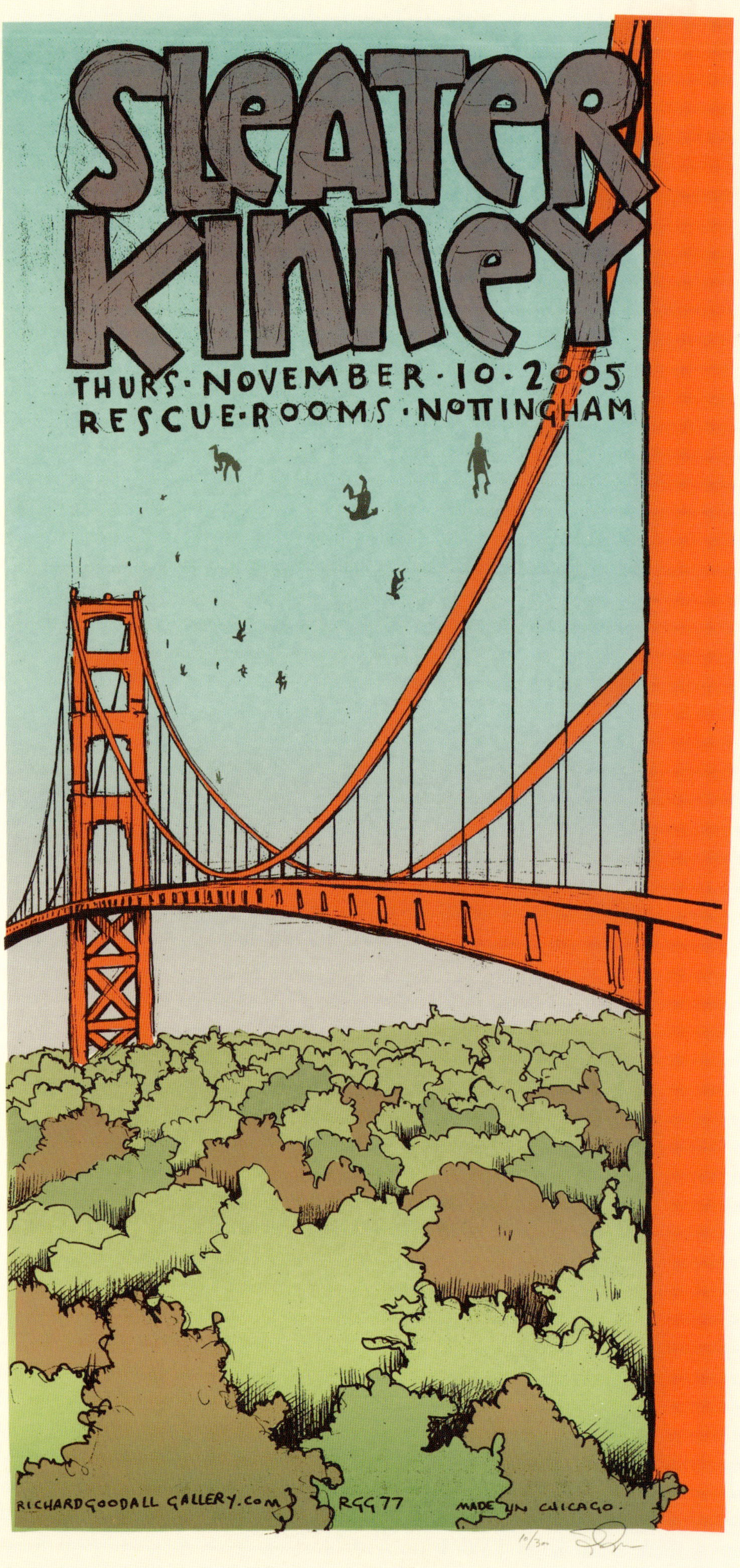
SLEATER
KINNEY
THURS·NOVEMBER·10·2005
RESCUE·ROOMS·NOTTINGHAM
RICHARDGOODALL GALLERY.COM
RGG77
MADE IN CHICAGO.
10/300

Sleater Kinney
2005
12 x 24 inches
4 screens

Another anti-gravity poster, based on the song "Jumpers" from the album *The Woods*.

Shellac (West Coast Tour)
2005
26 x 40 inches
9 screens

"The End of Radio" is a Shellac song which, to me, sounds like a rambling monologue, broadcast out over a darkened city by the last man on Earth. The ninth screen of this poster was printed on the reverse of the paper.

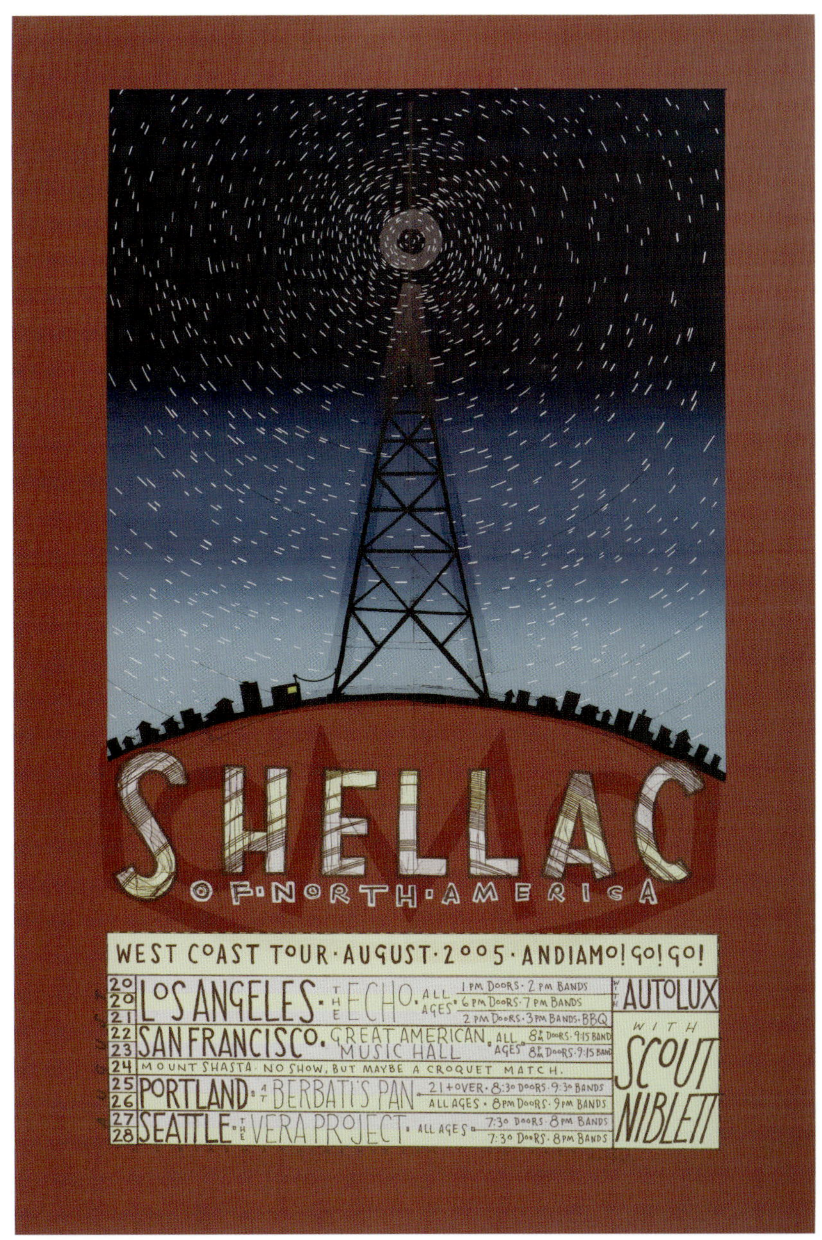

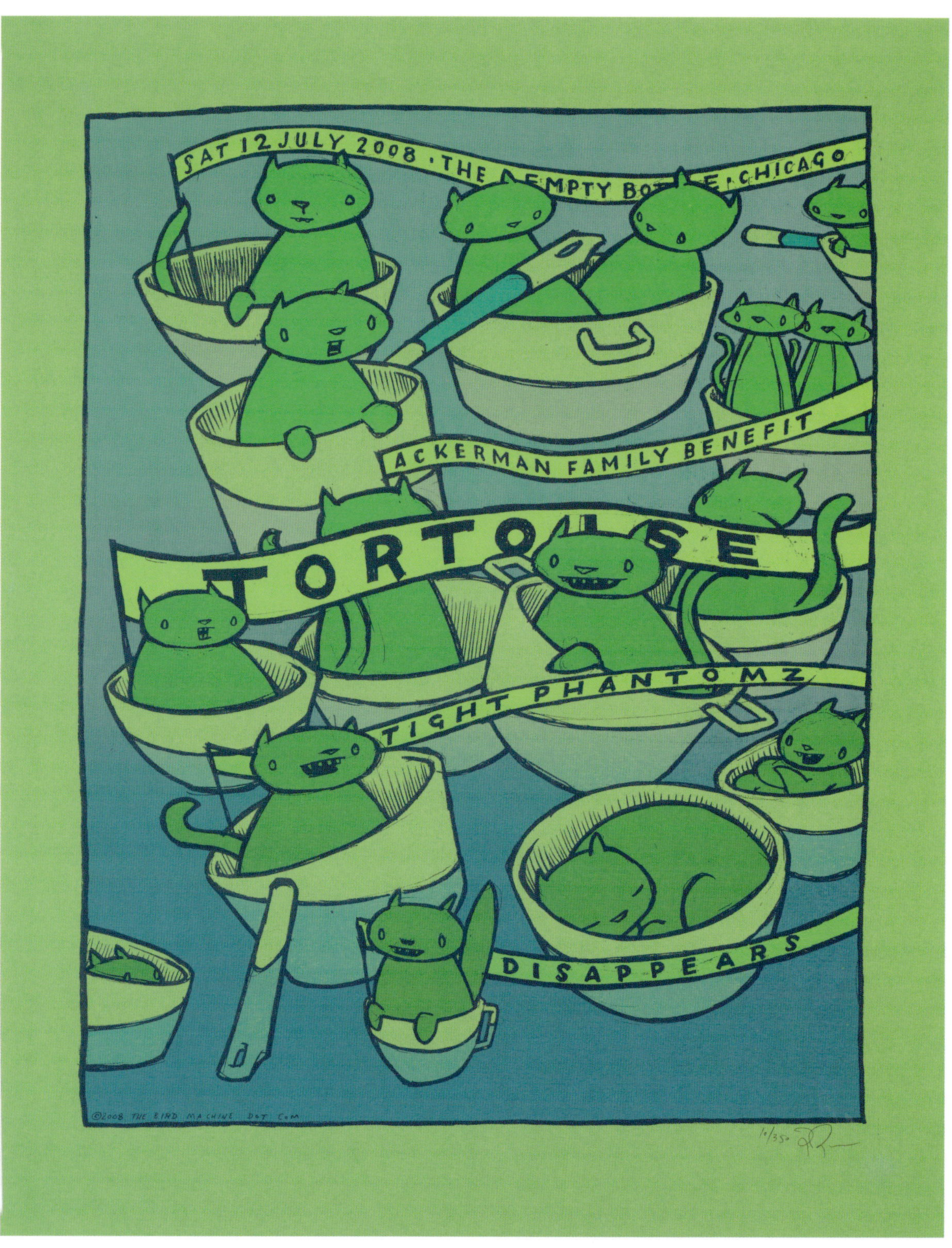
SAT 12 JULY 2008 · THE EMPTY BO E · CHICAGO
ACKERMAN FAMILY BENEFIT
TORTOISE
TIGHT PHANTOMZ
DISAPPEARS
©2008 THE BIRD MACHINE DOT COM
10/350

Tortoise

2008
20 x 26 inches
4 screens

These three bands played a benefit show for some friends, a family with a little girl who was ill. The cats are also concerned, and are slowly making their way to the little girl's house to see her.

The Sea and Cake

2008
20 x 26 inches
6 screens

Even though they're from Chicago, the Sea and Cake has always had what I imagined to be a vaguely European feel to their music. Their albums are Vespas on thin brick streets. Here, the band is a series of canals, surrounded by a small non-specific Dutch town.

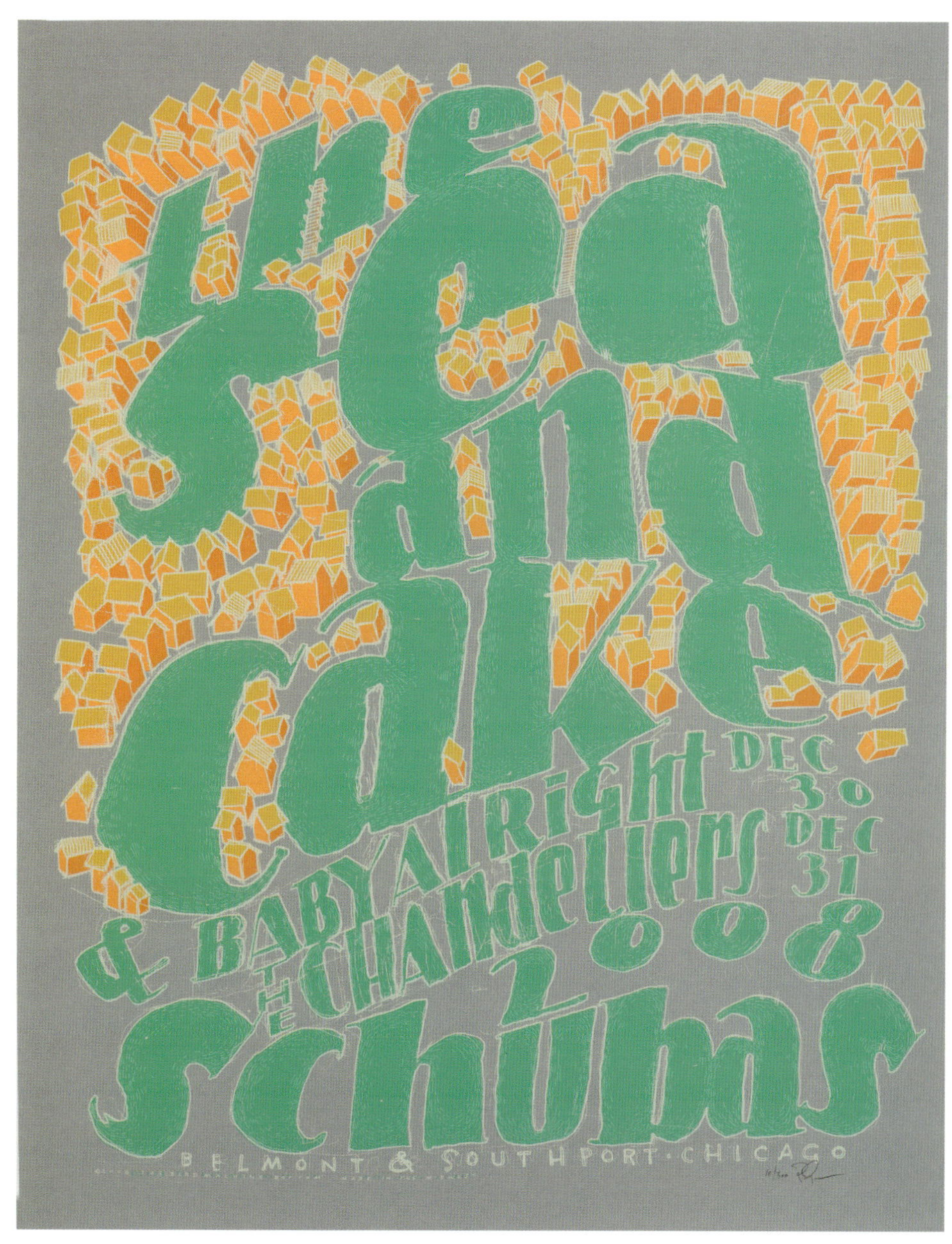

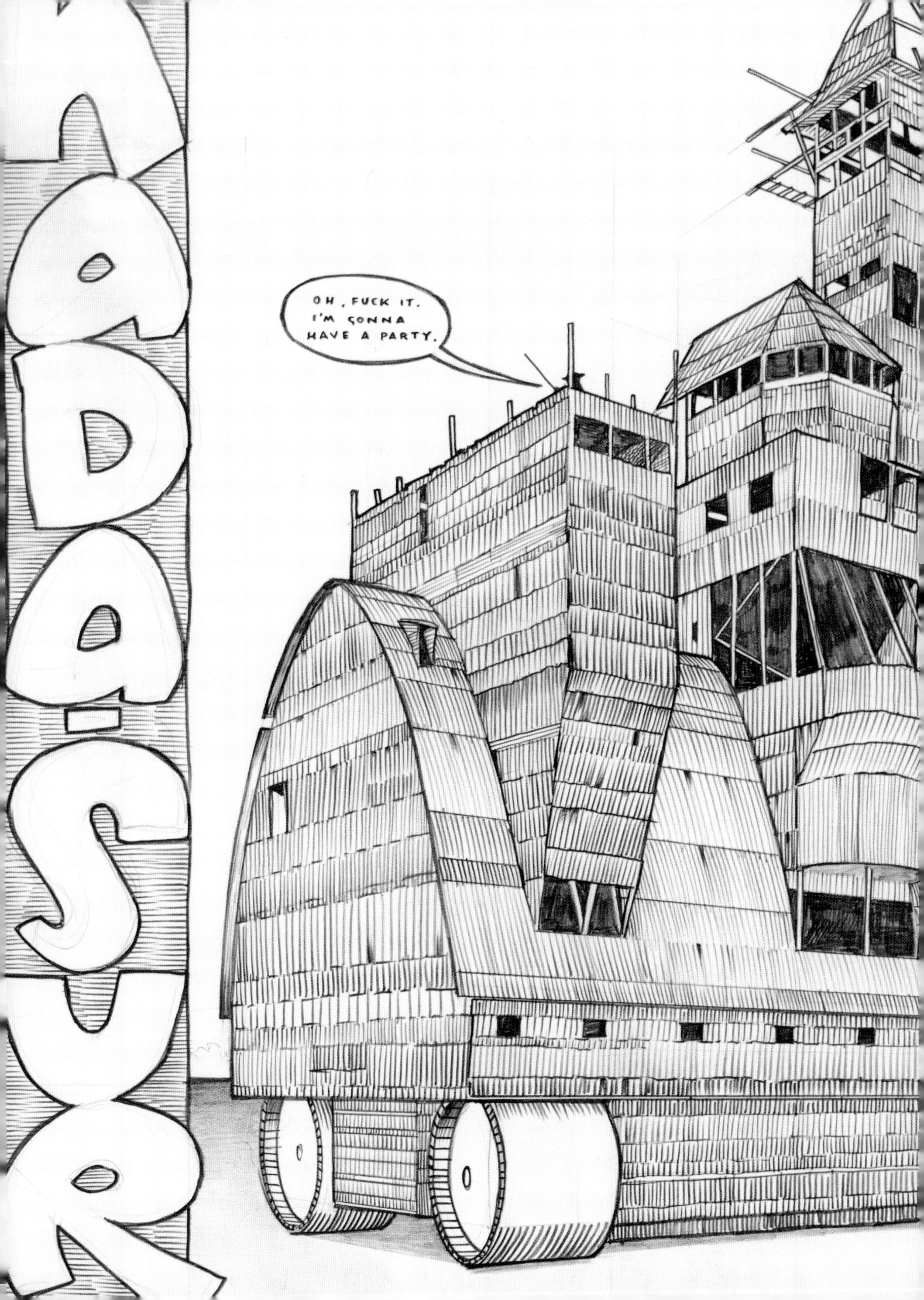
OH, FUCK IT. I'M GONNA HAVE A PARTY.

Nada Surf

2007

20 x 26 inches

5 screens

This print hung in the international terminal at O'Hare Airport for a while, until someone noticed that the little dude on top of the weird wooden castle-barn was quoting the slightly profane chorus of Nada Surf's song "Blankest Year."

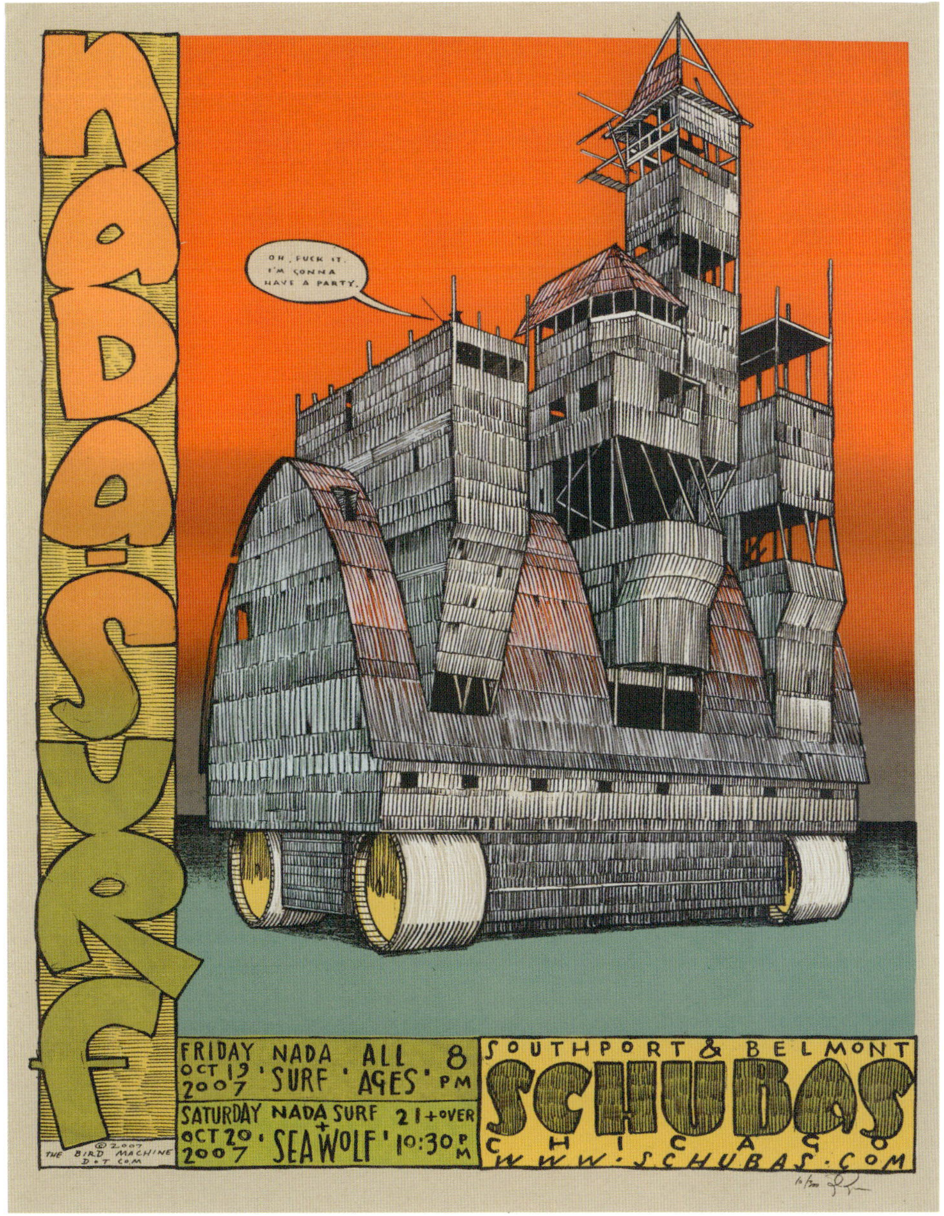

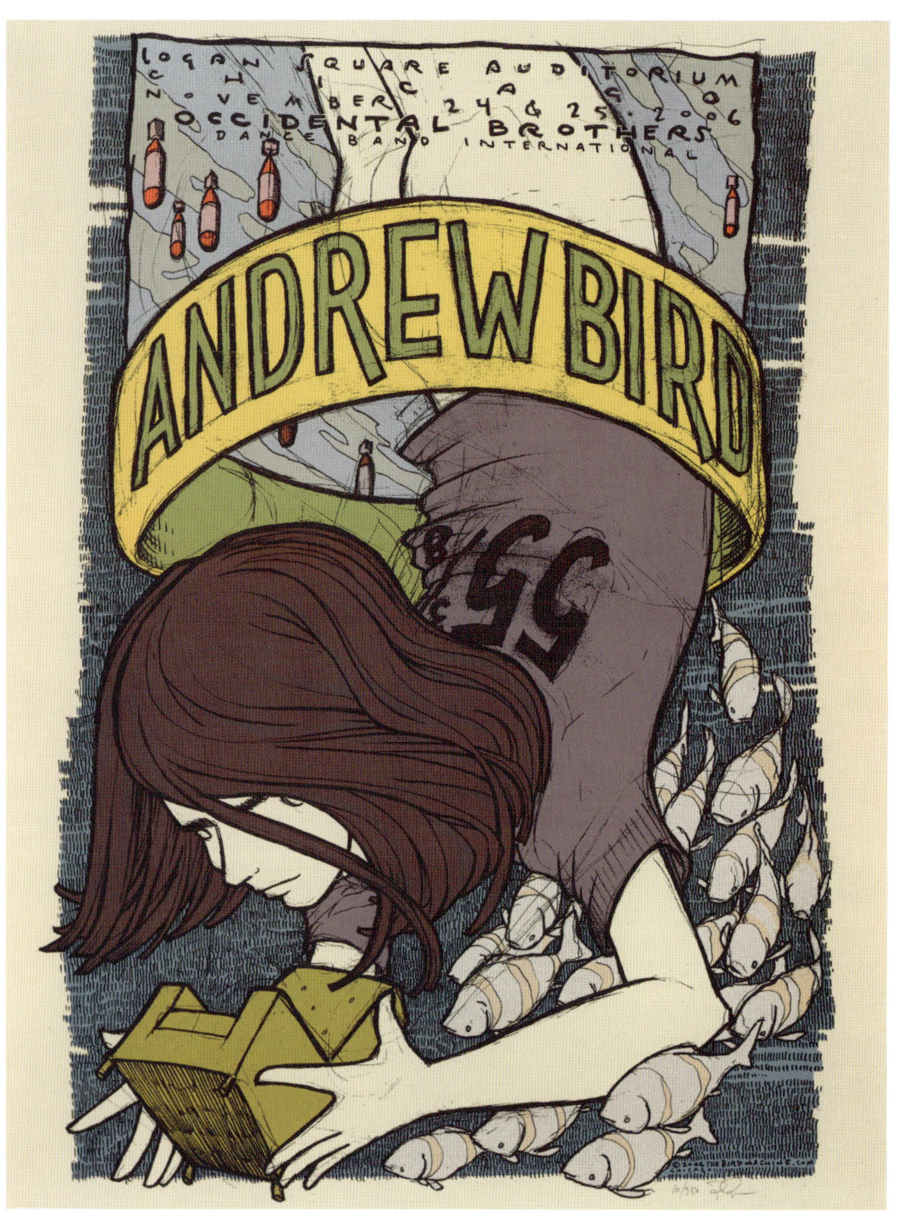

Andrew Bird
2006
18 x 24 inches
6 screens

I started with "the tangles in your hair," and moved outward from there. "Someday we'll get back at them all."

Jeff Tweedy
2007
12 x 24 inches
4 screens

I've been a fan of Jeff's music since seeing Uncle Tupelo during my undergrad days in Champaign, Illinois. This was the first of three prints I've done (to date) for an annual series of shows put on by a group of Wilco fans who pool their resources to win a benefit auction Jeff offers annually. The prize is a living room concert for 30 people, and all the previous posters have depicted Jeff. I wanted to include him, but couldn't get his face drawn correctly—thus he sits in this lazy boat, floating with the fish and whatever else might be in the water.

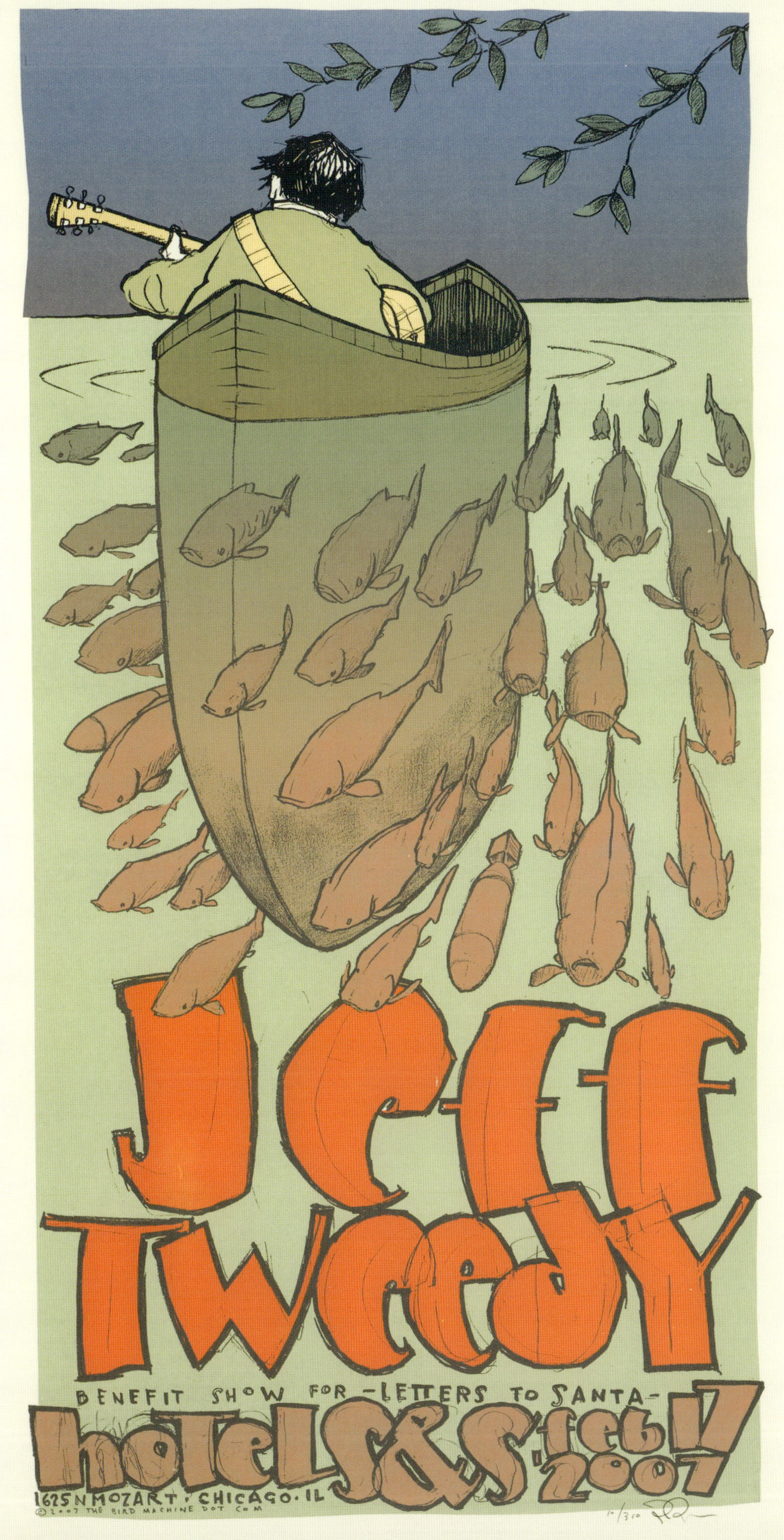
JEFF
TWEEDY
BENEFIT SHOW FOR -LETTERS TO SANTA-
hotel S&S · feb 17 2007
1625 N MOZART · CHICAGO · IL
©2007 THE BIRD MACHINE DOT COM
10/310

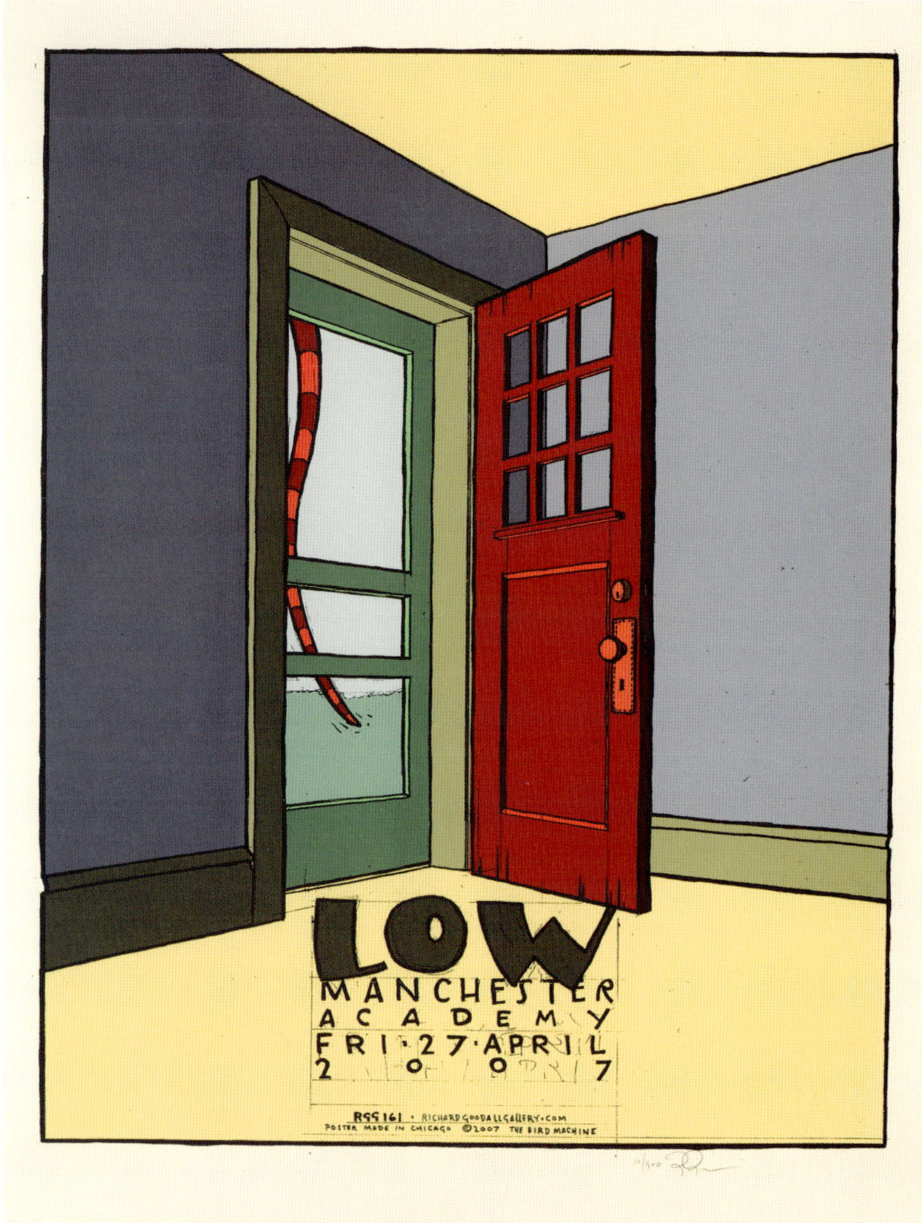

Low
2007
18 x 24 inches
7 screens

Low's music can be comforting, like a familiar living room, such as this one in Austin, Texas. Low's music can also be sinister, like something lurking just outside.

High on Fire
2006
18 x 24 inches
5 screens

The members of the band High on Fire are polite enough to have told me that they liked this print. In hindsight, it's not really appropriate for the band at all, and they were just being nice.

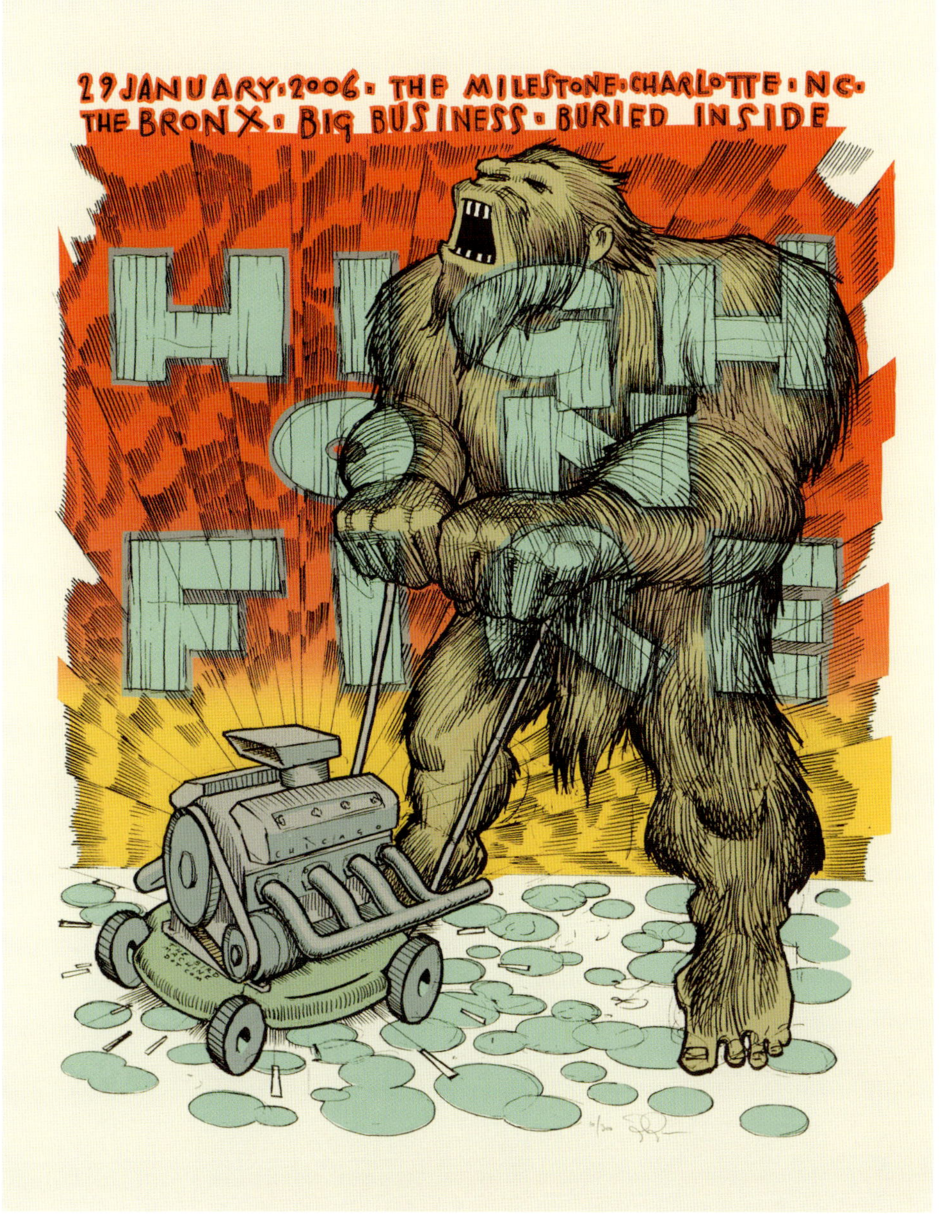

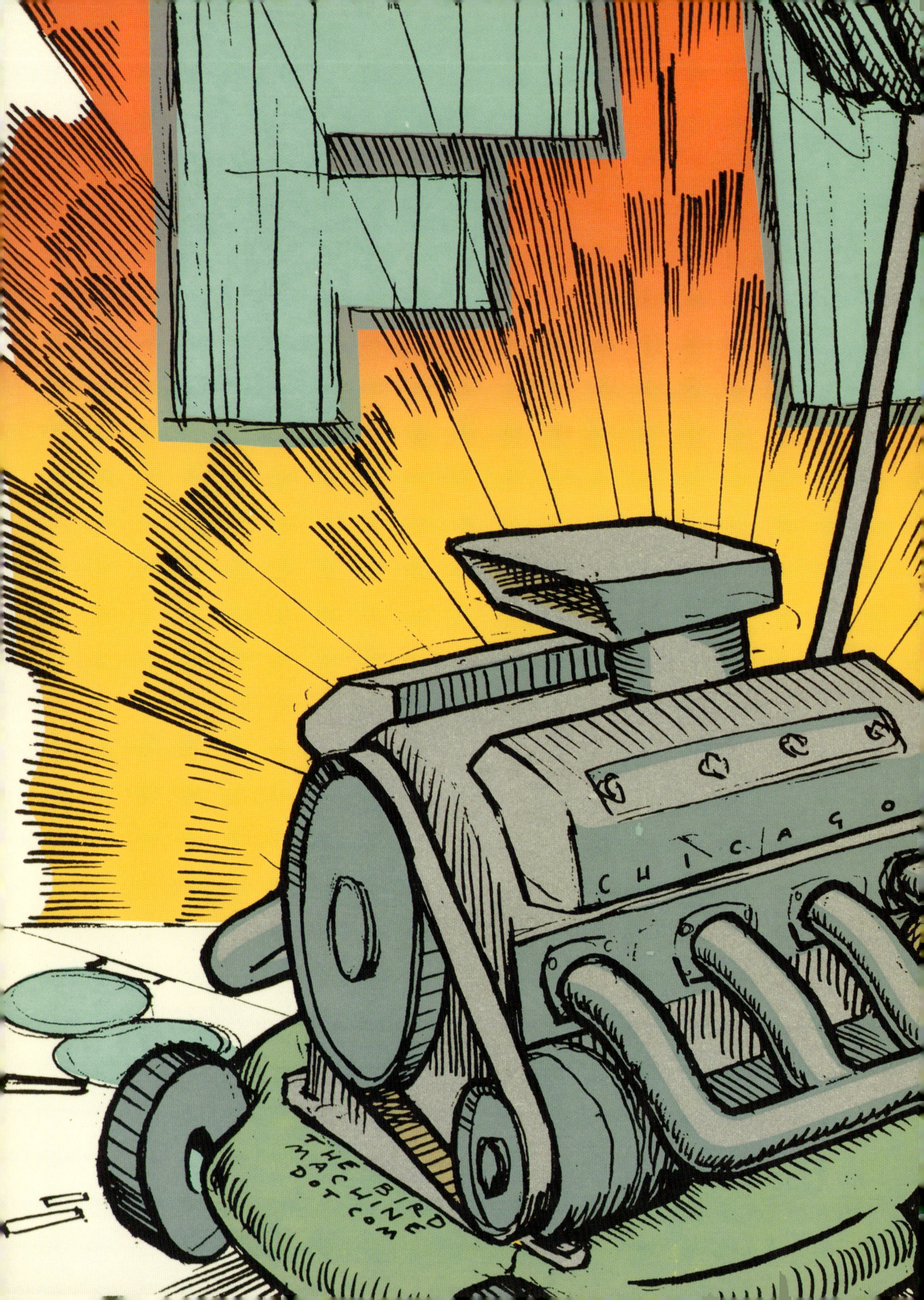
CHICAGO
THE BIRD
MACHINE
DOT COM

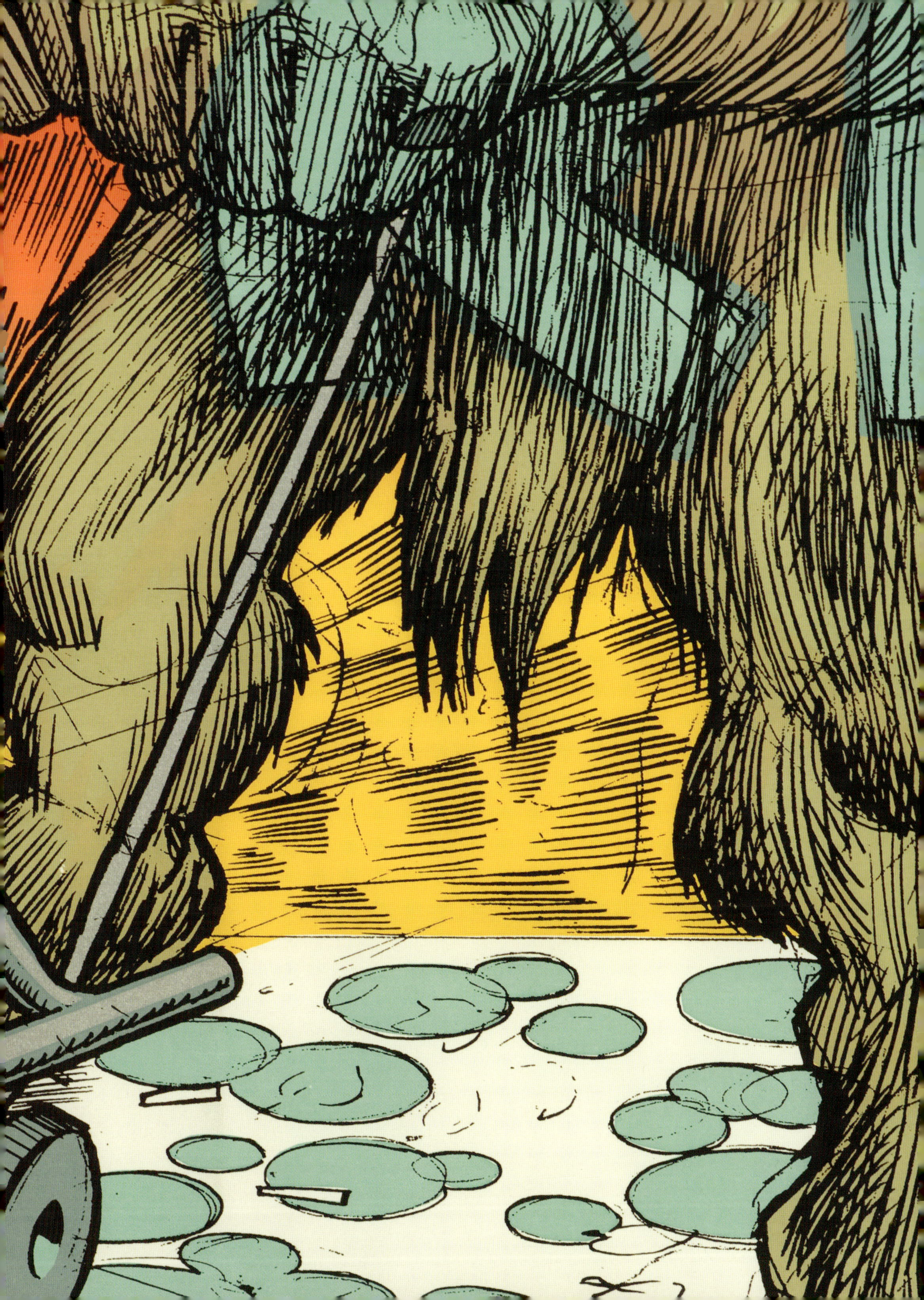

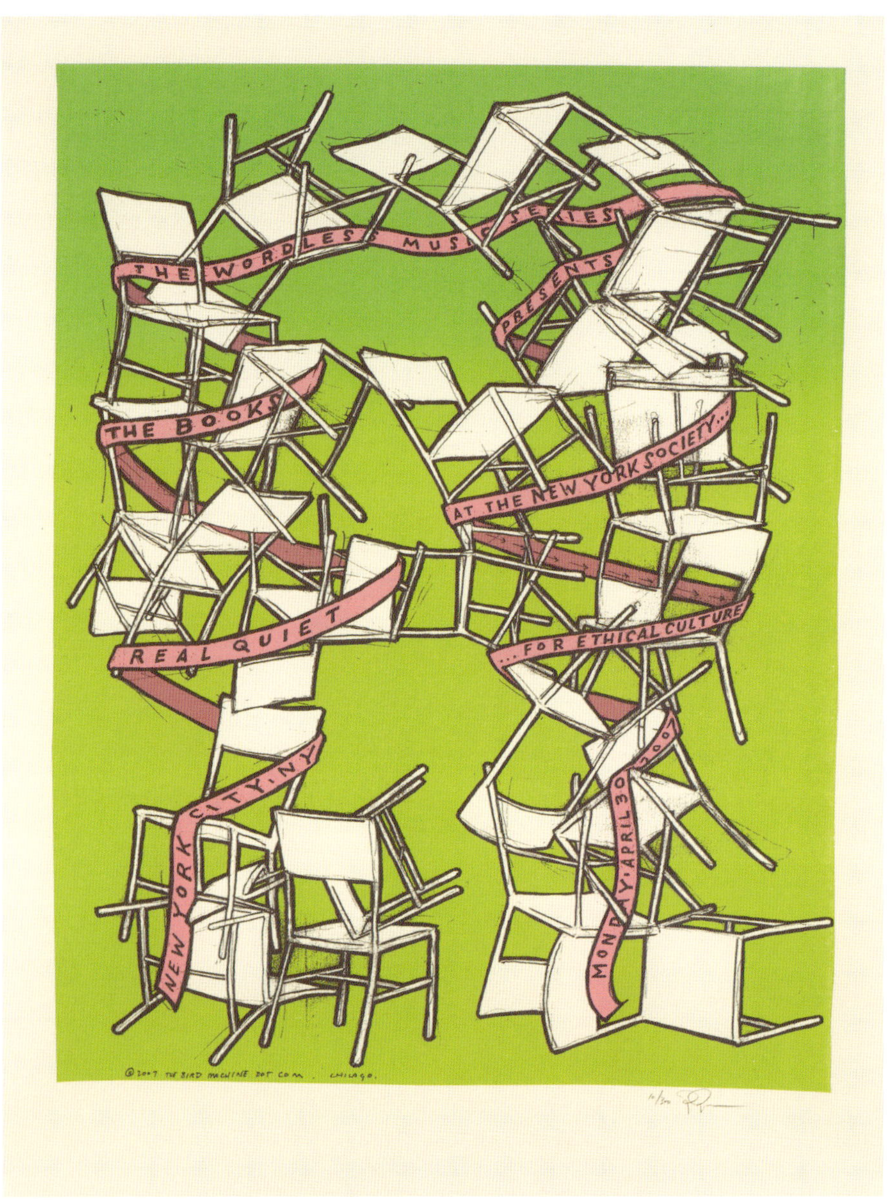

The Books

2007

18 x 24 inches

3 screens

The Books make music, then reassemble their own songs with well-executed samples integrated into the lyrics. Wait, no: this is a pile of chairs I drew in a log cabin in the Cascade Mountains. There it is. That's the picture. You can see it for yourself.

About the Size
2006
23 x 35 inches
5 screens

"That's about the size, where you put your eyes, that's about the size of it."

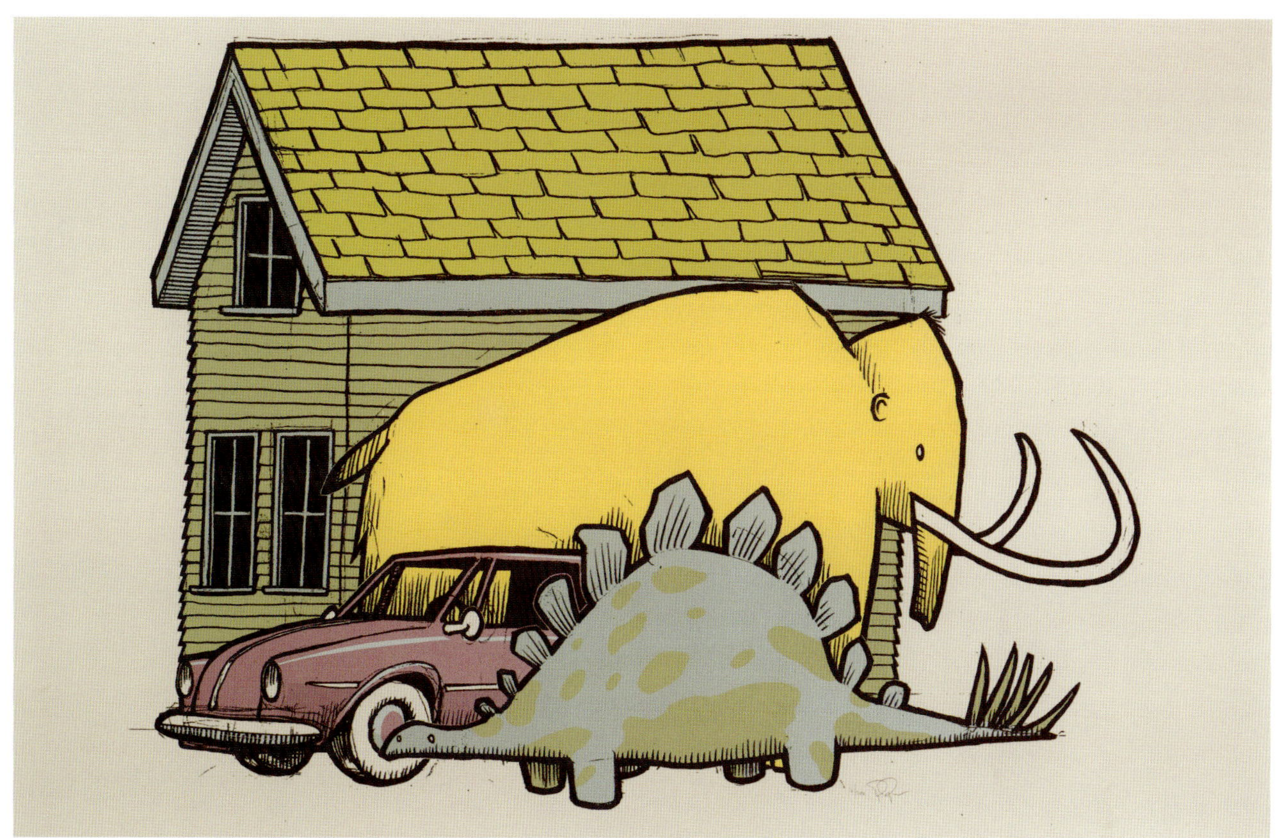

The Evens
2006
18 x 24 inches
3 screens

The Evens, from Washington, DC, are an often politically oriented two-piece band who operate by their own rules, touring with their own sound system and lights, playing only untraditional venues such as community centers and parks. I was asked to make prints for their Chicago shows while I was in Germany, and had to turn the prints around very quickly. I was flying home on a Friday, and the show's organizer needed the prints to hang the next day, Saturday. I downloaded some reference photos while at the Berlin airport, and drew this on the flight home. The subject matter can be read in a variety of ways.

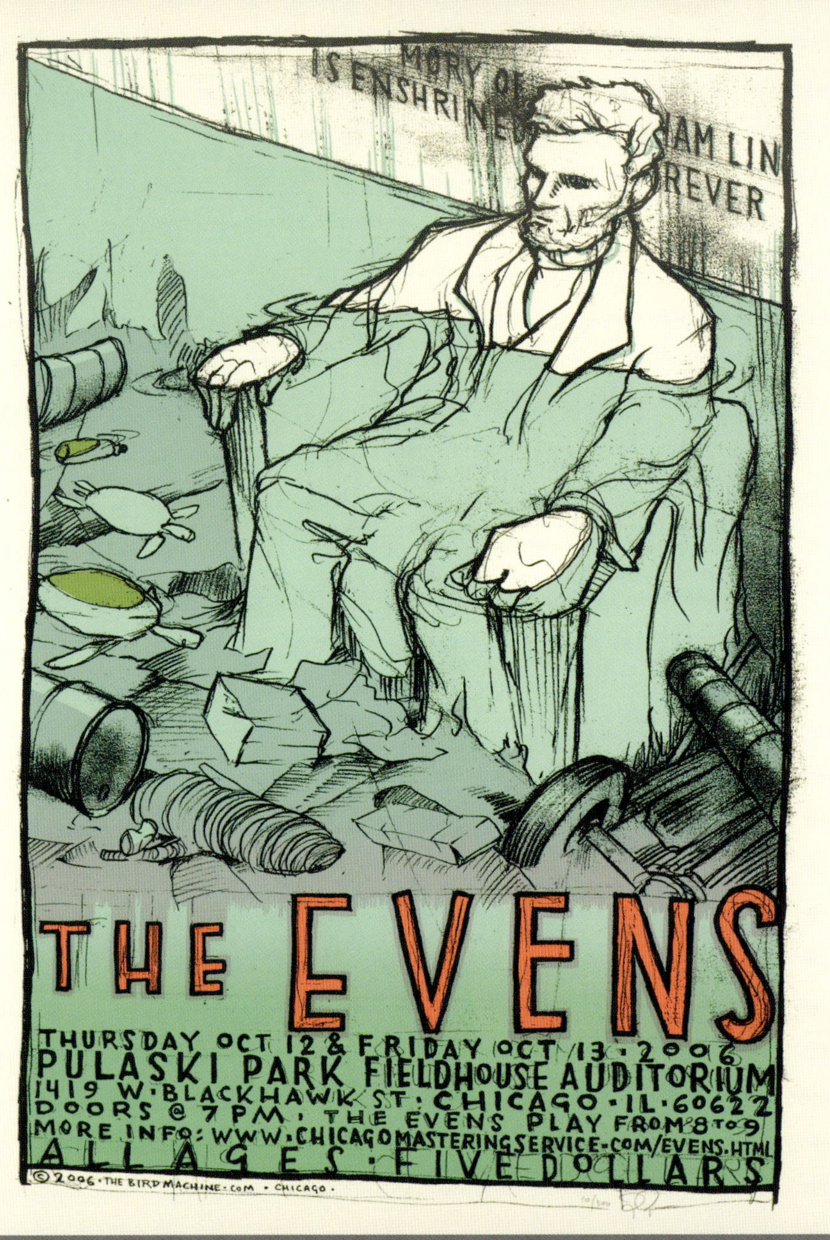

Touch and Go 25th Anniversary
2006
22 x 40 inches
4 screens

Touch and Go records celebrated their 25th anniversary in conjunction with the Hideout's tenth annual Block Party, and this festival provided some of the most amazing and memorable concert experiences I've ever had:

- a chance to see Girls Against Boys (including Johnny Temple, publisher of the book you hold in your hands) play *Venus Luxure No. 1 Baby* in its entirety.
- the members of Silkworm perform "LR72" one last time without their missing drummer, my late friend Michael Dahlquist.
- my first and only chance to see a longtime favorite, Big Black, reunited for 15 blaring minutes.

As of this writing, Touch and Go records has recently announced that they will be ceasing operations after over 27 years as probably the best independent record label in rock music history.

The print was made as a diptych, with Kathleen Judge providing the right half of these L tracks.

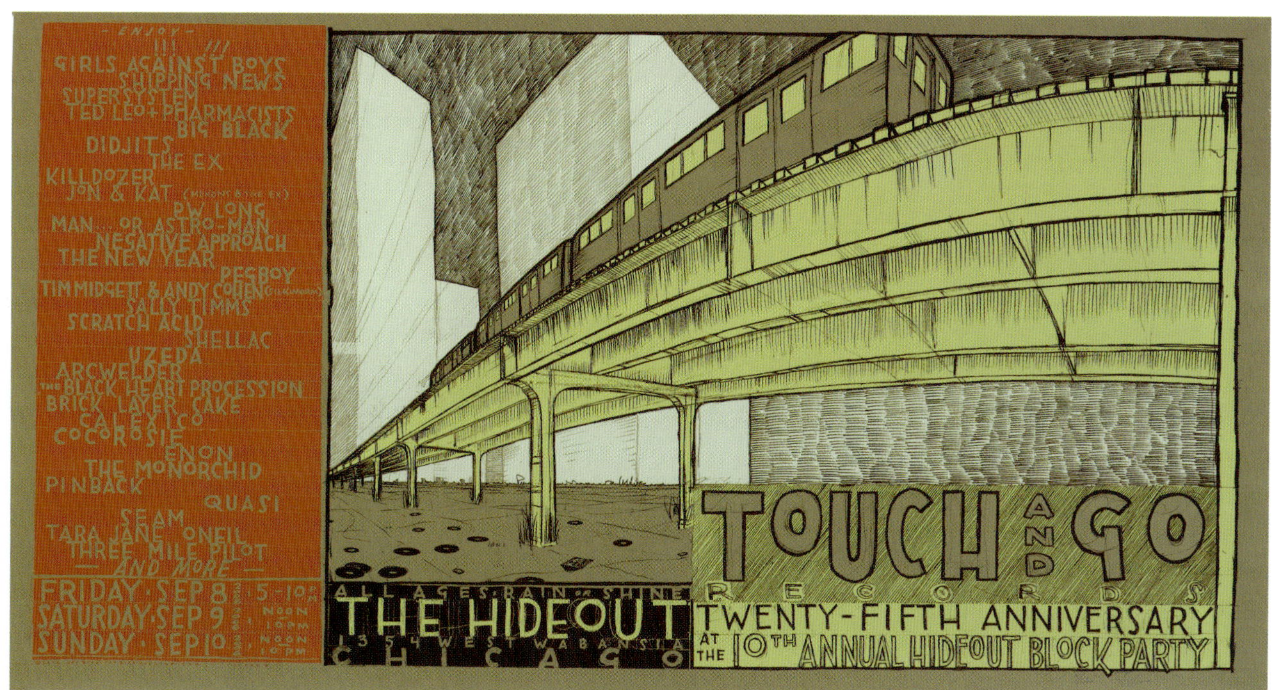

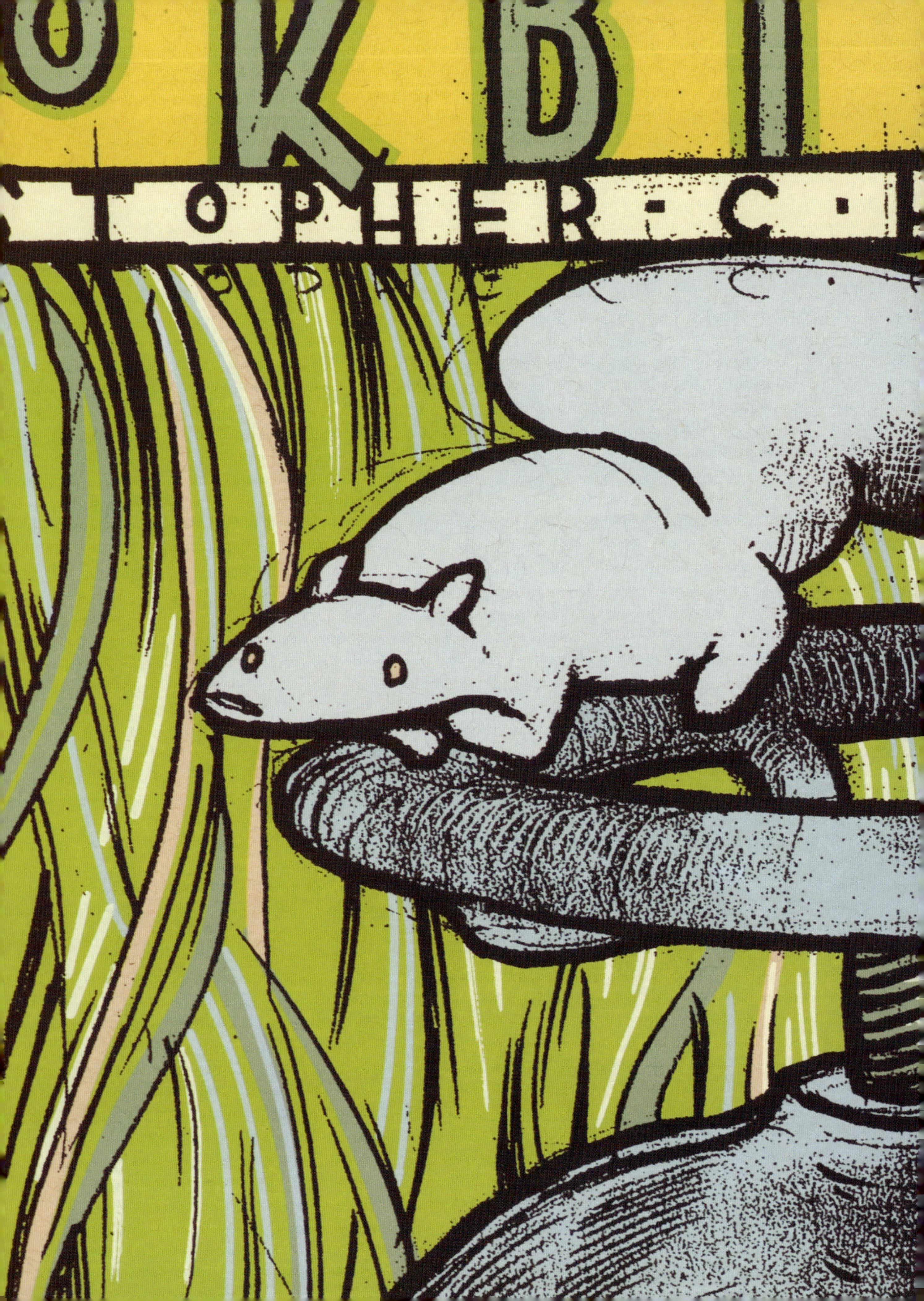

The Lincoln Bookbindery
2008
20 x 26 inches
6 screens

I've been taking projects to the Lincoln Bookbindery in Urbana, Illinois since I was an undergraduate there in the painting program. They celebrated their 30th year with some of the animals which frequent the yard around the shop.

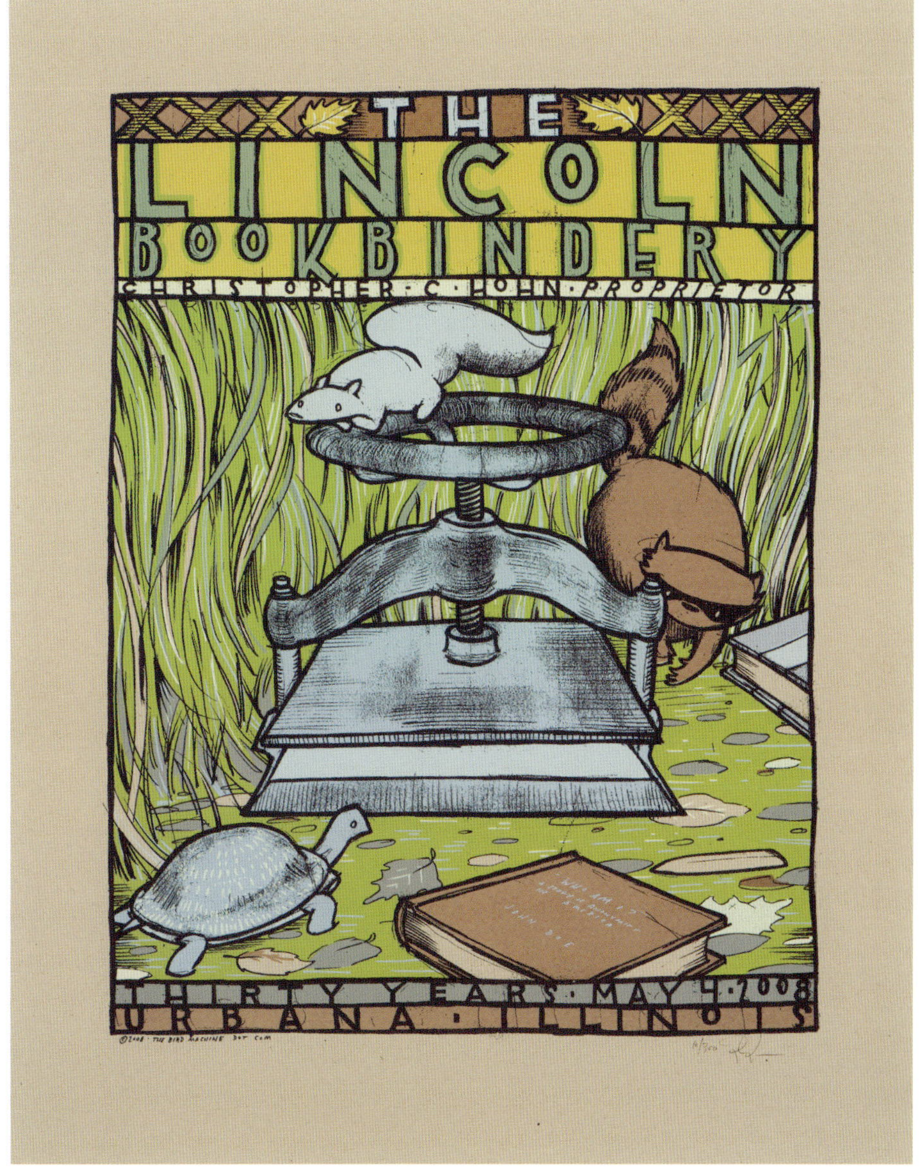

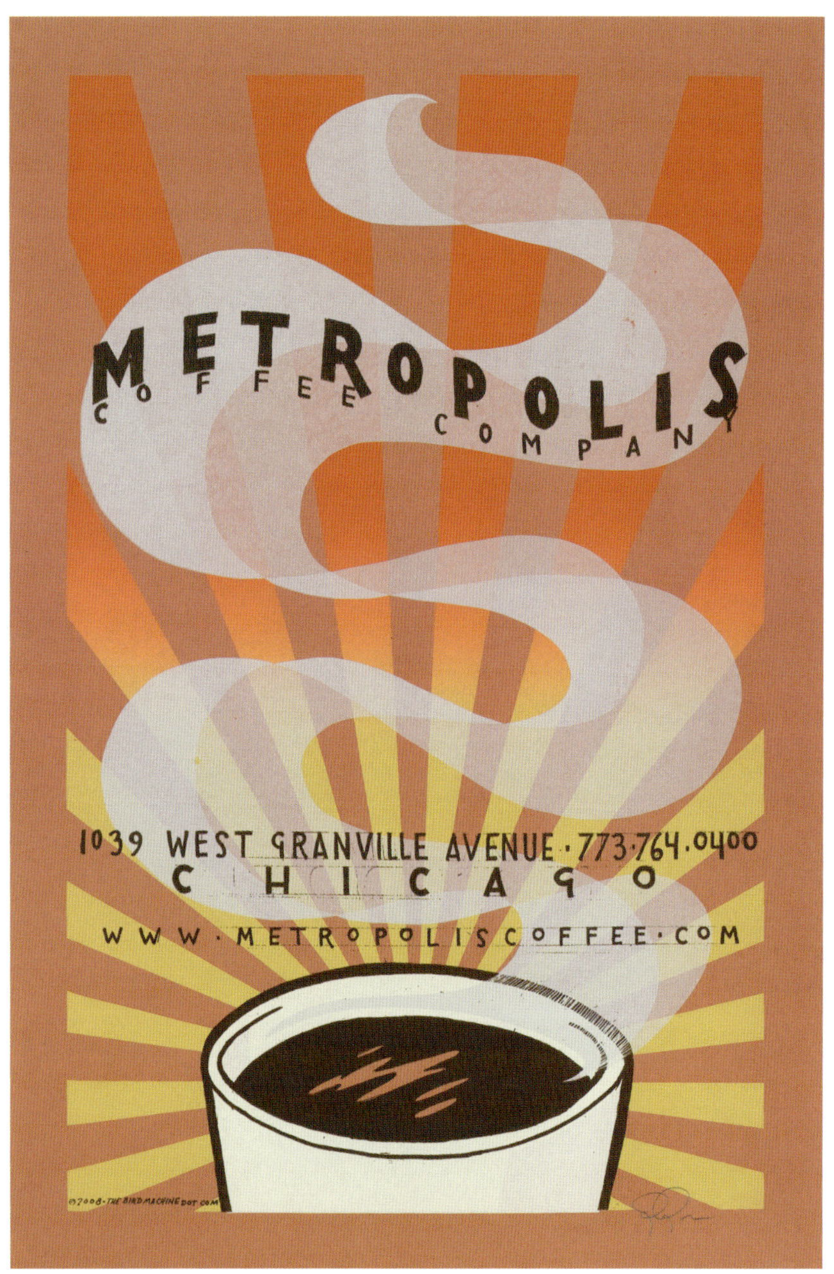

Metropolis Coffee Company

2008

13 x 20 inches

5 screens

Metropolis Coffee is a great family-run roaster on the north side of Chicago, owned by some friends of mine. I made a print for them when they opened their shop a couple years ago, and this second promotional print hangs in many of the cafés and restaurants which serve their fine coffees.

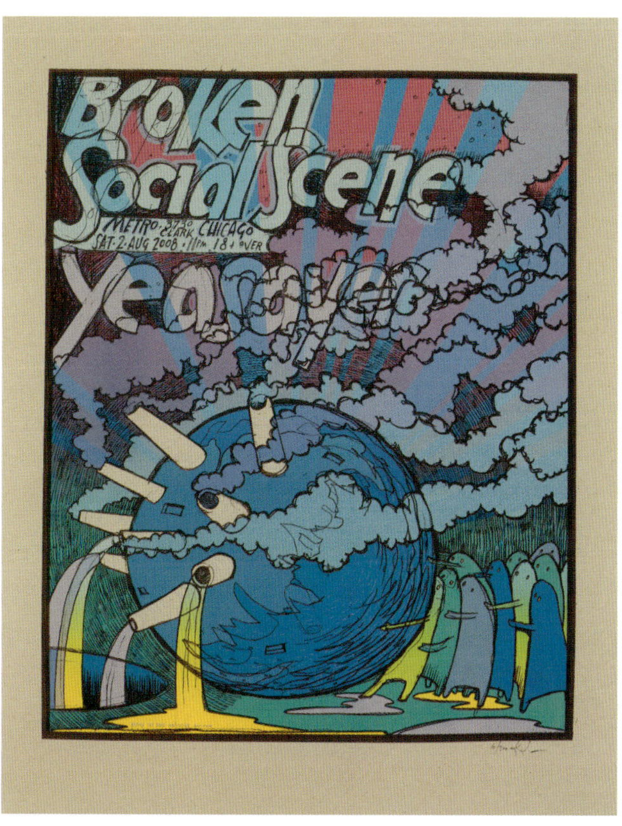

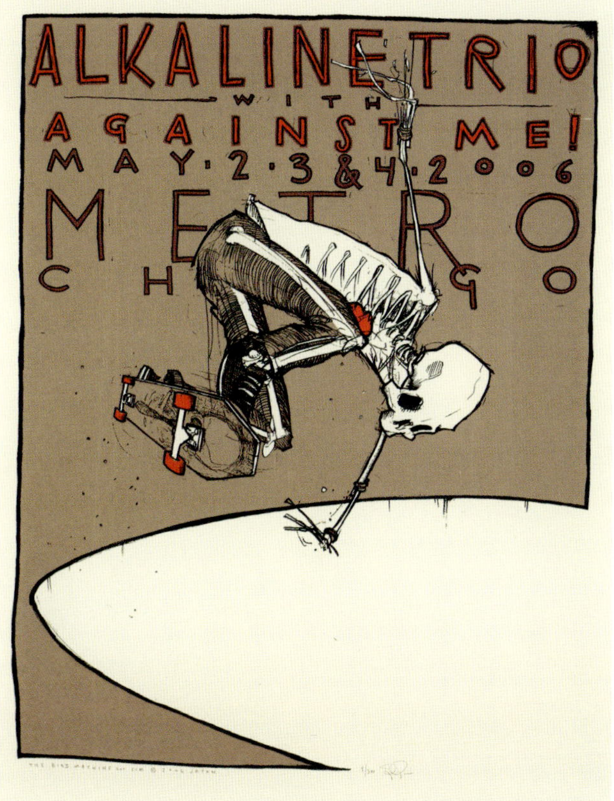

Broken Social Scene
2008
20 x 26 inches
5 screens

I'm still not sure exactly what is happening in this print, but the colors are pretty good. "It's a cruel world, and it's time..."

Alkaline Trio
2006
18 x 24 inches
3 screens

The story may not be entirely accurate, but as I understand it, Matt Skiba, singer/guitar player of the Alkaline Trio, was skating at the Wilson skatepark in Chicago and broke his wrist. This injury prevented the band from recording their *Crimson* record. Once he healed and the record was released, the band prepared to tour, but Matt broke his other arm, while skating at the Wilson skatepark. Again, Matt healed (thankfully), and they prepared to play these three shows at the Metro in Chicago. The venue contacted me to make these prints, and I promptly fractured my wrists while skating in a ditch in Denton, Texas. I drew this backside ollie (loosely based on a photo of Mike Mcgill) while my wrist was in a splint, and made the skeletal scarecrow arms bound together with twine.

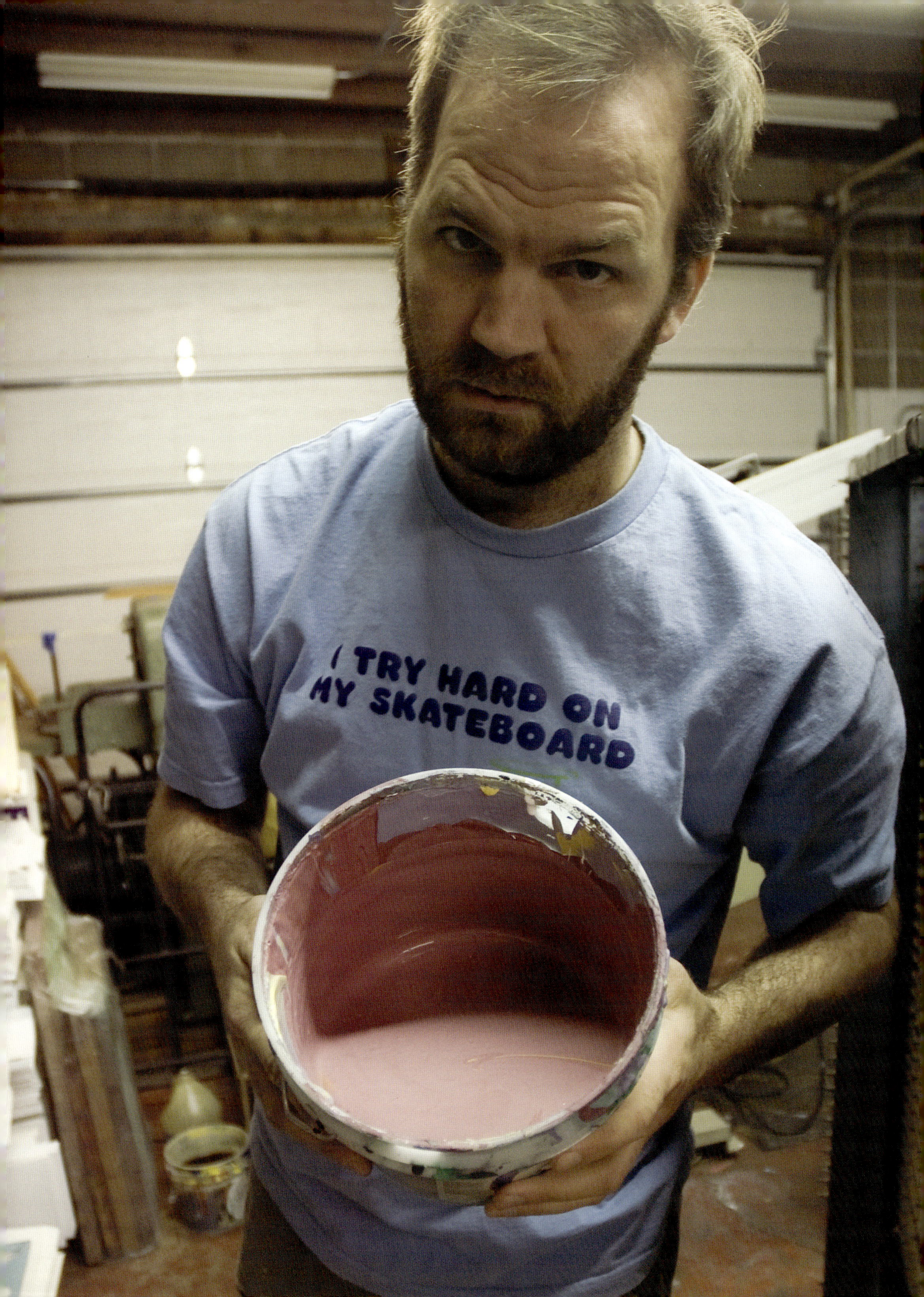
I TRY HARD ON
MY SKATEBOARD

Jay Ryan

by Joe Meno

Jay Ryan (born June 15, 1972) is an American artist and musician. He is most famous for his poster art, which features thought-provoking and absurd images.

Life

Ryan was born in St. Louis, Missouri, to Jack Ryan, a bicycle manufacturer, and Nancy Ryan, an amateur pianist. Ryan was raised in Northfield, Illinois, in a typically suburban cul-de-sac where he was forced to invent his own games to while away the boredom. He built his own musical instruments, selecting elements from the nearby Northfield Landfill, the largest garbage dump of its kind in the Western Hemisphere. Here the young artist would fit and weld and solder the working parts of a sousaphone to a harmonica, for example, and create intricate sounds that were largely influenced by the recordings from his mother's classical records. His proudest musical invention at the time was the Automatic Bass Flute, a reed instrument with an impossibly deep vibrato and ear-piercing resonance.

On the afternoon of September 13, 1982, Ryan slipped out of his house as his mother entertained the local gardening club and marched up and down his street while piping his Automatic Bass Flute, sending the neighborhood dogs and cats into a howling frenzy, shattering the windshields of passing automobiles, and killing a trio of newborn robins, piercing their miniscule hearts with the low, earthy warble of his self-made instrument. Standing beneath a birch tree in his front yard, he watched in horror as the mother bird returned to her newly dead young. Ryan immediately disassembled the Automatic Bass Flute and vowed to never experiment with music again. He buried the dead birds in his backyard beside a stand of poplars and thereafter visited them ritually. "It was the first time I discovered that sound is the most powerful force in all the world," Ryan later remarked.

Though most of his childhood was upsettingly tranquil, a strange turn of events occurred when Ryan was eleven years old. He was particularly close to a neighbor girl his exact age, named Holly Lamb, who lived on the other side of a white wooden fence. Together the two children would play in the nearby woods, building fantastic machines out of parts scoured from the local landfill. These devices never quite worked, however awesome their intention: a Cloud-Bicycle, a Bubble Chair, a Motorized Bathtub. One such device, the Bird Machine, which young Ryan and cohort Lamb spent several months perfecting, was built from the remnants of a fireplace bellows, a ruined Xerox copier, and an enormous—though cracked—magnifying glass. Once completed, Ryan exhumed the bodies of the three dead birds he had accidentally killed the summer before and placed their tiny, nearly featherless corpses in the tray of the copier and began to work the bellows. In an instant the three birds sprung back to life, their lidded, reptilian eyes blinking, their beaks squeaking for nourishment. In later interviews, Ryan said he was not entirely certain if what occurred that afternoon was an actual memory or a dream, though when he returned to those same woods years later, he found the machine standing exactly where they had left it.

A few days after the successful revitalization of the birds, on May 7, 1983, Ryan was detained by his mother and forced to endure an afternoon of piano lessons. Tragedy struck the young artist's life once again when his playmate Lamb, unaccustomed to wandering in the woods on her own, went missing. Days later, on May 16, 1983, it was young Ryan himself who, joining the frantic search party of policemen, neighbors, and relatives, pointed to the heavy boughs of a gigantic white oak tree, spotting his young friend's foot dangling nearly thirty feet in the air. Several ladders were brought to the scene to help retrieve Lamb's body from the uppermost limbs of the tree as Ryan looked on. The odd mystery of the young girl's demise befuddled all of Northfield, and this scene had a major influence on Ryan's graphic work, even years later, though he denies it.

After the death of the young girl, Lamb's grieving parents gave Ryan a set of art supplies—objects secured in a small wooden box—which included a sketchbook, paintbrush, palette, pencil, ink pen, and colored chalk. The box had, of course, belonged to Holly Lamb. Ryan mourned in the shade of the woods, sketching frantically with pencil and chalk. His first drawings at this time are now understood as attempts to make sense of the mysteries of his young life:

here were the animals who frequented the nearby woods, here were the strange machines of his own design, here was the frightening tree were he had found his young friend draped, looking strangely peaceful, forever asleep. Many of these images resurface in the artist's later work, themes and figures he revisits time and time again.

At the age of 13, like most children of Northfield, Ryan was sent to boarding school—St. Florian's in nearby Hasketville, Illinois. He was a member of the Artistic Society as well as the school's marching band, where he played mellophone and the timpani. He excelled at cricket and croquet. Remarkably, his first year at school passed without incident. Then at age 14 the young man was stricken with Sudden Colorblindness Syndrome. Ryan lost all sense of color for periods of several days or weeks at a time. Within months the rare disorder was so persistent that he became unable to distinguish between white, black, and gray. The boy's father—using materials from his bicycle factory—manufactured enormous and costly eyeglasses so the boy could continue his schooling.

At the age of 15, an experimental drug was administered with the hope of reducing the symptoms of his colorblindness. The drug, the now infamous Cloudal developed by British scientist Gabriel Gabrielle, seemed to work overnight, though there was one startling side effect: young Ryan lost his sense of smell. Treatments ceased but his ability to detect odors never returned, much to his parents' dismay. Even worse, his colorblindness soon returned.

Unable to further pursue the visual arts due to his colorblindness, Ryan's interests turned to contemporary music—a medium that would exert a lifelong influence on his visual work. His favorite group at the time was the popular English band Genesis. A disturbing 3-year period followed, from 1987 to 1990, during which Ryan strongly identified with the band's lead singer, Phil Collins, going so far as to turn in his classwork at the rigorous private school under the musician's name, demanding that his teachers and schoolmates address him as *Phil*. Photographs from this era show him wearing several scarves and turtlenecks in imitation of his new idol.

It was during these awkward teenage years that Ryan returned to writing and performing music, a craft he had only a few years prior sworn to abandon forever. He purchased a harmonium from a local antique store and a flock of parakeets from a pet supplier and set about acquiring several used birdcages from area garage sales. His plan was to convert his dormitory room into an enormous musical device. Searching the attic of the school building, he dragged many lengths of pipe back into his room and wired the cages with nearly a dozen microphones, creating the world's first fully functional electric bird-note organ. Ryan composed numerous songs based on daily weather, as the elements themselves had the single greatest effect on the birds' tone and pitch. His most famous composition from this period is "Autumn Day, Partly Cloudy Sky, Wind Coming from the Northeast, Humidity 15%." In later interviews, Ryan has referred to this device as The Bird Machine as well, though no record of it remains.

When Ryan was 18, another experimental drug, Pylar, was administered, permanently relieving the young artist of his colorblindness on July 17, 1990. His passion for visual art was reinvigorated and he constructed a bicycle made entirely out of candy; though while riding it, Ryan was attacked by a flock of grackles and was forced to wash his hands of it. Soon after, he devised a bicycle of birdseed which he imagined could be used to fly, also referred to in his notes as a Bird Machine. He believed that hungry birds would lift the bicycle from the ground and propel him through the air. On its first test flight, August 23, 1990, a sortie of manifold birds swept Ryan into the sky and tore the bicycle to pieces. Ryan was hospitalized for minor injuries.

Ryan attended the University of Illinois in Champaign-Urbana from 1990–1994, where he majored in Painting and minored in Impossible Physical Gestures. His junior thesis, "Ghost Riding Bicycle at 3:00 a.m.," was critically lauded though under-appreciated by his peers. It was during this period that Ryan yet again experimented with music. The nascent Champaign-Urbana punk, post-punk, and indie rock scene had just begun to take shape. Ryan quickly became adept at the bass guitar and featured in a number of local bands: Hubcap, Furniture, Furniture-Store, Furniture-Movers, Furniture-Fever, Furniture-Outlet, Furniture-Salesman, Furniture-Forever, and Braid.

While at college, Ryan was known to dress as the subjects of his paintings in public and ride his bicycle along the busy college streets. He believed it was necessary to truly understand that which he was attempting to depict. It was during one such jaunt that he met fellow student Diana Sudyka, in 1992. Sudyka was on her way to class, walking with an oversized newsprint pad, when Ryan, riding his bike, dressed as a log, collided with her. Both temporarily lost conciousness and soon began dating.

In 1994, having finished his schooling, Ryan moved to Chicago and formed the band Dianogah with college friend Jason Harvey and provocateur Kip McCabe.

In 1995, Ryan started work with poster artist Steve Walters at Screwball Press. Ryan soon discovered that if he ran all seven of the print shop presses at exactly the same speed, at exactly the same time, the vibrations would cause the metal fillings in his teeth to act as a transmitter, picking up ham-radio signals from across the globe as well as radio reports nearly fifty years old. It was in one of these transmissions that Ryan first received a call of distress, tapped out in Morse code. Ryan, a former Boy Scout, recognized the repetitive series of beats at once. Riding his bicycle up and down the streets of the city, he followed the signal as it grew louder and louder, vibrating within his teeth.

It took nearly three months for Ryan to identify the source of the transmission, a tiny bird shop on Chicago Avenue. On the afternoon of May 7, 1996, Ryan entered the bird shop and discovered a rare Taiwanese parrot that had been trained in Morse code. The parrot was part of an illegal, exotic bird smuggling ring, and the animal had managed to chew through part of the wall next to its cage, reaching the telephone lines within. It had been tapping out a call for help in Morse code for months and was only days away from being sold when Ryan arrived with police. A substantial reward for the missing bird was paid to Ryan. He continued to use his fillings to locate other missing exotic birds with the use of a helmet-mounted antenna. Atop his bicycle, which he renamed The Bird Machine, he circled the city honing in on distress calls. After the successful rescue of several other birds, Ryan used the mounting reward money to open his own print shop.

In 1999, Ryan started The Bird Machine printing press in the basement of his apartment building in Chicago. His earliest employees were all neighbors of the building who would work shifts while tending their laundry. The majority of Ryan's artwork at this time consisted of rock posters. Providing promotional materials for such indie acts as the Flaming Lips, Shellac, and Guided By Voices, the Bird Machine enterprise soon flourished.

In 2000, Ryan wed longtime girlfriend Diana Sudyka.

In 2002, Ryan relocated his print shop to a commercial space in the Ravenswood neighborhood of Chicago. After years of successful business at this location, a series of odd events occurred, beginning in July 2006: pencils and other objects suddenly vanished, large reams of paper were mysteriously found torn to shreds, and terrifying sounds rose from the washroom with alarming frequency. It was revealed that a large family of nearly extinct red-throated whip-poor-wills had taken residence in the air ducts of the facility and Ryan, of his own volition, determined to vacate the premises, leaving the birds to enjoy their new habitat.

In December 2005, the Punk Planet Books imprint of Akashic Books released the first edition of his now infamous book, *100 Posters / 134 Squirrels*. Because of a rare printing error involving ferrous inks, several schoolchildren who purchased and enjoyed the book found themselves covered in a coarse, nearly invisible hair upon contact with its pages. No cure has been found to offset the symptoms, though all of the affected children report an increased sense of well-being.

In 2007, Ryan once more moved the printing shop to a nearby suburb of the city—Skokie, Illinois. Skokie is home to a wealth of artistic and industrial concerns, including Handley and Sons Prosthetics, Hair Masters, and Asbestos-Be-Gone! Incorporated. From this new location, Ryan's reputation and professional stature continue to grow.

In 2009, Mayor Richard Daley of Chicago named June 15 Jay Ryan Day. On this day children were encouraged to dress up as their favorite Jay Ryan animal and ride their bicycles up and down the streets. After several near-fatal accidents involving youngsters whose vision was obscured by variegated squirrel, fish, and greyhound masks (said children frequently collided with parked automobiles and trees), Jay Ryan Day was cancelled. There are no plans to reintroduce Jay Ryan Day in the near future.

Relationship to Popular Culture

Ryan is an accomplished craftsman and artist whose work provides an opportunity for viewers to contemplate the important intersections of text and image, humor and pathos, memory and dream. Ryan admits that his process for developing any given composition is oftentimes confusing and elaborate. He will get an idea for a sketch and then write that idea down on a piece of paper. He will then fold that piece of paper lengthwise and insert it in the leg binding of one of a dozen carrier pigeons he breeds for this sole purpose. Ryan summarily turns the pigeon loose. If the idea is a good idea, the bird will return with a white flower in its beak—a bad idea, a red flower. Ryan will then sketch the basic composition. He must always face a window during this initial phase. If a bird flies west across the window while he is working, he abandons the project. If the project continues, the hand-drawn sketch is placed in a tin box where it is soaked in an iodine solution. After all this, the sketch is mounted on a silkscreen. Ryan's silkscreens are made of the finest materials, imported from a tiny village in Malaysia named Luk Do. Once the screen has been created, interns are used to "pull" the ink. Ryan tends to use a highly toxic combination of inks that are beautiful to look at but deadly to the touch. After printing, the posters are hung to dry on a large, metallic, windmill-shaped device for a period of thirteen hours. Ryan's work is then shipped across the world and mounted in art galleries and on the walls of sundry alleys. Each poster is unique, due to the unpredictable nature of the ink on paper. Contained within these artifacts are the complexities of a modern world grown too modern, too fast. Scores of art critics, philosophers, scientists, and gadabouts have conducted a staggering amount of research concerned with Ryan and his work. In its most simple definition, Ryan's work can best be understood in the charts below and on page 137.

General direction of movement in poster composition in this book

‹43	40	24›
to the left	no movement	to the right

Incidence of text occurring on billowing ribbon-style banners in this book

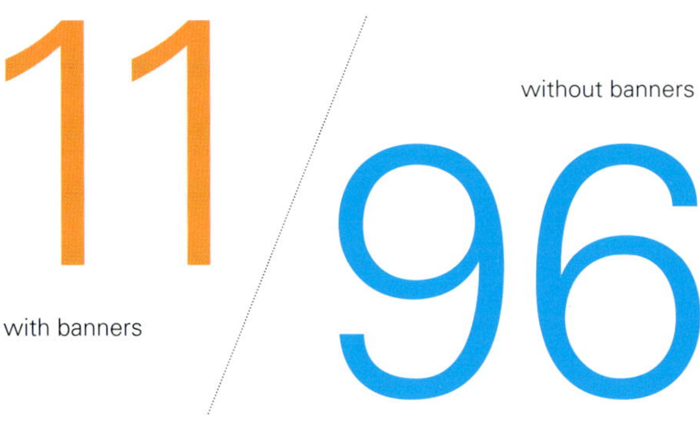

Incidence of squirrels in *100 Posters* book versus *Animals and Objects* book

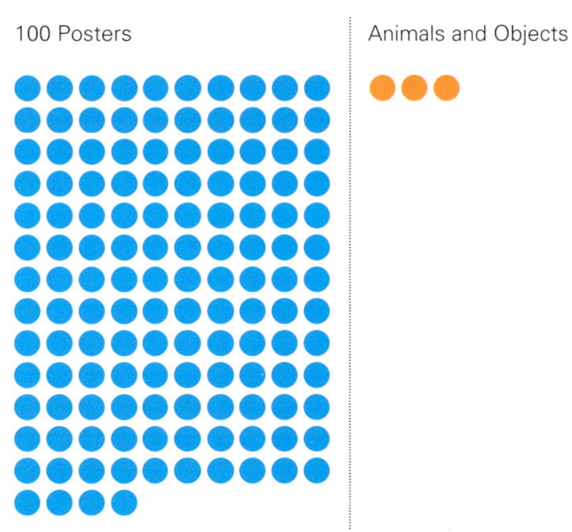

Total number of posters made per year, including work not featured in this book (according to www.thebirdmachine.com)

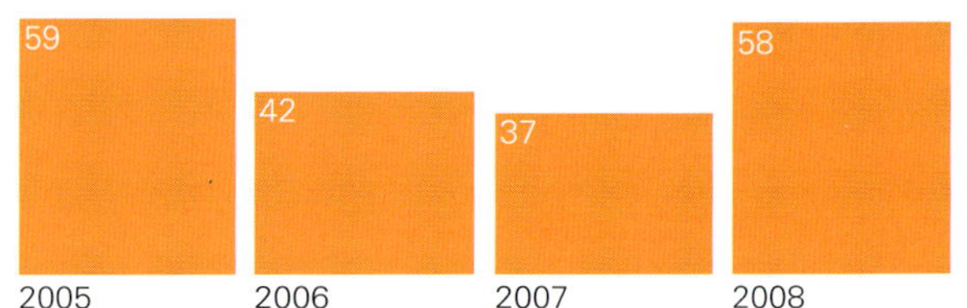

Relative incidence of different species in this book

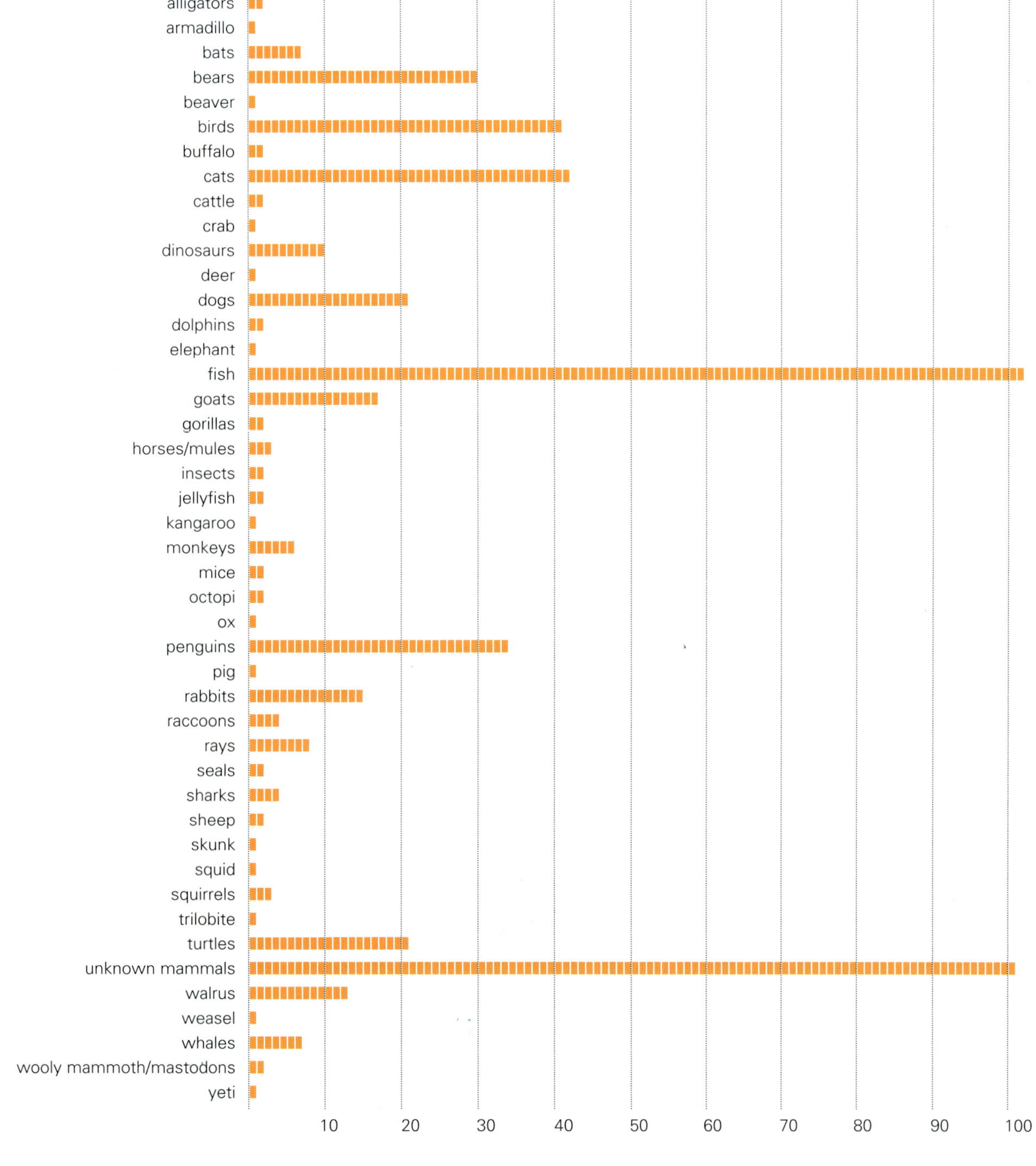

Additional Notes

Page 12. Dale Cabbot, inventor of the Hydrogen Fission Automobile, pioneered the harnessing of guano power, which is an effective gunpowder ingredient and fuel source due to its lack of odor and copious phosphorous and nitrogen content. This vehicle, nicknamed by the press as "The Nest," went on to win the advocacy of several environmental groups before its eventual adoption by failing automobile manufacturers. Today there are over 50,000 of these vehicles on the road.

Page 15. The eruption of Mount Pilate in Guam led to end of the island nation's plastic pool chair industry.

Page 27. It is a well-known fact that Malaysian honey bears, and most members of the ursine family, are solitary creatures. This pair, first documented by the naturalist Hans Schrieber, and later redrawn by the artist, has forced noted animal behaviorists and foremost biologists to reconsider their initial conclusions.

Page 30. The extraordinarily popular greyhound, Seth, has rescued over 30 men and women from a variety of serious tragedies including car accidents, fishing accidents, and accidents resulting from mistaken identity. The Italian Greyhound pictured here, named Uffizi, has similar accomplishments in the fields of military strategy and hair care.

Page 36. In summer, the polar bears of Rome, Nova Scotia, forced from their natural habitat, have been known to congregate in city parks, and have been conditioned by the singing chimes of local ice cream men. Passersby are routinely covered in blood.

Page 42. A composition taken from the final stretch of 2007's Fish Spectacular!, held annually on the outskirts of Reykjavik, Iceland. This particular participant did not win, thanks to its pervasive fear of success, typical to most endangered species.

Page 44. An interesting fact: the horse depicted here (left) is Goldie III, a direct descendant of Goldie, the steed made famous in many Western dramas and radio serials.

Page 51. This school of sting rays are of a rare breed known as the Choral Ray, whose songs most closely resemble the voices of prepubescent girls and boys. Sailors have famously tossed themselves to sea in search of the source of this magical singing.

Page 54. The strength of the Roman Empire lay in its exclusive use of terrapins for military strategy. Before them, the Greeks and the Mesopotamians were also known to use all manner of reptiles and amphibians.

Page 55. Another turtle, this one appearing off the Azore Islands, probably in search of a mate. Notice its tumescent sex organ, known as a cloaca.

Page 62. Originally, a sixth animal—a Siberian tiger—was to be included in this composition, but it was detained in customs as its owner, the Russian heiress Alana Krusknev, was caught trying to flee her homeland without consulting the proper authorities.

Page 67. In captive experimentation, this specimen has not been known to understand aural and visual cues. "Oscar" is depicted here in a sketch from 2006, moments before escape.

Page 75. The fuzzy marmot at rest. What has not been explained is its preference for smooth jazz.

Page 77. The North American cicada, which appear every seventeen years, was thought to be harmless until the incident of 1974 in Poland, Illinois, involving several schoolchildren who were carried bodily away in a swarm the size of a modest house. Seventeen years later, in 1991, all of the children returned to the small farming town, though many had forgotten their full names.

Page 90. These houses span the entire length of Nottingham Canyon, though what is most notable is their lack of use. Originally built by millionaire industrialist Clinton Reeves as a private refuge and sanitarium for his ailing son, Randall, "Hidden Canyon," as the property was once known, was abandoned upon the younger Reeves' death after a prolonged struggle with sepsis. Ironically, these deserted cabins have become a refuge for the grey-specked swallow, a species originally displaced by Clinton Reeves' immensely successful salt mines.

Page 95. Accidentally created by Swedish scientist Hans Rohmler in 1977 during the worldwide fuel crisis, the Dolphin Ghost Generator was first deemed a drastic failure. A decade later it was discovered that these non-corporeal creatures possessed an extremely attractive odor and were thus bottled and marketed as a world-famous Swedish perfume.

Page 119. Another little-known fact: the fish depicted in this image are Paratherina labiosa imported from Indonesia. After the drawings for this poster were completed, the species was accidentally released into the Chicago River, where it quickly upset the local fish population. Declaring a bounty on Paratherina labiosa, the mayor suspended the usual fishing regulations and called in sharpshooters.

Page 131. Due to overpopulation, pollution, rising ocean temperatures, and radiation poisoning, Earth has slowly begun to slip from its permanent axis over the last decade. Already several outposts and scientific research centers located along the North Pole have noted a substantial change in the atmosphere, which has led to the near-extinction of myriad Arctic species, including Arctic Squab, Snow Lemur, and Arctic Mouse.

Index

About

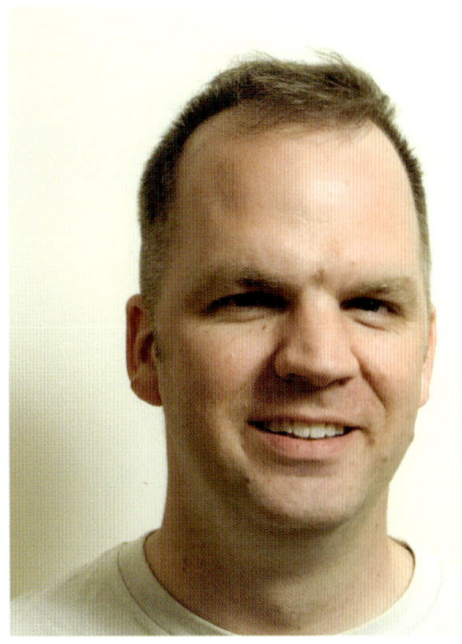

Jay Ryan has been making screenprinted concert posters and related items since 1995, first at Screwball Press, then (since 1999) at his own shop, The Bird Machine. Since graduating with a degree in painting from the University of Illinois (Urbana) in 1994, Jay has played bass guitar in Dianogah, and spends the rest of his time splitting firewood or thinking about bicycling. Jay was vice-president of the American Poster Institute from 2003 until 2007, was named to *Crain's Chicago Business Magazine's* "40 under 40" list in 2007, and was cited as one of *Time Out Chicago's* "cultural heroes" in 2008. Jay shows his work at Flatstock poster conventions four times a year, and travels extensively to talk about his work at universities. He is represented in England by Richard Goodall Gallery and in Germany by Feinkunst Krueger Gallery. Jay is married to illustrator Diana Sudyka, and lives in Evanston, Illinois, with Seth the greyhound and two cats. This is his second book, after 2005's *100 Posters / 134 Squirrels: a decade of hot dogs, large mammals, and independent rock.*

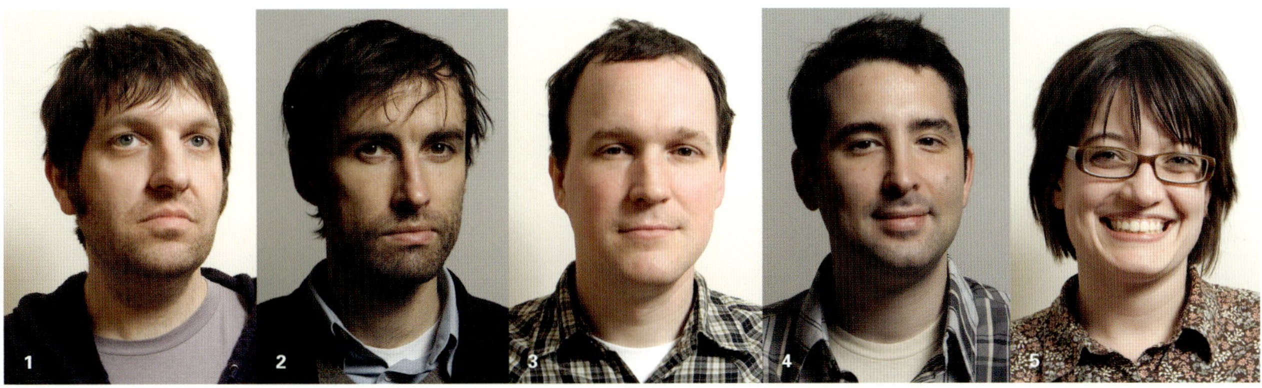

Akashic Books is a Brooklyn-based independent company dedicated to publishing urban literary fiction and political nonfiction by authors who are either ignored by the mainstream, or who have no interest in working within the ever-consolidating ranks of the major corporate publishers. www.akashicbooks.com

Fred Sasaki is a writer and editor living in Chicago. He publishes in or works with *Poetry* magazine, *Stop Smiling, ACM, MAKE, THE2NDHAND*, and other places.

Nathan Keay (1) is a photographer who grew up in St. Louis, but now lives in Chicago. He is known for his distinctive portraits, quirky art. He is lucky to be the husband of Stephanie Morris. www.nathankeay.com

Andrew Bird (2) is a multiinstrumental musician from Chicago, who spends most of his time playing concerts around the world at night, and riding his bicycle during the day. www.andrewbird.net

Jason Harvey (3) is a graphic designer in Chicago, with a focus on book design. Jason plays bass guitar in Dianogah, and lives in Evanston, Illinois, with his wife and twin boys. www.jhbookdesign.com

Joe Meno (4) is an award-winning novelist (*Hairstyles of the Damned, The Boy Detective Fails, Demons in Spring*) who lives in Chicago with his wife and daughter. He teaches writing at Columbia College Chicago, and his most recent novel is *The Great Perhaps.* www.joemeno.com

Sara Parker (5) moved from Thomson, Georgia, to study textile screenprinting at the School of the Art Institute of Chicago, before being hired to print at The Bird Machine in January 2008. Sara is married, teaches screenprinting at the Lill Street Art Center, and lives in Chicago. Sara printed many of the posters, and assisted Nathan with the photography of the work for this book. www.simonsara.etsy.com

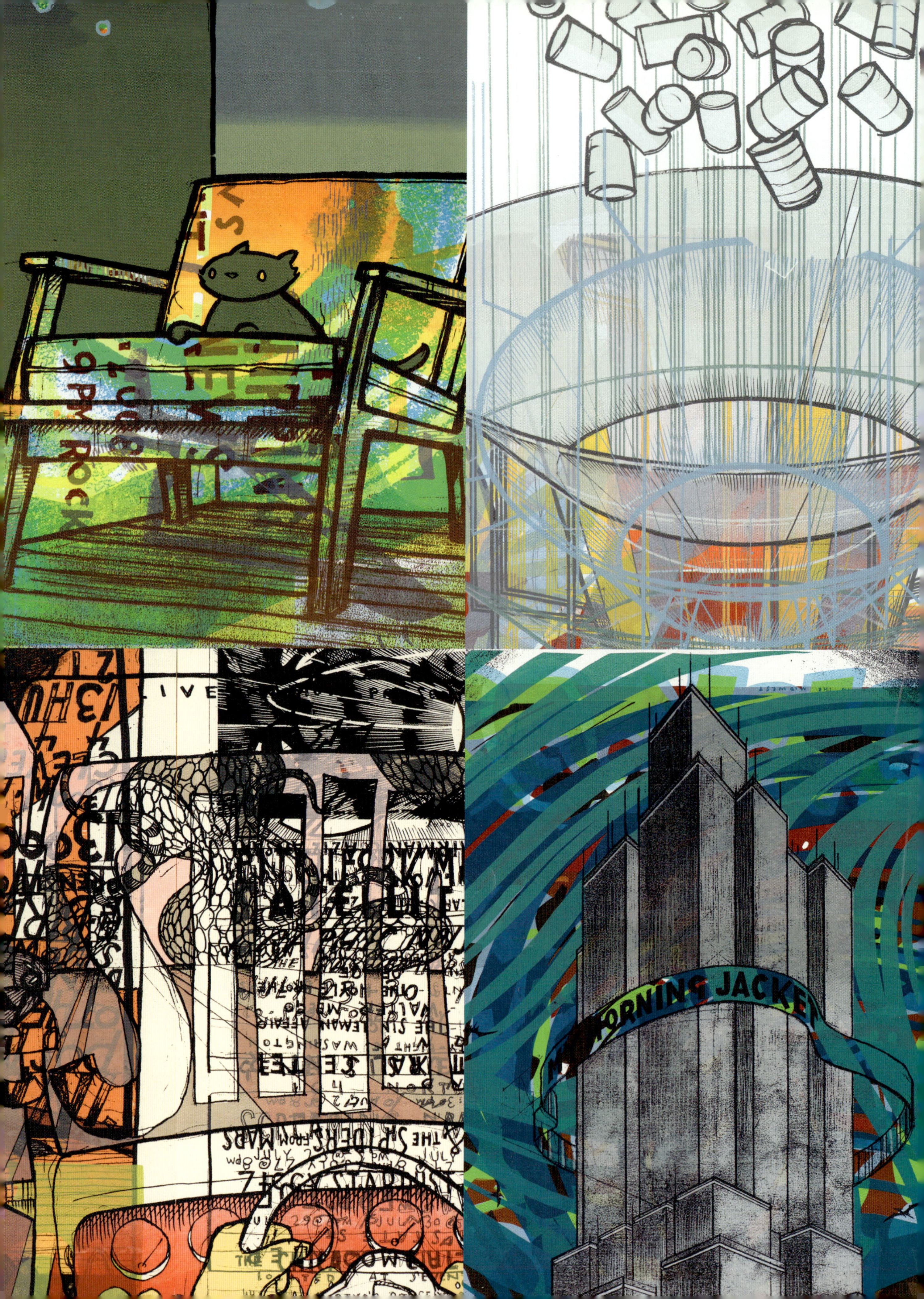
LIVE
JACKET

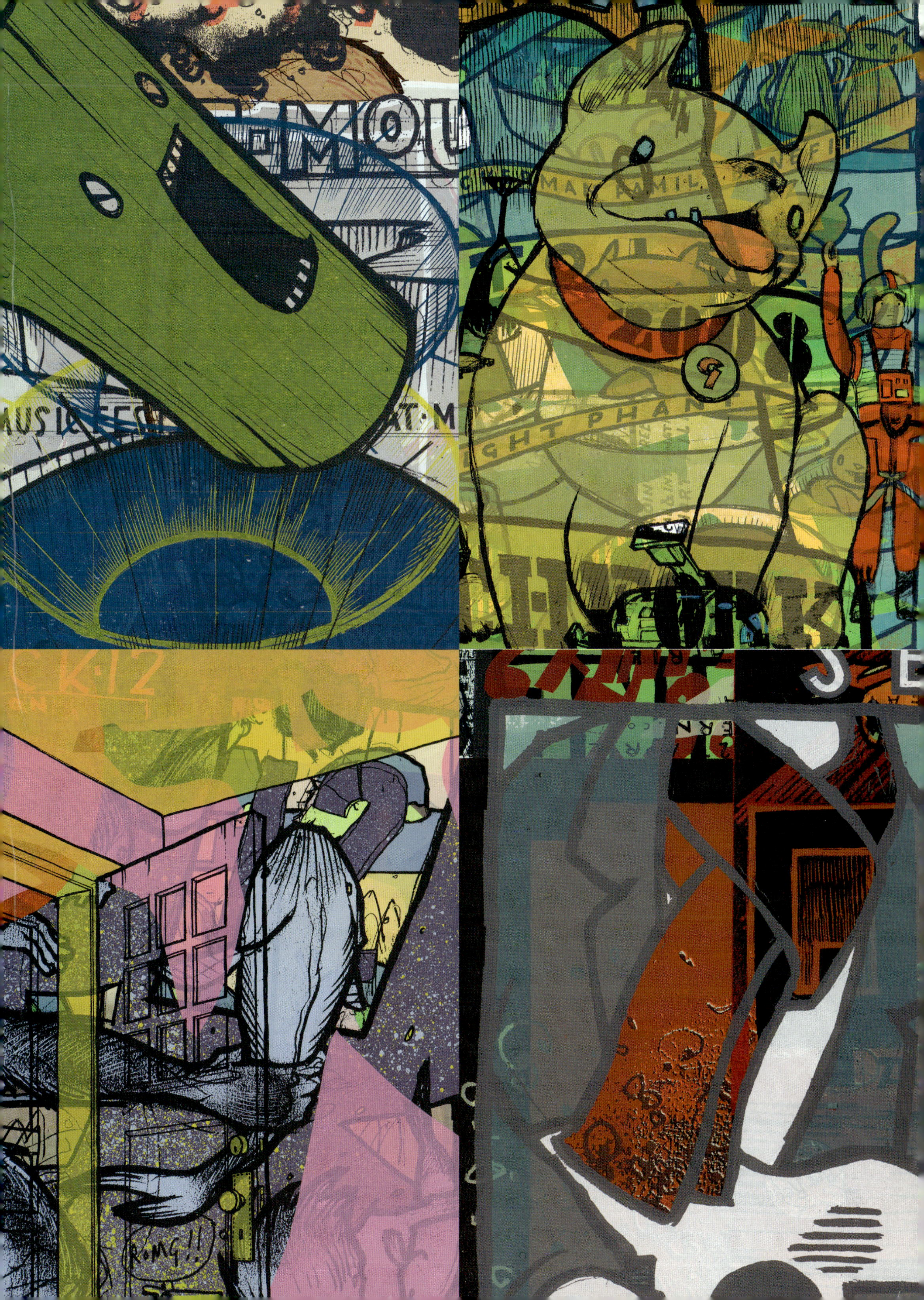
ROMG!!

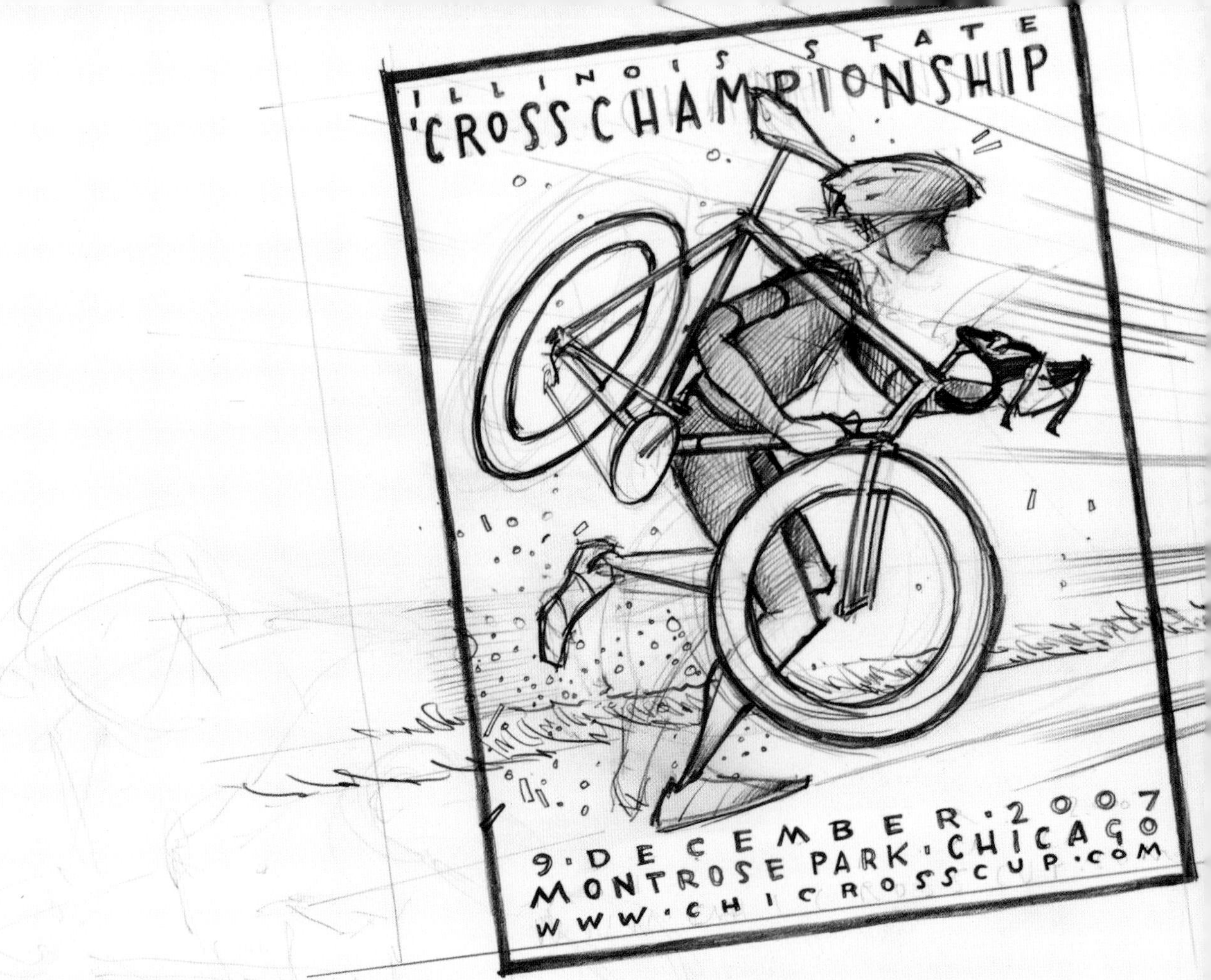
ILLINOIS STATE
'CROSS CHAMPIONSHIP
9·DECEMBER·2007
MONTROSE PARK·CHICAGO
WWW·CHICROSSCUP·COM